COGNITIVE
THERAPY

COGNITIVE THERAPY

A Practical Guide

DEAN SCHUYLER, M.D.

W. W. Norton & Company
New York • London

Production Manager: Leeann Graham
Manufacturing by Haddon Craftsmen, Inc.

Library of Congress Cataloging-in-Publication Data

Schuyler, Dean, 1942–
    Cognitive therapy : a pracical guide / Dean Schuyler.—Rev. ed.
        p.   cm.
    "A Norton Professional Book."
    Rev. ed. of: A practical guide to cognitive therapy. 1st ed. c1991.
    Includes bibliographical references and index.
    ISBN 0-393-70432-7 (pbk.)
1. Cognitive therapy   I. Schuyler, Dean, 1942–. Practical guide to cognitive
therapy.   II. Title.
[DNLM: 1. Cognitive Therapy—methods.   2. Professional-Patient
Relations. WM
425.5.C6 S397c 2003]
RC489.C63 S34   2003
618.89′142—dc21   2003054051

W. W. Norton & Company, Inc., 500 Fifth Avenue, New York, N.Y. 10110
www.wwnorton.com

W.W. Norton & Companhy Ltd., Castle House, 75/76 Wells St., London
W1T 3QT

1   2   3   4   5   6   7   8   9   0

Dedication

To a group of young Charleston psychiatrists whose out-standing work in cognitive therapy merited inclusion in this book:

Nikki Brannon, M.D.

Jeff Cluver, M.D.

Marc Dalton, M.D.

Susan Douglas, M.D.

Andrew Kozel, M.D.

Chris Pelic, M.D.

Katherine St. Germaine, D.O.

Lisa Sebotnick, M.D.

Samantha Symons, M.D.

Stephanie Thomas, M.D.

Daniel Varon, M.D.

CONTENTS

GUIDE TO CASE EXAMPLES

ACKNOWLEDGMENTS

Twelve years have passed since the publication of *A Practical Guide to Cognitive* Therapy in 1991, and life has changed utterly. Gone is the "big city" of Washington, D.C., and life is now dominated by the small, delightful city of Charleston, South Carolina. Gone is my private office practice, with occasional opportunities to teach. Life is now dominated by diversity: supervising third year psychiatry residents learning cognitive therapy, treating terminal cancer patients on a brief cognitive therapy protocol to aid their adjustment, consulting and teaching in a Primary Care Clinic. My new world is awash in ideas, stimulation and new challenges.

I am grateful to Drs. Ben Clyburn and Kim Davis for allowing me to be an "attached psychiatrist" in the Medical University of South Carolina (MUSC, Charleston) Adult Primary Care Clinic. I appreciate Dr. Glen Askins and Mr. Arnie Metz for encouraging me to teach a highly motivated group of physician assistant students. I want to thank a wonderful doctor, Frank Brescia, for introducing me to the world of cancer and its treatment, in a way both humane and challenging. Dr. Len Egede has stretched my knowledge of cognitive therapy by encouraging me to help him decipher how diabetics become depressed, and why depressives so often become diabetic. My daughter, Amy Schuyler, has been a constant source of stimulation, and a loving fountain of support.

Dr. Sloan Manning responded to a short article on doing brief cognitive therapy by providing me a vehicle to encourage and reward successful resident psychotherapy with publication. This has been a wonderful spur to teaching and writing. My daughter, Rachel Heaney, an advanced practice nurse in pediatric oncology, peppered me with questions that spawned an interest in cancer, which led to my association with Dr. Brescia. Dr. Ray Greenberg, the president of MUSC, has been continually encouraging and interested in my career. Dr. Marilyn Laken has provided opportunities and stimulation and friendship

when the prospects looked most bleak. Dr. Charles Kaiser, chairman of psychology at the College of Charleston, offered a whole new audience when he invited me to teach a section of abnormal psychology to undergraduates.

The MUSC psychiatric residents who agreed to teach undergraduates with me, and who taught me and learned cognitive therapy from me, are the professionals to whom this book is dedicated. Deborah Malmud of W. W. Norton and Co. invited me to lunch in Philadelphia in May, 2002. What she had in mind was unclear. In November, she contacted me to suggest this revised and expanded book. Lunch was good, but the invitation to update my life's major work was an unparalleled opportunity.

Finally, I am grateful to my wife Terry, who has walked this unpredictable career path alongside me, willing to take uncertain turns to unknown destinations.

Dean Schuyler
Charleston, South Carolina.
November, 2002.

PREFACE

Over the past twelve years, cognitive therapy has achieved a larger and more central role in the development of a practical and effective psychotherapy. The American Psychiatric Association has mandated that resident trainees become proficient in delivering the cognitive model. The application of cognitive therapy beyond acute depression, to chronic depression, generalized anxiety disorder (GAD), obsessive-compulsive disorder (OCD), posttraumatic stress disorder (PTSD), phobias, and social anxiety has been well documented. The cognitive model has been successfully applied to schizophrenia, bipolar disorder, eating disorders, anger management, and substance abuse as well.

The advent of managed care, with its many abuses and ill effects, has nonetheless supported cognitive therapy as a cost-effective and brief approach to some difficult emotional problems.

Personally, my course at the annual meetings of the American Psychiatric Association ("Cognitive Therapy: The Basics") has continued to be offered to enthusiastic clinicians in each of the past twelve years. Presentations of cognitive therapy at the CME, Inc. Psychiatric and Mental Health Congresses have continued annually, aided enormously by the support and encouragement of Mrs. Diane Turner. Invitations to teach the cognitive model continue at a significant rate. In the interim, I have been elected a Founding Fellow of the Academy of Cognitive Therapists. I have been invited to write an article on the treatment of dysthymia with cognitive therapy by a new journal, *Current Psychiatry*. Most important, since I arrived at Medical University of South Carolina (MUSC, Charleston) in 1997, I have continued to treat outpatients utilizing the model of cognitive therapy. In addition, a Department of Defense research grant enabled me to test my ideas within a population of cancer patients.

It is my hope that these opportunities and developments are reflected in this revised and expanded version of *Cognitive Therapy: A*

Practical Guide. Books and journal articles that have contributed to
our utilization of cognitive therapy are included in the bibliography
at the end of the book. Cases that have benefited from cognitive
therapy make up the significantly expanded final section: The Model
in Practice. The book has been edited to include the latest information that the author has found useful in presenting the cognitive
model to today's clinician in training.

Many workshop participants have told me enthusiastically that *A
Practical Guide* enabled them to not just learn about cognitive therapy, but to do cognitive therapy. It is my hope that this edition will
continue and further that tradition.

Dean Schuyler
Charleston, S.C.
November, 2002.

P<u>————</u>I
Preliminary
Issues

1

The Active Ingredient Question

My curiosity about why psychotherapy works when it does is not new. Its roots were planted in 1981. I felt bored, stale, waiting for some stimulation to break the sameness of each day. As a faculty member in the department of psychiatry at Georgetown, I taught the residents the course on affective disorders. I was a cognitive therapist in a world of psychodynamic thinkers. When I began to believe that nothing was likely to present itself, I decided to form the Psychotherapy Idea Group (PIG).

Brief letters were sent to four other members of the university family asking them to "join an elite group to study the process of psychotherapy." In contrast to the university's emphasis on strict hierarchy and role definition, PIG would attempt to stress equal status for its members. A graduating psychiatric resident, a fourth-year and a third-year resident were invited to join the senior members, a psychiatrist and a psychologist. Two were women; three were men. All but one accepted and we began meeting for 90 minutes twice monthly during work hours.

Initially, the sessions were informal and the focus was fixed on "identifying the active ingredients in successful psychotherapy." Whether the group member had seen two patients/clients or had "years of experience," his or her hypotheses were solicited and regarded equally. Most proposals for added structure (e.g., a journal club) were turned down. Articles passed freely among the group, but quoting from the writings of others was often received negatively unless accompanied by a novel idea.

Someone suggested that we invite guests, a kind of "PIG-of-the-Month." For the return of a pastrami sandwich, impressive guests joined our group: Morris Parloff, Leon Salzman, John Wiley, and

3

Loren Mosher were early invitees. Subsequent "Guest PIGS" included Paul Chodoff, Al and Carol Levinthal, Ted Beal, Irene Elkin, and Barry Wolfe. The question posed to them was always: "When your patients succeed in making changes, what are the active ingredients?"

Shortly after the group's first birthday, we began to meet monthly in the evenings at a member's home. A couple of original members dropped out, some to return subsequently. There were new people added, but the group never exceeded six in number and retained its mix with regard to age, gender, and background. Topics discussed ranged from schizophrenia and obsessive-compulsive personality to cognitive therapy, psychoanalysis, and psychotherapy research. As several of the group were not in the mainstream of the university's psychoanalytic orientation, PIG served to support and encourage dissenting views. Foremost, however, it stimulated a group of clinicians to think about their work as a process separate from considerations of theory.

Mark well that the following does not represent original research. It is instead the result of study group conversation over a four-year period, complemented by active reading of the psychotherapy research literature. Precise assignment of acknowledgment for any original ideas is blurred by the process of the group. Members over the four years were: Dean Schuyler, Bart Evans, Art Behrmann, Bob Hedaya, Marcia Chambers, Ellen Liebenluft, Dan Levine, Diane Arnkoff, Carol Glass, and Morris Parloff.

We began by artificially separating factors into three groupings: those relevant to the therapist, the patient, and the process. We began with three givens as fundamental parts of the psychotherapy transaction, as stated by Frank and Frank (1993): a healer, a sufferer, and a prescribed series of contacts.

THERAPIST VARIABLES

It has been written that the so-called relationship factors (i.e., warmth, acceptance, genuineness, empathy) may, by themselves, be the active ingredient in psychotherapeutic change. More likely, they may be necessary but not sufficient. Psychotherapy is a unique transaction, particularly when viewed in the context of medical care. An unwilling sufferer can be given an injection of penicillin to success-

fully treat a pneumococcal pneumonia. A medical specialist with a gruff and distant bedside manner may successfully diagnose and treat an obscure illness. There is, however, no analogy in psychotherapy.

Therefore, the first stage of therapy is often called *engagement*. The therapist's task is to form a bond with the patient that will facilitate the work they are bound to do. An atmosphere of warmth and acceptance of whatever the patient reveals of him or herself seems related to a positive outcome. The utilization of computers to simulate and deliver psychotherapy threatens the fundamental significance of the relationship factors. Can a distressed individual form a relationship with a computer screen? Will the patient fantasize a therapist behind or within the computer? Can psychotherapy carried out in this fashion be successful?

In 1974, I role-played a suicidal patient to test the adaptability of a simple computer program prototype at the University of Wisconsin. I took on the task with great skepticism but in the end felt that the computer had performed impressively well. Computers have not yet nullified the value of the human factor for me in the psychotherapy transaction, but with increasing computer sophistication will therapists someday be rendered obsolete?

A therapist who is genuine, real, and straightforward with his or her patient will usually find engagement an easy task. Psychotherapy consists of a purposeful oscillation between objectivity and comment, on the one hand, and feeling and empathy, on the other. *What the therapist says* can be taught through studying a manual and modeling after a supervisor. *What the therapist feels* may derive from a personality constellation that is difficult to acquire.

It seemed to us in PIG that it would be difficult for a therapist to help a patient he or she could not respect. The issue of *liking* seemed to be important, but not critical. Some of us endorsed the concept that the more nearly alike the therapist and the patient are, the easier it is for them to work together. Others said that there are blind spots where therapist and patient converge. Neither generalization seems warranted. Rather, a working pair that is on the same wavelength may have captured the necessary connection to facilitate change. Similarly, an experienced therapist may have an advantage with some patients and a clinician who is considered to be fresh or unspoiled might do better with others.

The polar opposite to the familiar concept of burnout in a therapist is motivation. When the clinician gets involved and shows interest, remembers details and demonstrates sensitivity, this requirement is seen to be met. It seems important that the therapist possess and retain a sense of optimism (the expectation that the patient will change). An element underlying self-confidence is the therapist's belief in the validity of his or her approach to psychotherapy.

It has been striking to me that some of my colleagues (who may be highly successful in their psychotherapy practice) can be absolutely tedious in a social setting. I always thought that interpersonal skill was a requisite for success in psychotherapy. Perhaps some "give at the office" and manifest less interest and enthusiasm elsewhere. When the group was challenged to examine skill in communication more closely, one's ability to admit being wrong or in error emerged as a useful trait. In addition, the capacity to use fresh, vivid language was seen to be an asset.

The therapist must be able to foster positive expectations in his or her patient. This entails providing encouragement, support, and the stimulus to risk trying something new. The ability to evoke an emotionally charged atmosphere (just enough; not too much) may be an element that fuels change. It was an observation that some clinicians have more tolerance for this element than do others.

The eight therapist variables that may facilitate change in the patient are summarized in Table 1.1.

TABLE 1.1: THERAPIST VARIABLES

1. Relationship factors
   a. Warmth, acceptance, genuineness, empathy
   b. Respect for the patient
   c. Liking the patient
2. Indications that therapist understands patient
3. Motivation
4. Optimism
5. Self-confidence
6. Communication (interpersonal) skill
7. Can provide support, encouragement to try something new
8. Ability to evoke (and tolerate) an emotionally charged atmosphere

PATIENT VARIABLES

Even the best of therapists don't help everyone. Conversely, some patients seem likely to succeed in therapy with almost anyone. Merely seeking help (sometimes just making the decision to do so) is enough to bring the sufferer some relief. He or she has decided to do something constructive about his or her difficulties. He has engaged an expert. He has begun to share a burden by unburdening himself.

It seems important for the patient to generate *hope for change* despite the symptom of hopelessness often encountered in the emotional disorders. The capacity to trust the therapist chosen appears to speed the process of psychotherapy. As a cognitive therapist whose referrals are often specifically for this model, I find that the shared belief in the method utilized seems to facilitate change.

Although psychotherapy has become much more broadly known through magazine articles and television talk shows, some patients still arrive expecting *instant change*. The patient's tenacity, persistence, or commitment is one trait that may separate those who gain from the rest.

We wondered why some patients have years of therapy with little change and then suddenly make rapid progress. We employed the term *readiness* to describe this state of a patient that seems to facilitate change. Then we tried to define it operationally. The *capacity to acknowledge distress* seemed to capture one aspect of it. Sufficient motivation to work hard was another factor. The *willingness to assume responsibility* for one's own behavior was the critical third feature.

Some patients orient themselves to the task of therapy by describing events in great detail, as well as the contribution and reaction of others to these events. They leave themselves out, accepting the role of observer instead of participant. It is possible, but unusual, to be able to change the behavior of another. With diligent effort, we seem to be able to make changes in ourselves. I recall a patient whom I had treated weekly for one year. She focused on "all the awful men who had mistreated her." One day, she decided to concentrate instead on herself (her beliefs and expectations of these men). We terminated successfully three months later.

Another factor that may contribute to readiness for change is the willingness to take prudent risks. Most striking in the chronically depressed, but encountered in acute depression as well, is the lack of *willingness to risk*. Compounding the problem is a risk-assessment approach that sees risk in places where others seem virtually certain of a positive outcome.

The patient's view of the therapist and their relationship incorporates several factors that seem to affect change. A positive view (the therapist is seen as confident, involved, likable) is felt to facilitate the therapeutic work. There is a similar effect when the relationship is felt to be warm, safe, and stimulating of the patient's thinking. Although perhaps obvious, it seems that nothing succeeds quite like success. The patient's awareness that he or she is making progress appears to facilitate further progress.

A summary of the ten active ingredient patient factors is found in Table 1.2.

THE MATCH BETWEEN PATIENT AND THERAPIST

While there seem to be "good" patients and "good" therapists, who are each more skilled than some of their peers, *goodness of fit* might be another active ingredient in change. Early in my training, I was taught (by Marc Hollender, at the University of Pennsylvania) that a

TABLE 1.2: PATIENT VARIABLES

1. Seeking help
2. Hope
3. Trust
4. Shared belief in therapist's method
5. Commitment (persistence)
6. Readiness
7. Sees therapist as confident, involved, likable
8. Sees relationship as warm, safe, stimulating
9. Experiences a sense of progress
10. Talks about him or herself, rather than circumstances or others

simple 2 × 2 table must be part of every patient evaluation (see Table 1.3).

In Box 1, the focus is on the personality styles of the therapist and the patient. The implication is that similarities in dealing with data and relating to others facilitate a good working relationship. In Box 2, the therapist's knowledge and familiarity with the patient's diagnosis and/or problem is spotlighted. I rarely treat schizophrenics, adolescents, or drug abusers. Most often, my patients are acutely or chronically depressed or anxious. Another group I work with has a rigidity of character style that impedes success or happiness. I try to refer the unmatched group to colleagues and to encourage referrals of the "good matches" to me.

Box 3 asks about the patient's expectations of the treatment. With dissemination of therapy-relevant information more widespread today, many patients choose a therapist at least in part for his or her model or approach. This box asks that the technique be one the patient believes is suitable for him or her. In the fourth box, the therapist is asked, "Is this technique likely to be useful for the patient's problem?" The attempt is made to challenge the notion that one approach works for everyone and to encourage the therapist to identify a match between technique and problem.

Given the strange (and occasionally wonderful) ways in which patient and therapist find each other, the notion of a match may strike some clinicians as arbitrary and unnecessary. Although there are additional active ingredient factors, I have found the match to be an important evaluation consideration. I have learned to refer those with whom I don't fit well to my colleagues.

TABLE 1.3: THE MATCH BETWEEN
PATIENT AND THERAPIST

	PATIENT	PROBLEM
THERAPIST	1	2
TECHNIQUE	3	4

PROCESS VARIABLES

This set of factors raises the question, "Does anything the therapist *does* make a difference or is the relationship the active factor in change?" I believe that the process contributes significantly to change. I also believe that some psychotherapies package the process factors more powerfully than others.

An early issue for the therapist to consider involves the patient's concept of what he or she must do in therapy. We believe that a clear understanding by the patient of his role facilitates change. Some patients referred for treatment have had substantial experience in psychotherapy. Some have read about it or heard about it from family or friends. Some still make the analogy to a doctor visit and expect to be the passive recipient of advice leading to relief. It has been shown that formal role induction instructions help to bring the less experienced patient up to speed.

Whatever the model of psychotherapy chosen, the patient is usually asked to become an observer of his or her own thoughts, feelings, and actions. No one model provided to explain the patient's distress has proven to be globally better than any competing model. More important, it seems, is to provide for the patient an explanation for

FIGURE 1.1: THE NINE-DOT PROBLEM

Connect the dots by four straight lines *without* lifting pencil from paper.

(Taken from P. Watzlawick, J. Weakland, & R. Fisch [1974]. *Change: Principles of problem formation and problem resolution.* New York: Norton.)

FIGURE 1.2: THE NINE-DOT PROBLEM SOLUTION

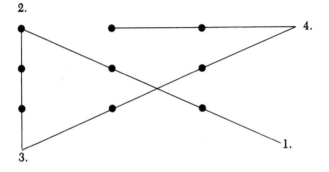

First-order change: One attempts to solve the task within the ("assumed") rectangle.

Second-order change: Examine not the dots, but the assumptions about the dots.

(Taken from P. Watzlawick, J. Weakland, & R. Fisch [1974]. *Change: Principles of problem formation and problem resolution.* New York: Norton.)

his or her distress. It is of interest that the provision of a myth seems more important than its content.

I have found it useful to inquire about my patient's concept of anatomy, physiology, and even "how the mind works" (where relevant). Often these ideas have proven factually false. Some relief and relearning can be provided with simple, direct, corrective information. For some (e.g., depressed) persons, certain functions (e.g., expressivity, assertion, independence) are lacking because the necessary skills to perform them are lacking as well. These individuals need to be taught—by modeling, reading a book, suggestion and practice—how to add a lacking skill to their repertoire.

Three technique-based interventions that are a part of most psychotherapies are modeling, exposure, and mastery. Behavior therapists have described each of these most clearly. Watching the therapist engage in a behavior or approach a problem may overcome some

patients' resistance to risk. For fears and phobias, actually confronting the feared object or situation may be a central ingredient in change. For the depressed, the experience of mastering a task or assignment in therapy may begin to challenge their belief in their own ineffectiveness.

For us, reframing as a process seemed to capture the essence of what therapists and patients do in addition to what they are for each other. Reframing is defined as: changing the conceptual and/or the emotional setting or viewpoint with which something is held, seen, or understood. Placing the interpretation of an event or relationship in another framework may change its consequences and its meaning for the individual.

The cognitive therapist often calls this *breaking the set* or *shifting the set*—for example, the negative cognitive set that dominates thinking in depression. Watzlawick, Weakland, and Fisch (1974) note how Tom Sawyer reframed the drudgery of whitewashing a fence into a pleasure for which participants had to pay. They discuss first-order change as a process of rearranging variables in the same field into different sequences. All factors remain within the original system. (My grandmother would compare this concept to housecleaning as a process of "moving the dust from one place to another.") In second-order change, however, there is a shift in the premises (rules) on which the system is based. This is the essence of reframing.

The nine-dot problem will be familiar to some readers (see Figure 1.1). The problem is insoluble given the assumption that all lines must originate and terminate within a mythical rectangle drawn around the

TABLE 1.4: PROCESS VARIABLES

1. Role induction
2. Patient becomes an observer
3. Providing an explanatory system
4. Providing corrective information
5. Teaching new skills
6. Facilitating perspective
7. Modeling
8. Exposure
9. Mastery
10. Reframing

dots. Once you challenge this assumption (free yourself from this limitation), many solutions present themselves (for one solution, see Figure 1.2). Focusing on the assumptions about the dots, rather than on the dots themselves, leads to the solution. This notion of reframing may be the process the patient describes when he says: "I still have some of the same problems I had when I began therapy, but I feel (think) differently about them."

The process factors are summarized in Table 1.4.

2
P̲ractical
Psychotherapy

I have been fortunate to be invited to many lecture halls to speak about cognitive therapy over the past 32 years. Several of my hosts have taken the liberty of suggesting titles for my presentation. Their suggestions (most of which I have taken) illustrate the understanding they have (with variable exposure to the system) of the cognitive model for psychotherapy.

I was invited to Memphis to lecture by Hagop Akiskal, professor of psychiatry at the University of Tennessee. Finding traditional psychotherapy ideas to be too often muddled, he asked me to speak about "Practical Psychotherapy for Depression." Barney Carroll, soon after becoming chairman of psychiatry at Duke, asked me to speak about "Psychotherapy in the Real World." His concern was that some academicians had lost touch with the systems guiding some private practitioners in their outpatient work. In Buffalo, Murray Morphy adapted a version of the old campaign slogan of Adlai Stevenson, coming up with "Cognitive Therapy: Talking Sense to the American Patient." He expressed the worry that psychotherapy was often too jargon-filled for his taste.

Psychotherapy is a process for educating (or sometimes reeducating) the patient. Bearing in mind that most patients present for therapy because of distress, and not to educate themselves, psychotherapists must offer the hope of relief from distress. If not cure, which I believe is a rare outcome, psychotherapy must help the patient. The patient seeks change. This acknowledged, there are certain practical considerations that I believe are necessary for any psychotherapeutic system to work. Systematization of these ideas was stimulated by Dr. Akiskal's suggested title for my talk.

PRINCIPLES OF PRACTICAL
PSYCHOTHERAPY

*1. Educate the Patient About His or Her
Clinical Condition*

Patients have brought to my office a wide range of approaches to understanding the nature of their distress, from the curse of the Devil or the will of God to chemical derangement, hereditary taint, parental models, lack of necessary skills, laziness and ineptitude, and more. One task of the psychotherapist is to present a clear understanding of the psychopathology to the patient. This may serve to challenge and counteract the patient's attempt to attribute his or her distress to an external, irreversible source.

2. Educate and Engage Significant Others

Traditional psychotherapy has taught that interaction with someone other than the identified patient may dilute the effectiveness of the treatment. Family systems approaches have argued that the *patient* is only the system's way of defining the problem. Since the *distress* is in the system, several persons may have to be involved in the therapy to achieve change.

I have taken a middle route. I don't believe it is necessary to see everyone in the patient's family in every case. However, significant information is often forthcoming from someone other than the patient. I encourage gaining access to this information by meeting with a significant other, either accompanied by or in the absence of the patient him or herself. The configuration is often dictated by the level of trust within the family system. The need to maintain the patient's confidentiality may make this meeting a difficult, one-way transaction, but for me it has nearly always been worthwhile. Family members frequently have questions about anxiety or depressive syndromes that can be answered in a straightforward fashion. Commonly, they want to know how they can best help. Sometimes they reveal their own distress or shed light on how they may contribute to the patient's problem. In this instance, a referral for help can lead to major familial gain.

3. Maintain Your Optimism and Mobilize the Patient's Hope

I have often been asked, "Since you seem like such an *up* person, how do you do it, seeing so many depressed people and listening to their problems all day?" My optimism is rooted in the belief that depressive and anxiety disorders are two of the most responsive conditions to treatment. At some point, I usually tell my patients that I have seen many like themselves change markedly in a short time.

Mobilizing hope, particularly in someone who is depressed and hopeless, seems like a contradictory expectation. The contradiction is resolved if you consider hope in a narrow, defined sense. It is possible, I have found, for a depressed person to maintain simultaneously a pessimistic outlook on the future and an attitude of hope about the likelihood of the therapy to achieve a desired result.

4. Identify and Utilize the Patient's Resources

At the risk of reducing to the concrete some of the abstract aspects of change in psychotherapy, I have often presented their task to my patients as "using the practical, goal-directed approach you have applied in the past to such tasks as fixing your car to the problem of fixing your thinking." Certainly, some people are clinically depressed or anxious because they lack a skill that would enable them to be more effective. In these cases, that skill may be *taught* to them in the therapy. In many cases, however, the necessary skills are already present, but the patient is *obstacled* from utilizing them. Identification and removal of these obstacles enable the patient to put his or her usual resources to work on the problem. This may be, for some, the definition of the cognitive work of therapy—removing the obstacle.

5. Teach Skills When They Are Lacking

My mother told me many years ago that she strongly preferred that I never become a teacher (like her). I guess I both followed and abandoned her advice. Cognitive therapy has been fairly called a *psychoeducational treatment*. At its most specific, it may identify a skill that is lacking and devise a way to teach that skill to the patient. Some skills that come to mind are assertiveness, expression of feelings, and

decision-making. Methods to convey those skills include modeling by the therapist, assignment of relevant readings, and the generation of appropriate alternatives in a specified situation.

6. Accept the Patient

Early in my career, I injudiciously told a bright and prolific supervisee that I felt that I could help any patient whom I liked. While I have learned from experience that the statement is naive (and that I might at least have specified *any motivated patient*), I believe this quality of acceptance is central to a successful therapeutic outcome. Experience has taught me that I can find *something to like* in many patients. When first impressions are negative, I sometimes grow to like a patient over time. When I believe a patient and I are a bad match, I make an effort to refer him or her to someone more suitable.

7. Encourage the Patient to Become Self-Observant

Beck and colleagues (1979) have written about the patient's adopting the orientation of viewing himself as the object of scientific inquiry. In point of fact, the patient in cognitive therapy is encouraged to identify relevant thoughts and to analyze them by noting errors in thinking. This capacity of "taking distance from oneself"and viewing thoughts, feelings, and behavior more objectively may be a central feature of all psychotherapy.

8. Provide Structure When Needed

Particularly for the acutely anxious or acutely depressed person, the defining of limits or the establishment of an approach to a problem may, by itself, bring some relief. Often the capacity to establish and utilize structure is lost early in a crisis situation. The methods of successive approximation or modeling may help the patient regain a lost sense of mastery and lead to the discovery of solutions to problems.

9. Discourage Major Decision-Making

It is a tenet of traditional psychotherapy that the period of treatment is often ill-suited to the making of major decisions. The cognitive model suggests that thinking in acute emotional states may be

distorted and, therefore, unrepresentative of the patient's usual cognitive output. It stands to reason that, under these conditions, decisions reached may not reflect the patient's so-called usual values, priorities, or choices. Therefore, it is recommended that major decisions (e.g., leaving a job or spouse) might better be postponed until the distortions are no longer dominant.

10. Encourage Appropriate Risk-Taking

Particularly among the depressed and the chronically passive, there is often a reluctance to take risks. The probability assessment that ordinarily precedes risking may be wildly distorted. Ask, for example, a person phobic of flight travel what the probability is of his or her plane crashing. Ask the socially anxious man or woman what the probability is of being turned down when he or she asks someone out on a date. Ask the anxious parent what the probability is of his or her child's accepting advice or a limit. Ask the timid employee what the probability is of the boss granting his or her request for a raise. Often I have found it helpful to identify with the patient some serious, some middling, and some minor risks. Then the clinician can discuss the restrictions imposed by the refusal to risk and the benefits that may result from taking reasonable risks.

11. Provide the Patient With
an Explanatory System

Although Frank (1974) maintained that the content of the explanation is secondary to its provision, I believe it is critical for the system to be one that the patient can comprehend. I have found that the notion of cognitions driving affects and behaviors is a simple one for most patients to grasp. The mastery that often results from viewing thoughts objectively, defining errors consistently made, and trying out alternatives forms for me a solid endorsement of the cognitive model.

12. Encourage the Generation
of Alternative Beliefs

All psychotherapies do this. Cognitive therapy perhaps approaches it most directly. Critical beliefs are identified; consistent errors in thinking are pointed out; then new options or alternate choices are

found, and their consequences are examined. Experiments may be done to test the new choices.

13. Encourage (Provide) Mastery Experiences

Again, successful psychotherapy will either present or lead to opportunities for mastery. Cognitive therapy does this directly in the psychotherapeutic work. When an individual no longer feels himself a prisoner of his or her distorted thinking, a sense of mastery over one's thoughts may lead to powerful changes in feelings and behavior.

14. Facilitate the Regaining of Perspective

This is the central principle of crisis intervention treatment. In most short-term psychotherapy, the regaining of lost perspective is one way of looking at a successful outcome. Once more, cognitive therapy approaches this practical need concretely. This may take the form of a shift of priorities, the acceptance of a limit, or the acknowledgment that outcomes cannot be controlled.

WHAT DOES A COGNITIVE THERAPIST TREAT?

Cognitive therapy began as a model for the treatment of unipolar depression (Beck, Rush, Shaw, & Emery, 1979), and then acute anxiety disorders (Beck, Emery, & Greenberg, 1985). It has since been applied to chronic depressive disorders as well. What began as individual psychotherapy has been applied in work with groups (Sank & Shaffer, 1984), and what began as a short-term model has been extended for long-term, character problems (see Chapter 9).

When I mentioned at a lecture that schizophrenia is not usefully approached with this model, I was given a reference challenging this notion (Perris, 1989). I believe that the borderline patient is often beyond the reach of cognitive therapy; however, others routinely employ the language of cognitive therapy in these cases. Marsha Linehan (1993) has developed a systematic approach to the borderline patient that relies substantially on cognitive therapy principles.

Although all of my work has been with outpatients, cognitive ther-

apy is used with inpatients; in fact, many psychiatric hospitals have established inpatient units that employ the cognitive model.

Although I have worked exclusively with adults, there are reports of successful outcomes with children and adolescents (Wilkes, Belsher, Rush, & Frank, 1994). There are reports of successful cognitive interventions to treat phobic patients, substance abusers, and those with sexual dysfunctions (Emery, Hollon, & Bedrosian, 1981). Beck (1988) has written about using a cognitive approach to explore relationship problems among couples, as have Dattilio and Padesky (1990).

WHO IS A CANDIDATE?

Clinicians frequently hope that an alternative model will provide a framework to approach those patients they find most difficult to treat. While cognitive therapy has been applied in some of these cases (particularly when the patient has derived little benefit from psychoanalytic treatment), in the main a good candidate for traditional therapy will be a good candidate for cognitive therapy as well. The capacity to be introspective (or psychologically minded) is one requisite. If the patient can't identify automatic thoughts or can't work on a conceptual level, this approach will usually not be fruitful. The patient expecting magical answers or demanding that the therapist do the work will usually not succeed with this model.

It is clear to me that age, in and of itself, predicts neither success nor failure in psychotherapy. The patient who fails to engage does no better in cognitive therapy than elsewhere. Those unmotivated to change offer the same challenge to the cognitive therapist as to more traditional clinicians. I know of no answer for them.

THE COURSE OF THERAPY

It seems to take about three to five sessions to teach a motivated patient the cognitive model. For a few, this will suffice as treatment, since the structure of the method will support hope and a sense of mastery. Using the techniques may combat demoralization and help these patients regain perspective. Their own resources will then take over to help them deal with the problems they face. For them, therapeutic contact ends at this point. They may call or return at a later date.

For most patients, short-term cognitive therapy is prescribed to deal with acute depression or anxiety. Therapy may last from three to six months, involving 10–20 (weekly or biweekly) sessions. Antidepressant medication may accompany treatment in appropriate depressed patients.

For character (personality) problems, long-term cognitive therapy may require several years of work. The frequency of contact is typically once weekly. A focus on schemas replaces that on cognitions in the short-term'model. Relationship elements receive special consideration (see Chapter 9).

For both short- and long-term courses, follow-up visits at increasing intervals (usually beginning at one month and preceding to three to six months) may be scheduled subsequent to termination (see Chapter 12).

TRAINING IMPLICATIONS

It is the job of the good teacher to engage his or her students. I have found this to be most challenging in those settings in which psychodynamics are taught as basic to all psychotherapy. This problem is compounded by a course placement late in the student's training. My first opportunity to teach cognitive therapy at Georgetown was with fourth-year psychiatric residents. Subsequently, second-year residents were presented with the model at a time before their views of intervention choice had hardened. This was more enjoyable (for both teacher and students) and more successful.

One engagement technique is to demonstrate the method by having the students apply it to a problem in living of their own. Once they demonstrate the capacity to frame a personal situation in cognitive language, the application to patient issues is facilitated.

A frequently encountered problem for me as a teacher has been the opposition provided by some psychoanalytically oriented supervisors. Since the supervisory group often wields considerable influence with the trainees, engaging this group may be a prerequisite for a successful learning experience with the students.

There is little that can aid the trainee in visualizing the technique of therapy like viewing the teacher behind a one-way mirror or on videotape. An opportunity to ask questions or generate alternative approaches following the demonstration complements this approach.

The up-to-date clinical program, whether in psychiatry, social work or psychology, should present the model early, provide role models of cognitive therapists as teachers and supervisors, require that some patients be treated and reviewed, assign representative readings, and convey an acceptance of the cognitive model as "one of the roads to Rome."

My arrival at the Medical University of South Carolina in 1997 coincided with a departmental effort to revise the curriculum for teaching psychotherapy to psychiatry residents. The outcome of our deliberations provided me with the opportunity to prepare trainees optimally to deliver cognitive therapy.

Two 60-minute presentations in the PG (post-graduate) I year introduced the model. Four 90-minute slots in the PGII year provided cognitive conceptualizations of anxiety syndromes and depression. Four 90-minute classes in the PGIII year were devoted to case presentations: typically major depression and dysthymia, panic disorder, specific and social phobia, and obsessive-compulsive disorder. Elsewhere in the curriculum, the resident was exposed to cognitive therapy for substance abuse, eating disorders, and posttraumatic stress.

In the trainee's second year, a 26-week course with half the group (repeated each semester) reviewed elements forming the Foundations of Psychotherapy. The class read *Persuasion and Healing* (Frank and Frank, 1993), considered boundary and confidentiality issues, the therapeutic relationship, the concepts of reframing and exposure, issues relevant to self-help, the impact of childhood on adult problems, and issues of particular relevance to women. Each trainee presented a case, with class discussion focused on how psychotherapy would be prescribed or planned for the patient.

The centerpiece for learning cognitive therapy in psychiatry residency training is individual supervision. I met with PGY-III trainees once weekly for periods varying from six months to a year. Although there have been chapters of the book assigned earlier, all were expected to read and master the *Practical Guide*. Questions were formulated and discussed, additional readings were assigned, but the hallmark of supervision was a session-by-session review of the trainee's doing cognitive therapy.

Through the generous encouragement of Sloan Manning and the *Primary Care Companion to the Journal of Clinical Psychiatry*, a resident who successfully treated a patient utilizing cognitive therapy was rewarded with an opportunity to publish his or her case report.

The—II
Cognitive Model

3

Prelude to the Cognitive Model

Psychotherapy is traditionally considered to be a long-term venture. Meaningful changes made by patients are thought to involve character structure (or personality). The therapist, in psychodynamic psychotherapy, serves as a passive guide for the patient, who seeks illumination of the present in understanding events of the past. A prominent role is assigned to the unconscious. In this place, to which access is available via dreams, free associations and inferences, reside the thoughts and feelings that conflict with the realities facing the distressed individual.

The relationship of patient to therapist, if kept sufficiently free of realistic details, is thought to serve as a mirror into the determinants of significant relationships in the past, as well as a reflection of the formulations governing relationships in general. This has been called transference. Its counterpart in the therapist (thoughts and feelings about the patient that divert his or her attention from the task at hand) has been called countertransference.

The testing of assumptions and the "working through" of feelings about the therapeutic relationship are seen by many psychodynamic therapists as an important road to change for the patient. These characteristics associated with psychodynamic psychotherapy are summarized in Table 3.1.

BRIEF THERAPY

The assumption that therapy must be long-term has been challenged effectively by Budman (1985) and others. In brief therapy, the therapist and patient agree to a contract specifying termination after about three to six months (10 to 20 sessions). This is a *prospective*

TABLE 3.1: AN OVERVIEW OF CHARACTERISTICS
OF PSYCHODYNAMIC PSYCHOTHERAPY

1. Long-term
2. Oriented to character change
3. Often dwells in the past
4. Often prescribes a passive role for the therapist
5. Assigns a prominent role to the unconscious
6. Emphasizes the therapist-patient relationship (so-called transference)

judgment made during the evaluation phase of psychotherapy (not a retrospective judgment made after therapy ends prematurely!).

Some have suggested that one factor determining the lengthiness of psychotherapy is "psychotherapeutic perfectionism" (Budman, 1985). Psychotherapy, the argument goes, aims at *cure* or *complete change* and anything short of this is unacceptable. The counterargument asks of therapy that it "be helpful," that it facilitate relief from distress. Consumer demand and third-party payment have supported more focal and less lengthy psychotherapies.

With this shift in emphasis has come a move away from the psychodynamic perspective on growth and development (psychosexual stages, regressions, and fixations) and a movement toward a life-cycle concept of development (Erickson, 1963). In this approach, critical periods of development are identified throughout the life cycle in which *ego qualities* emerge. These so-called eight ages of man begin with basic trust and proceed through autonomy, initiative, industry, identity, intimacy, generativity, and ego integrity. This approach leads to treatment that is periodic (rather than continuous), emphasizes follow-up (even when well), and offers the therapist's long-term availability for future consultation.

What does this brief therapy look like? Most often, it is time-limited. Goals are discussed and agreed upon by therapist and patient during the evaluation. The focus is maintained in the here-and-now, with only occasional brief forays into the past for some specific purpose. The therapist's role is active, with the interaction more often a dialogue than a patient monologue. A premium is placed upon rapid

assessment, therapeutic flexibility, and careful patient selection. The characteristics of brief therapy are summarized in Table 3.2.

Cognitive therapy is but one model among several that qualify as brief therapy. Behavior therapy was a predecessor, now firmly established as a useful approach to habit change. The work of Wolpe (1958) is generally credited with stimulating clinicians to apply the principles of learning theory to help clients change behavior. Applying laboratory findings from studies of lower animals to their human analogues led to the formulation of techniques and strategies for treating clinical anxiety, depression, sexual problems, and substance abuse. In addition, so-called habits like cigarette smoking, stuttering, and overeating have been approached by behavioral analysis and intervention.

Systematic desensitization, a technique derived from classical conditioning that combines deep muscle relaxation with graded exposure to an anxiety-evoking stimulus, was an early suggestion for treating anxiety disorders. The token economy system, derived from operant conditioning, was adopted as a structure for the inpatient treatment of some severe emotional disorders.

The brief behavior therapy approach stressed an initial behavioral analysis to identify antecedent and consequent conditions of the behavior to be changed. Then a baseline measure was made of the behavior before therapy began. Finally, a paradigm or strategy derived from

TABLE 3.2: CHARACTERISTICS OF BRIEF THERAPY

1. Time-limited
2. Goal-oriented
3. Here-and-now focus
4. Active role for the therapist
5. Rapid assessment
6. Therapeutic flexibility
7. Opportunity to ventilate
8. Rapid formation of a therapeutic alliance
9. Careful patient selection

Derived from S. Budman (1985). *Forms of brief therapy.* New York: Guilford.

learning theory was designed as a basis for intervention. Careful measurements were made to document change when it occurred. Booster sessions were available should problems recur.

Social skills that were lacking were taught by didactic presentation, reading assignments, modeling, coaching and roleplaying. Written materials were employed to chart activity, monitor mood, track changes, and provide reinforcement for change.

Behavior therapy principles emphasized structure, applied theories of reinforcement, encouraged self-monitoring, and focused on goal attainment. Adherents initially stressed the necessity for all variables considered to be observable. By definition, this requirement excluded cognition. Over the past several decades there has been a convergence of cognitive and behavior therapists, as a willingness has developed to consider thoughts as "acceptable data" for psychotherapy.

Interpersonal psychotherapy (ITP) was developed by Klerman and Weissman (see Klerman, Weissman, Rounsaville, & Chevron, 1984) in the late 1970s. It aims to provide a short-term interventive focus for problems related specifically to grieving, the resolution of role disputes, role transitions, and interpersonal deficits. Initially designed for the depressed patient, this system emphasizes the relationship of disruption or deprivation of attachment bonds to the onset of depression. Through a renegotiation of the interpersonal circumstances relevant to the individual's emotional state, practitioners seek to reduce depressive symptoms and improve functioning. There is liberal use made here of both cognitive and behavioral principles and techniques. Sessions are held once weekly, and therapy is planned to last for three to four months.

Approaches to the identified interpersonal problems include outlining the issues, expectations, wants, options, and resources of the patient and his or her spouse. Parallels with previous relationships may be drawn. The *interpersonal strategy* of each individual may be discussed and contrasted. Finally, alternative approaches and their consequences are considered.

In response to the stress on shorter and more focal psychotherapy in the 1970s and 1980s, the psychodynamic schools developed delivery systems to compete with the brief therapies. Sifneos (1972), Mann (1973), Malan (1973), and Davanloo (1976) are among the major contributors in this regard.

COGNITIVE THERAPY

Cognitive therapy was formulated in the early 1960s by Beck at the University of Pennsylvania. Contributions were made by Mahoney (1974) and Meichenbaum (1977). There are many similarities and overlaps between this work and the rational emotive therapy (RET) approach of Ellis (1962). Furthermore, students of each of the above have written and extended the model and its usefulness.

A comprehensive review of the many streams of cognitive therapy is available elsewhere (Dobson, 1988); here I will concentrate instead on presenting the system as it was taught to me by Beck in 1969–1971 and as I have employed it in my practice of psychotherapy.

As a model for psychotherapeutic intervention, cognitive therapy (Beck, 1976) seeks to:

1. Identify cognitions relevant to the presenting problem
2. Recognize connections among cognitions, affects, and behaviors
3. Examine the evidence for and against key beliefs
4. Encourage the patient to try out alternative conceptualizations
5. Teach the patient to carry out the cognitive process independently

Beck (1976) elaborated specific changes in the form and content of thinking for a broad range of clinical problems. He then applied the model to clinical depression, hypomania, anxiety, phobia, paranoid state, hysteria, obsessions, and compulsions. Because the earliest applications concentrated upon clinical depression (Beck, 1961, 1963, 1967), let us follow the elaboration of the model with depression as an example (see Beck, 1967).

A COGNITIVE MODEL
OF DEPRESSION

It is said that a depressed person's thinking more closely resembles that of another depressed person than it does his or her own thinking prior to the onset of the depression. In form, conceptualization becomes more global, universal, and all-encompassing. There is a dominance of *shoulds* that has been called moralistic. In content, the depressed individual usually sees the disorder as an *irreversible* change.

As the depression extends and deepens, he or she views the world more and more narrowly, constricting his or her focus to *personalistic* concerns. A tendency, sometimes present in the premorbid state and sometimes new to the depressed condition, is to think in a *dichotomous* fashion. People, events, and situations are seen as black or white (polarized). There is no middle ground—no grays, no alternatives to the categorical extremes. Some qualities of thinking in depression are noted in Table 3.3.

As a depression develops, predictable distortions occur in the patient's thinking. A hypothetical look at the evolution of depression in an individual will illustrate one application of the cognitive model to help understand a clinical problem. Two predisposing factors mark the starting point of development. The first is early loss (e.g., of a parent who dies or leaves) or rejection. The second is the learning of perfectionistic standards that limit later adaptability.

Two kinds of precipitating events may mark the onset of the depressive disorder. The first is some significant subtraction from the patient's personal domain (the sum total of traits, values, and issues considered important by the patient). The second is a chronic gap between the patient's expectations and outcomes.

Initially, the meaning assigned to the precipitating event is *polarized* by the depressed person. The patient's focus narrows to the negative aspects of the event, to the exclusion of the positives. Finally, the focus shifts to (and gets stuck on) the self. The depressed person "jumps to negative conclusions" about him or herself. These have been called *arbitrary inferences* or conclusions derived from insufficient data. Selecting one detail out of context and magnifying its sig-

TABLE 3.3: QUALITIES
OF DEPRESSIVE THINKING

1. Global
2. Moralistic
3. Irreversible
4. Personalistic
5. Dichotomous

Derived from A. T. Beck (1967). *Depression: Clinical, experimental, and theoretical aspects.* New York: Harper & Row.

nificance is a second common cognitive error; this has been called *selective abstraction*. The self-view of the patient is modified to see him or herself as deficient or defective.

Now depressive schemas dominate the patient's thinking. A schema is a unit of belief, a principle or main organizing idea. Schemas are formed early in life through the influence of role models, direct feedback, cultural factors, and early experience. When depressed, these negative schemas (like large "pipes") hypertrophy, so that much of the data input is filtered through them. The result is a broad range of *negative generalizations* about the self. These generalizations support a growing tendency to personalize events and situations, to become extremely self-critical and self-blaming. They are soon extended to encompass input about the world and the future as well as the self.

This globally negative cognitive set (negative orientation of the patient's thinking) leads to behavioral *withdrawal*. Apathy and *loss of motivation* follow. Physical symptoms of depression appear: disrupted sleep, appetite loss, constipation, low energy, easy fatigue, poor concentration, and diminished attention span. A *feedback loop* in which the patient's appraisal of his or her own negativity creates more negativity, now worsens the condition. Low self-worth, pessimism, and helplessness are common cognitive consequences. Suicidal ideas may be organized around a theme of escape, cessation (relief), or punishment.

Withdrawal is often complemented by *passivity* (e.g., unwillingness to risk, little behavioral initiative) and an increase in escape and

---

TABLE 3.4: DEVELOPMENT OF A DEPRESSION

1. Polarization of key event
2. Selective focus on the negative
3. Focus stuck on the self
4. Negative generalizations about the self
5. Negative generalizations about the world and the future
6. Behavioral withdrawal
7. Loss of motivation
8. Physical symptoms of depression appear
9. Feedback loop worsens syndrome
10. Passivity and escape and avoidance behaviors increase

Derived from A. T. Beck. (1967). *Depression: Clinical, experimental, and theoretical aspects.* New York: Harper & Row.

avoidance behaviors. Now, the patient's usual activities and obligations cannot be undertaken. He or she is often out of work, functioning poorly in relationships, and extremely dissatisfied with him or herself. The downward slide into depression is summarized in Table 3.4.

Understanding clinical problems like depression within the framework of a cognitive model prepares the therapist-patient team to attack the problem with cognitive therapy. The model will be explained in detail in Chapter 4. A broad range of therapeutic techniques will follow in Chapter 5.

4

Cognitive Model: The Basics

It is my hope that the readership of this book includes clinicians of differing backgrounds in training and some students who are not committed yet to psychology, medicine, or social work. If this hope is borne out, these opening words will have relevance only to those committed to some other system (e.g., psychoanalytic, behavioral) but not to the truly open-minded (whether they're eclectic clinicians or students not yet paying their dues to one system of psychotherapy).

If you have joined a particular school of thought, I ask you now to attempt to lay aside its basic assumptions (for a while). If you don't, you face the danger of trying to learn the cognitive model within the language you already use. For this reason, a paradigm shift is in order for those already committed to a system other than the cognitive one.

Attempting such a paradigm shift raises questions of motivation, flexibility, and security. Motivationally, why do you need to consider an alternative way of understanding people and problems? Is there something in it for you? For your patients or clients? For the clinician seeking to add some techniques to his or her armamentarium, I believe that the interventions are of little value alone, without their theoretical underpinning.

Particularly for those of us who have been doing therapy for quite a while, it is difficult to retain the flexibility that permits looking at a problem in a different way. There is a tendency to say that the alternative represents nothing new or to translate it into more familiar concepts. Finally, many of us seem to require the "membership" that accompanies belonging to a particular "union," whether it be behavioral, analytic, or biological. Over time, we make this a part of our identity, so that suspending it, even for a brief time, may be an overwhelming challenge.

Now that we have set aside restricting assumptions, let us proceed with the four components of the cognitive model: basic principles, the automatic thought, cognitive errors, and cognitive schemas. I will discuss each in turn.

BASIC PRINCIPLES

The cognitive therapist understands the person as an information-processing organism, one who takes in data (from both outside sources and inside readings) and generates appraisals. The individual's feelings and behavior are seen to be influenced in the here-and-now by one's thoughts. Most patients come to my office wishing to change some element of how they feel or what they do. If one of the therapeutic pair doubts that thoughts, feelings, and actions are related, it is likely that changing the latter two by working with the former won't make much sense. Here is one point at which a shared belief in the therapist's method truly comes into play!

The cognitive therapist believes that humans are capable of altering their thinking by dealing with conscious processes. A question commonly asked by psychoanalytically oriented colleagues is, "Do you believe in an unconscious?" In fact, I believe that the concept is a useful one, but it plays no role in the psychotherapy I do.

A second question, often posed from the analytic viewpoint, concerns the importance and therapeutic utility of exploring the past. The cognitive model does not dwell on the past. It is evident that cognitions (e.g., thoughts, assumptions, expectations) must have their origins prior to their emergence in the present. Indeed, some beliefs are seen to be learned quite early in life. However, one's cognitive set (the totality of an individual's beliefs, values, and appraisals) is constantly subject to modification. Surely, those beliefs held longest and given the most support will be the most difficult to dislodge. The original "learning" of these cognitions occurs by role-modeling, by feedback from significant figures, by the powerful effects of culture, and by experience. It seems logical that cognitive distortions (which form the basis for clinical problems) are learned the same way.

While the first set of principles of the cognitive model relates to our understanding the patient and his or her problems, the next group focuses on the process of psychotherapy itself. Therapy attempts to harness the patient's usual problem-solving skills. When certain skills

are absent (e.g., assertiveness, expressivity, independence), these may be taught as part of the treatment.

Psychotherapy is an active, collaborative venture between therapist and patient. The story is told that an analytic failure is typically assigned to the patient, while a behavior therapy failure is typically seen as the responsibility of the therapist. In cognitive therapy, the collaborating pair takes the credit for success or the blame for failure.

Psychotherapy remains rooted in the here-and-now. Although an initial history may examine the origins of some key beliefs in the past, and some patients insist on tracing a relevant cognition back to its root, the active ingredients for change are seen to exist in the present. The therapist may reorient the patient to the present with comments such as, "Of course the idea came from somewhere. Our task now, however, is to determine what you want to do about it, and then to develop some alternatives."

One of the code words of the analytic method is *transference*. For a while, the reverence with which it was treated in conversations among clinicians convinced me that it had some mystical meaning. I ventured one time to suggest to an analytic colleague that it meant that the sum of thoughts and feelings attached to a significant figure in the past forms the basis of appraising a person in the present. When he seemed nearly satisfied, I wondered why such a to-do was made over a concept that seemed so obvious.

Change in cognitive therapy is not understood in terms of transference. The therapeutic relationship may serve as a vehicle for examining beliefs and appraisals, but more often the subject is another relationship of the patient or the patient himself. The therapist is active and collaborative, hardly the traditional *blank screen*. Self-disclosure, when done within limits (see Chapter 5), is not proscribed in this model. A summary statement might be that in cognitive therapy change can occur without dealing with transferential material directly.

THE CENTRAL CONCEPT
OF THE AUTOMATIC THOUGHT

For many of you, an understanding of the core concept in the cognitive model will involve a trip back to the teachings of college psychology. A basic learning principle was taught to me in terms of

stimulus-response. This was illustrated (in my day) with the example of Pavlov's dog. The dog would salivate in response to the presentation of the stimulus of food. You could elicit the same response (e.g., salivation) to a different stimulus (e.g., a bell) if you paired the ringing of the bell (e.g., conditioned stimulus) with the presentation of the food (e.g., unconditioned stimulus). After a few trials, the dog would respond with salivation to the sound of the bell alone.

The stimulus-response learning paradigm we will focus on concerns stimulus events or situations. The responses are feelings (reactions) or behaviors (actions). For example, if you went to your boss this morning to ask for a raise and he or she said, "no," you might be angry. But you also might be sad, relieved, or anxious. There are several likely responses to the same stimulus event. A clue to the response is available in the variable that occurs between stimulus and response—the intervening variable (see Figure 4.1).

Since this intervening variable is not directly observable, it has been called a *private event*. It is elicited by asking the patient or client to examine his or her thinking and to supply it for the therapist. It has been referred to as the "silent statement people tell themselves" (Meichenbaum, 1974). Using this formulation, Meichenbaum explains how people describe, elaborate, or appraise a situation before they react to it. This intervening process between event and reaction has also been called *self-talk*. In plainest English, this process supplies the meaning to the stimulus, guiding the selection of a re-

FIGURE 4.1: THE AUTOMATIC THOUGHT STIMULUS RESPONSE

STIMULUS	intervening variable	RESPONSE
event	intervening variable	reaction
situation	private event	action
	black box	
	meaning	
	silent statement	
	self-talk	
	automatic thought	

sponse. Beek has defined the intervening variable as the *automatic thought* (Beck, 1967).

My wife has occasionally awakened me in the middle of the night with the question, "Do you hear that noise downstairs?" Whether I do or do not is immaterial. Next she says, "Please go downstairs and see if there is someone in the house." My immediate response (usually unstated) is, "If there is someone in the house, what good would it do for me to go downstairs?" Protests rarely neutralize the urgency of the request. Most often, sleepy and skeptical, I comply and get out of bed. As I reach the top of the stairs and hear the noise, my palms are wet, my heartbeat is apparent to me and rapid, and my thoughts center around the themes of danger, unpreparedness, intrusion, and fear. Can you guess a few of my automatic thoughts?

I never quite know whether or not to turn on the light. If I am surprising an intruder, this act would surely compromise the element of surprise. On the other hand, my general clumsiness at this hour and under these circumstances has undoubtedly already announced my impending arrival on the scene. So I turn on the light. At the bottom of the stairs, I hear the noise again. Looking out the front window, I can see the shutter being blown by the wind. When the shutter hits the siding of the house, the noise is produced. Very rapidly, I think, "It's harmless. There is no danger. I'm relieved." By the time I reach the top of the stairs, my heart rate has returned to normal, my hands are dry, and I am anxious to return to sleep. Armed with a different set of automatic thoughts, I return to bed, often annoyed at being awakened "for nothing." Note how the testing of my original assumptions facilitated their rapid replacement by a more rational set of beliefs.

Have you ever been in a country where the native language is one other than your own? Once, in that situation I walked past a group of eight young guys on a street corner and they instantly burst out laughing. I thought, "Must be doing something wrong here; something funny; look out of place." I felt anxious, uncomfortable. Most likely, it occurred to me later, someone among them had told a joke and they had all laughed. My behavior was probably not significant to anyone but myself.

This is an everyday experience and not just for travelers. For the hearing impaired, it is common to be unable to receive the usual

auditory cues available to anyone within earshot. Typically, the individual fills in the blanks as best he or she can. Sometimes the guesses are wrong, with embarrassment, humiliation, or occasionally, humor resulting. For one patient of mine, this led to social anxiety and avoidance of situations in which people would gather. He admitted sadly that he could not go to parties. The fundamental problem was not in the party, or in the real hearing impairment he suffered; rather, it was in the self-talk: the silent statements he was making to himself; his automatic thoughts. With diligent cognitive work aimed at identifying and challenging the relevant beliefs, this man was able to make a different adaptation to a social situation. It enabled him to attend, even to enjoy, a party for the first time in years. The change involved accepting his limitations and quieting his concern about the expected reactions of others to his request to "listen to something again."

In summary, the same stimulus can give rise to different responses depending upon the meanings assigned. In rational emotive therapy (RET), a similar system is described in terms of ABC: the stimulus event (A), the automatic thought (B), and the response (C). At workshops, psychoanalytic colleagues often say that the automatic thoughts are familiar to them in their work with patients, then they suggest that they are unconscious. My standard response is that we can be made aware of this channel of self-talk merely by having our attention called to it -the accepted psychoanalytic definition of *preconscious*, not unconscious.

Characteristics of automatic thoughts have been described by Beck (1976). Automatic thoughts are specific and discrete. They often occur not in full sentences but in a kind of shorthand, telegraphic form. Invariably, they are seen by the patient as plausible. Their content is idiosyncratic to the individual person having them, but there are similarities among patients with similar conditions (e.g., anxiety, depression, paranoia). They may provide clues, without invoking unconscious mechanisms, to unexpected reactions in individuals. And so, one way to understand such phenomena as *success depressions*— depression after childbirth, or emotional reactions to moving—can be to investigate the relevant automatic thoughts.

This might be a good time to pause and recall a situation you have recently been in that has evoked a powerful reaction, feeling, or behavior. Try to identify the automatic thoughts associated with your

reaction. If this is difficult, and you are a good *imager*, conjure up an image of the situation. This sometimes brings back the associated silent statements in people to whom automatic thoughts do not come easily. Alternatively, recall an issue being discussed in your office by a patient. Try to infer the automatic thoughts of your patient from the presentation. Cognitive therapy does not have a monopoly on the appearance of, or work with, automatic thoughts. It is likely that you can find a referent for this in your own work or in your own life.

In the frequent presentations that I do, often I begin with evident speaking anxiety. Usually this reaction disappears as soon as I get engaged in my talk and connect with my audience. On one highly memorable occasion, this didn't happen. I was invited to share a workshop on cognitive therapy in Savannah, Georgia with a good friend and colleague. He suggested that I speak for the first hour, and I readily agreed to lead off. I noticed the usual anticipatory butterflies as I was being introduced and the usual initial performance anxiety as I began to speak. ("Would they think that my talk was worthwhile? Would they form a positive impression of me?") I had planned to tell a joke as an *engager*. I told my story, and there was utterly no response. ("Must have been Northern humor," I thought, but didn't say.)

My anxiety level leaped several notches higher. I could hear my voice shake, began to feed back to myself how anxious I felt, and noticed that, instead of getting better, the nervousness was getting worse. I knew that getting involved in my talk would help me turn the corner; however, having failed to do it in the way I had planned, I was at a loss for how to proceed. Meanwhile, I was proceeding with my presentation in a shaky and unsure tone. I decided next to interrupt the flow (such as it was!) by pausing for a long drink of water. As my mouth was uncommonly dry (a typical anxiety symptom), this seemed like a good idea.

I was aware of speaking on one channel, having automatic thoughts on a second, and recording them on a third. ("What will they think when I stop? Do they know how nervous I am? What if I can't continue? This isn't going according to plan. Never happened to me quite like this before.") When I resumed, I made an offhand comment and noted an affirming look from a young woman sitting in the front of the audience. I began to speak directly to her, ignoring for the moment the other ninety-nine or so participants. I guess I got into my

talk, because before long the audience was nodding, laughing, and clearly attending to my words. The hour passed quickly, so that I was almost reluctant to give up the floor to my colleague. Rational responses had replaced the anxiety-evoking and anxiety-affirming automatic thoughts. ("They didn't like my joke, but they did get involved in my talk. They looked like a group interested in the topic and motivated to learn. My bout with anxiety was a small initial problem, eventually dealt with in the usual fashion, by engagement. The presentation, in the end, was little different from most others I have done.") Anyone who has done more than a little bit of public speaking has probably had a similar experience.

COGNITIVE ERRORS

The identification of automatic thoughts forms a large part of the initial work in cognitive therapy. Once known, they are worked with in a variety of ways. One way is to identify the consistent errors in thinking that lead to the production of cognitive distortions that lead to symptomatology. These errors can be found in the everyday thinking of healthy individuals, but in the emotional disorders, they dominate the cognitive set and are applied uncritically to most incoming data.

Commonly we see three major errors, and four more specific distortions (see Table 4.1). *Polarization*, or dichotomous thinking, refers

TABLE 4.1: COGNITIVE ERRORS

MAJOR:
Polarization
Personalization
Overgeneralization
SPECIFIC:
Selective abstraction
Discounting
Arbitrary inference
Catastrophizing

Derived from A. T. Beck (1976). *Cognitive therapy and the emotional disorders.* New York: International Universities Press.

to assigning meanings in polar opposite categories. It is the first major error. Everything is understood as either black or white. There are no grays. If you don't fit on one extreme, you must belong in the only other category-its opposite. A grade of 95–100% is an "A"; anything below 95% is an "F." Your appearance is perfect or terrible. There are no gradations, no middle ground. Thinking is categorical, not dimensional.

The second major error is *personalization*. The individual can only think in terms of him or herself. When this person looks at his television screen of life, he sees only himself, taking up the entire screen. Ask him about a relationship between two people he knows and he will tell you how they each relate to him. It is difficult for him to remove himself from the situation and give you an impression of his observations.

Overgeneralization is the third major error: drawing conclusions beyond the substance of the data. When someone is criticized for a specific action and responds that he or she feels like a failure, this is the error being made. When an individual performs below his or her level of expectations and assumes that he or she can never do better, this may be overgeneralization as well.

Specific errors in thinking include *selective abstraction*: focusing on one detail out of context. When an individual who receives an excellent performance appraisal with one area of suggested improvement makes this error, he conveys the criticism but ignores the overall evaluation. Discounting refers to an inability to accept praise. A common response to a compliment is, "Anyone could have done it," or, "The accomplishment doesn't mean much, really." Making an *arbitrary inference* in common language is called "jumping to conclusions." Finally, *catastrophizing* (a term from RET) occurs when a person thinks in terms of the worst possible outcome.

COGNITIVE SCHEMAS

A schema is a relatively enduring unit of belief from which moment-to-moment cognitions are derived. These schemas are the *rules* that govern how an individual assigns meanings. Ellis (1962) compiled a list of irrational beliefs that he believed occur with a high frequency in our population. Some of these common rules or schemas are presented in Table 4.2.

TABLE 4.2: COMMON SCHEMAS, WITH PARTICULAR
RELEVANCE TO DEPRESSION

---

1. In order to be happy, I must be successful.
2. In order to be happy, I must be accepted by all people, all the time.
3. In order to be happy, I must have a husband (wife).
4. My worth depends upon what others think of me.
5. I cannot work, therefore I am inadequate.
6. I've made a mistake, therefore I am inept.
7. If someone disagrees with me, he doesn't like me.

Derived from A. Ellis, (1962). *Reason and emotion in psychotherapy.* New York: Lyle Stuart.

Given time and motivation, the basic rules that govern the thinking of each of us could be identified and described. These building blocks of a person's thinking are analogous to the framework of a house. The structure in which you live is laid on top of, and within this framework. In the analogy, that structure refers to the automatic thoughts that lend meaning to everyday life.

In the practice of short-term cognitive therapy, automatic thoughts form the basic data of treatment. The schemas from which they derive may be evident or they may be elusive. Identifying these rules may not fall within the scope of a brief therapy. Even if identified. schemas are not often a subject of therapeutic work, due to the limitations of time and the goals set for change.

In long-term cognitive therapy, rather than aiming at achieving insight, resolving conflict, or making conscious the individual's unconscious wishes or fears, we attempt to identify these schemas and to make them the focus of the therapeutic work (see Chapter 9). As the central rules that guide an individual's thinking, the schemas are enduring and are anchored by a host of derived cognitions applied to daily experience. The work entailed in change, therefore, is lengthy and often tedious; it may require considerable perseverance by the therapist-patient team.

For example, the schema of "I require the approval of significant others before I can accept myself as adequate" is frequently held by chronically depressed individuals. The therapeutic task may be conceptualized as one of challenging the individual to develop an alternative rule to guide the determination of self-worth. This may entail a con-

TABLE 4.3: MAJOR FEATURES OF COGNITIVE THERAPY

1. An active, structured dialogue
2. Focus on the here-and-now
3. Goal-directed, problem-solving collaboration
4. Often time-limited
5. Assumes that affect and behavior are affected by how one thinks
6. Use of homework assignments
7. Interpretations of unconscious factors are not made
8. The "transference neurosis" is neither encouraged, assumed, nor interpreted as such

sideration of the models provided by significant others, multiple examples of feedback elicited by the patient in a wide range of situations over time, and his or her appraisal of performance. Guidelines for self-appraisal may have to be developed in those for whom seeking approval has obviated the necessity for self-evaluation.

THE MAJOR FEATURES OF COGNITIVE THERAPY

To highlight those aspects of the cognitive model that distinguish it from alternative ways of understanding a patient and a problem, let me now abstract these characteristics from the four components of the model. In addition, let us make the transition from a model of understanding to a structure for intervention.

On the basis of the theory, what does cognitive therapy look like? The transaction between therapist and patient is an *active, structured, collaborative dialogue*, as opposed to a passive patient monologue. The focus is set on the *here-and-now*, rather than concentrated upon the identification of origins in the past for problems in the present. Therapeutic talk is *goal-directed and problem-solving in orientation*, rather than aiming at achieving insight, resolving conflict, or making conscious the individual's unconscious wishes or fears.

Often the therapy is a time-limited venture, with weekly or biweekly meetings and a planned number of sessions agreed to at the outset, rather than an open-ended, continuous exploration requiring more frequent sessions over a lengthy period of time. The assumption

is made that *affect and behavior can be changed by gaining mastery over one's assumptions, beliefs, and appraisals.* Homework assignments usually complement the work done during the sessions, providing an opportunity to generate data, test automatic thoughts, or practice suggested alternatives. Interpretations of unconscious factors are not made. The so-called transference neurosis is *neither encouraged, assumed, nor interpreted as such.* These characteristics of cognitive therapy are summarized in Table 4.3.

5

Techniques of Cognitive Therapy

While Director of Continuing Education (CE) in Psychiatry at Georgetown, I once invited a highly esteemed psychoanalyst to speak about the "Treatment of the Adolescent Patient." He spent the better part of an hour roaming through psychoanalytic concepts of adolescence and anecdotes of patients he had treated. The audience appeared to be listening, but also seemed somewhat restless. Finally, one of my CE regulars interrupted the speaker with a question, "The title of your talk was the '*Treatment* of the Adolescent Patient.' When are you going to tell us something about *treatment*?" The speaker quickly lit and chainsmoked three cigarettes. When he replied, "That would be a whole other talk," I looked for the trapdoor that CE directors keep for occasions like these. This impression is indelibly marked on my brain and I try to honor its lesson whenever I speak to my colleagues: Clinicians often find models to be academically interesting; however, their prime investment is in learning something they can use with their patients.

Before turning to treatment techniques, let me address your (the reader's) expectations. It is generally accepted that behavior therapists, in discussing technique, have helped to define what many therapists (behavioral and nonbehavioral) do. So too, you will see, with cognitive therapy. Much of what is discussed in this chapter is, therefore, not likely to be brand-new. Many of you will have referents for these techniques in your practice; some of them are firmly grounded in common sense.

Perhaps some of the approaches that follow will capture for you the essence of the active ingredients of psychotherapeutic intervention, as discussed in Chapter 1. And, perhaps not. For me, cognitive therapy approaches what I believe to be the active process ingredients in their purest form.

An attempt has been made to categorize the interventions in a temporal way. Early in psychotherapy, the techniques that help to *provide structure and gain mastery* for the patient often dominate the treatment. Cognitive therapy progresses next toward interventions to help *shift the set* (alter the determining viewpoints) of the patient with an emotional disorder. Finally, a patient, now open to new considerations, will begin to *generate alternatives* (novel ways to view situations and events relevant to the presenting problem). Another supplement to this chapter on cognitive therapy techniques is available in McMullin's handbook (1999).

TECHNIQUES TO PROVIDE STRUCTURE AND GAIN MASTERY

This initial group of interventions borrows liberally from the behavior therapy arsenal. They are particularly useful for patients who are severely withdrawn and lack access to the introspective resources needed to do basic cognitive work. If vegetative signs of depression are prominent (e.g., sleep disorder, loss of appetite, weight loss, lack of energy, and extreme fatigue or lethargy), antidepressant medication is often the first order of the day.

We still lack a clear delineation of symptoms in depression that respond differentially to drug therapy and psychotherapy. The suggestion even has been made (Simons, Garfield, & Murphy, 1984) that acute depression as a syndrome clears similarly, whether treated with drugs or with psychotherapy. If this proves true, the rationale for psychotherapeutic treatment of depression may shift to the prevention of relapse and the attenuation of the course of this problem over time.

Response to drug therapy may return to the patient his or her capability to utilize the problem-solving approaches used prior to the onset of the illness. Then, a focus on the cognitive elements may usefully begin. For a patient with major depression for whom drug therapy is contraindicated for some reason, behavioral techniques may constitute the sole initial treatment. Additionally, behavioral approaches may be employed to engage the patient in the tasks of change and to demonstrate his or her capacity to be effective before cognitive therapy begins.

Record keeping is often an initial assignment. To provide a base-line measure of activity or thoughts, a daily log may be kept and reviewed at each session. For the severely withdrawn patient, structure may be developed by prescribing activities to be engaged in and then recorded in the log. Psychotherapy to aid in weight loss or smoking cessation often begins with records kept of caloric intake or the number of cigarettes smoked. In later stages, cognitions maintaining the habit will be identified and challenged. Records of automatic thoughts play a prominent role in later stages of therapy.

In taking a history, the cognitive therapist is oriented toward identifying problems that cluster around organizing themes. When difficulty is noted in different situations, identifying a common thread may permit *problem reduction*. Often, the automatic thoughts in situations as diverse as consulting with one's legal clients, talking on the phone with mother, and negotiating a decision with one's spouse may be reduced to a common pathway with similar cognitive elements (e.g., a fear of confrontation). The patient may be shown early in psychotherapy that a change in his or her thinking, therefore, may bring widespread benefits.

In attaching meanings to events or situations, patients commonly mislabel or fail to label. *Accurate relabeling* may, by itself, provide significant relief. During my residency days at the University of Pennsylvania, I encountered a patient whose presentation illustrated a mislabeling problem. This 39-year-old man from a Middle Eastern country was a student at the business school. One month prior to coming to outpatient clinic, he experienced a series of episodes of chest pain and difficulty breathing. His father and a brother (each back home) had died of heart attacks at the age of 40. The patient went first to medical clinic, presenting himself as a man with coronary artery disease. A physical exam, electrocardiogram, and blood enzyme studies failed to support the diagnosis. He was referred to psychiatry and, upon arrival, assigned to me.

An alternative (and more accurate) explanation for his symptoms was that they were manifestations of an anxiety reaction. Since death is an infrequent outcome of anxiety, this relabeling brought some relief to the patient. The next task was to gather data that would form a plausible context for his anxiety and help in the identification of the belief system relevant to his symptoms.

Certainly, the majority of time in cognitive therapy is oriented to the *identification of, and then the evaluation of, automatic thoughts.* Once a problem focus is established, how does the therapist guide the patient in locating the relevant cognitions? Frequently, the therapist asks questions. These questions may focus on the meaning of an event or situation. With a patient who has difficulty identifying cognitions, imagery may be useful. When the patient is directed to picture the situation as it occurred, associated thoughts may become evident to him or her. Alternatively, mind pictures may be investigated just like automatic thoughts, as elicitors of feelings and behavior.

When the concept of an automatic thought is unclear, asking the patient to recall a strong past emotion and then to search for the thinking associated with it may clarify the matter. If none of the above is successful, role play and role reversal may prompt an awareness of cognitions. Once the problem of *no thoughts* is encountered, a strong case can be made for the patient's keeping a daily log of situations, feelings, and automatic thoughts. This record, maintained between sessions, is often helpful even for patients who can identify cognitions easily. It may bridge the gap of elapsed time effectively and permit the patient to work with you today in terms of yesterday's thoughts. Finally, everyone has cognitions related to the situation of attending and participating in a psychotherapy session. Asking about these may facilitate the patient's understanding of this basic concept.

Once you've identified the automatic thoughts, what next? One approach is to *focus on the errors* in thinking (e.g., personalization, polarization, overgeneralization). This is particularly useful when the patient can become aware of making an error consistently, across a variety of situations. A format to do this involves the use of the *triple column technique*: a listing of situation, feeling, and automatic thought. The patient may keep a memo book that forms the basis for working with automatic thoughts between sessions (on his own), as well as during sessions (with you).

In addition, visual confrontation by means of a blackboard can facilitate sending a double-barreled message to the brain: auditory and visual. The *triple column* may, at a given time, actually consist of as many as five columns: situation, feelings, automatic thoughts, cognitive errors, and alternative responses.

FIGURE 5.1: TRIPLE COLUMN TECHNIQUE

Situation	Feeling(s)	Thoughts
left husband	sad, depressed	1. My husband doesn't want me to leave. It's my fault that he's unhappy.
		2. He will probably have to live the rest of his life alone.
		3. A loving wife would stay with a man who loved her.

A young woman came to see me shortly after she had separated from her husband of five years. Soon after leaving with her two young children, she had become seriously depressed. She discussed the three reasons that summarized why she had left. She believed that these needs, which had gone unmet, warranted her leaving the marriage and "trying again." I asked her to pinpoint the meanings related to leaving that might underlie the depression. I then formed three columns on the blackboard and wrote her responses in the third column under *Thoughts* (see Figure 5.1).

I then asked her to check the logic of her thinking, to see if it made sense or if there was an error. She believed that her first thought assigned responsibility for her husband's happiness to her. Since she felt that she had adequate reasons to leave, it seemed unreasonable for her to shoulder all the blame. She felt her second thought represented a jump to an unsupportable conclusion. Her last thought reminded her of mother's cautions to her when she was younger. Mother frequently told her what she should do. In a fourth column, I noted the errors in her thinking (see Figure 5.2).

FIGURE 5.2: TRIPLE COLUMN TECHNIQUE

Situation	Feeling(s)	Thoughts	Errors
		1.	1. Personalization
		2.	2. Arbitrary inference
		3.	3. Should statement

Finally, we worked together to develop alternatives. She felt that she deserved some responsibility for leaving her husband: however, it would be up to him to choose a life path for himself. She would try to support him in this effort. She realized that she could not predict that path from the facts now available. He may choose to remain alone or he may over time form new relationships. Since she believed that her reasons for leaving were valid, a man's love alone did not constitute sufficient reason to stay. I wrote the alternatives in a fifth column on the blackboard (see Figure 5.3).

How much of this work is done in the office and how much between sessions depends upon the patient's capacity. The same person, with diminishing anxiety or depression, may do increasing amounts of the work by him or herself, using the sessions to review work with the therapist. The objective is to teach the method, review how well it has been learned, follow up on its use, and then to make yourself available for *booster sessions*. There are a variety of ways to challenge distorted automatic thoughts and to generate new conceptualizations. We'll return to these later in this chapter.

Homework assignments may take a variety of forms and be used for a variety of purposes. Patients referred for cognitive therapy generally expect to be assigned homework. An assignment helps to structure and formalize what is expected of the patient outside of the office. Together, you may anticipate an upcoming situation and prepare the patient to analyze it in a future session. Homework may also help in teaching the concept of the automatic thought.

A common cognitive technique used early in psychotherapy involves the *separation of the uncontrollable from the controllable*. Depressed and anxious patients frequently hold themselves accountable

FIGURE 5.3: TRIPLE COLUMN TECHNIQUE

Situation	Feeling(s)	Thoughts	Errors	Alternatives
				1. He must take responsibility for himself.
				2. I can't predict his future.
				3. A partner's love is not enough.

for *outcomes*. It is useful to point out that we cannot control outcomes, only devise alternative approaches if the result is not satisfactory. I sometimes make the analogy of giving a large party and worrying about the effect of a rainy day. Whether or not it will rain on a given day cannot generally be controlled (even its *prediction* is often not made with accuracy!). A depressed patient is apt to say, "If it rains, the party will be ruined. And, as my luck goes, it probably will rain." The arbitrary inference (jump to a conclusion) inherent in this formulation can be pointed out to the patient. The overgeneralization ("my luck . . . rain") can be noted as well. Then, I may call the patient's attention to *rain* as an uncontrollable factor. Often, however, provisions can be made (e.g., covering the party area, alternative date, bringing people inside the house) to deal with this uncontrollable contingency. Wonderful parties have been given despite the rain. When the uncontrollable comes up in a different context later on, I remind the patient, "You remember, you can't control the rain . . . ."

SHIFT OF SET

Beck (1963) used the term *cognitive set* to describe a person's immediate state of mind. This designation encompasses the rules (schemas), as well as the attitudes and expectations (cognitions, automatic thoughts), that comprise an individual's belief system. One generalization identifies the *negative cognitive set* of the depressed patient. Another might describe the anxious patient's belief system as one of "controlling the present and anticipating the future." In a patient with anger as a dominant theme, the cognitive set may center upon "the collection of injustices."

Once the relevant beliefs and rules have been identified, cognitive therapy proceeds into its second phase. The aim of the collaborating, problem-solving team is now to shift the set. It has been suggested (Hoehn-Saric, Liberman, Imber, Stone, Pande, & Frank, 1972) that, in the emotional disorders, a person's thinking becomes frozen in place. He or she applies (uncritically) the same stereotyped meanings to a wide range of situations and events, as well as to him or herself. The task is to *unfreeze* or dislodge these beliefs from their autonomous state and to subject them to the patient's inquiry. I sometimes refer to this process clinically as "putting your ideas on the table," so

that both patient and therapist can work with them. Another way to conceptualize the process of inducing cognitive change acknowledges that most patients have given considerable thought to their problems, without arriving at acceptable solutions. Therefore, continuing to work in the context of the patient's problem is likely to be fruitless. One approach that may work therefore, is to shift the set.

Three ways to shift the set involve the use of *analogies*, the power of *self-disclosure*, and the liberating potential of *humor*. Taken together, their success requires the engagement of the patient in the story that the therapist tells. With each technique, the relevance of the intervention to the problem being discussed is usually kept implicit. The patient's task is first to make the jump from his or her set to that of the protagonist in the story. Second, he or she must make the connection (see the relevance) of the story to the problem being discussed. Finally, the patient must come to some conclusion about the material presented and then, switching back to his own cognitive set, apply that conclusion to his or her own belief system. When this works, the patient will be led to examine more objectively one tenet of his or her own thinking. There are perils at every step, and the therapist must be prepared to guide, prod, actively challenge, or gently support the patient, as his or her instinct and experience dictate.

A patient presented the following problem. "Every time I have an intimate relationship with a man," she said, "I find a way to ruin it. It's because I'm damaged. I'm damaged by the effect my childhood had on me, and the devastating impact of my divorce. I try really hard to please a man so that he'll commit himself to me. But, they never do.

"When they don't comply with or anticipate a simple request or need, I get angry and feel failed. When the anger builds, I become convinced that they don't really love me. At that point, either the man leaves me or I decide to end the relationship. Either way, men seem to me to be miserable creatures and I end up alone again, proving to myself that I will never be loved. Most women I know get married and stay married. Some are less attractive than I am. Some are not very bright. A few are downright obnoxious. But, they're chosen and I'm not. What's wrong with me?"

There are many errors in thinking illustrated here. This woman saw herself as a "prisoner of her past" with little choice available to

her in the here-and-now. Most clinicians have seen this formulation in one of its many guises. Her schema requiring that she please a man, regardless of the consequences, is one she could not yet view objectively. It prohibited her from expressing a small anger.

Generalizations followed, with a resultant buildup of anger. The generalizations reinforced her negative self-view, which helped maintain a state of chronic depression. Another set of generalizations defined "all men as alike." Whether she took action to end the relationship or was the "passive recipient of being rejected," she concluded that she had failed again. The meaning of an acute failure reinforced her ongoing self-image as damaged or defective.

The task for the therapy now is neither to "cure" her nor to approach all of her cognitive errors in one fell swoop. Rather, the therapist will attempt, by means of an analogy, to target a critical assumption and encourage her to look at it more objectively. Once the negative cognitive set has begun to unravel, there will be more opportunities to attack its other aspects.

I heard her explication of the problem over several sessions. I thought about how I might demonstrate to her the errors (so apparent to me) in her thinking. Suddenly, the words of a popular song came to mind. Unfortunately, popular music was not this woman's favorite, but I was willing to bet she could overcome that and would hear a personal message in the lyric. I began:

"There is a song, popular now especially among the kids, called 'Paradise by the Dashboard Light.' It's recorded by a man who calls himself Meatloaf. [We both grinned at this.] It doesn't speak to you directly, but I'd like you to listen to it, and I'd be interested in your reaction." I played the tape through from the beginning to the end. The song presents an adolescent boy and girl in a parked car. He can "see paradise by the dashboard light." She is more reluctant to get involved in lovemaking with him. The song abruptly shifts into an allegorical baseball game, broadcast by the old New York Yankee radioman, Phil Rizzuto. This portion concretizes the notion of *scoring* by following a runner on the bases. As he heads for home plate, the baseball allegory ends and the story line returns to the two protagonists.

Now, the woman beseeches her male friend: "Will you love me forever, for the rest of your life? Will you never leave me? Will you

make me your wife?" He responds, "I'll give you my answer in the morning." The rhythm and tone of the song build to a number of climaxes, as the dialogue becomes more urgent. He finally promises to "love you 'til the end of time." At the end, both lament that they are now "praying for the end of time, so I can end my time with you." Tough stuff. And not recommended unless the trust in the relationship is such that the patient won't feel humiliated by the implications she may draw from your presentation of the song.

The song ended. I turned off the tape. She made the transition quickly from the situation of the song, the youthful age of the participants, and the off-putting (to her) rock beat, to her own system of meanings. "Do you think I come across that screechingly about commitment?" she said. "And maybe that, plus my overwhelming efforts to please, drives some men away." Her cognitive system relevant to relating to a man opened, just a bit. Over subsequent months, she found some alternative strategies. She became confident enough to risk a relationship again. She slid back and then advanced slowly forward. She ended a relationship prematurely and then allowed it to resume. It was clear, both to her and to me, that some basic attitudes had changed. This was accompanied by a change to a less depressed, more optimistic state of both thinking and feeling.

The preceding is a fairly dramatic use of an analogy to shift a cognitive set. Usually, a story about a friend, a recollection from the past, or the mention of a current news article makes for a gentler analogy. Whether the analogy is dramatically presented or not, however, the cognitive process is still the same.

Self-disclosure works in a way similar to that described for analogies. This time, the analog comes from the therapist's life, his or her own family, his or her own life experience. The clinical prohibition against self-revelation has frequently prevented psychotherapists from using this approach. And, it is fraught with dangers. As with the more general analogy, it may be seen by the patient as irrelevant and a waste of time in therapy. It may be seen as lecturing ("a late-night television monologue") or worse—as something done purely for the therapist's own gratification. Once again, the trusting nature of the relationship must provide the context within which it can succeed.

Once the caveats are identified and honored, however, one of the most unexpected gifts a therapist can confer upon a patient is a

glimpse into his or her own life, given for the patient's benefit. For this, we can thank the psychoanalytic tradition, which leads most patients to expect little if any self-revelation by the therapist. The active collaborative quality of the relationship in cognitive therapy forms an effective framework for the successful use of self-disclosure.

For example, a patient recently eased out of a job was confronting the meanings and consequences of unemployment and jobseeking. For several hours, I listened to the explication of his concerns. I was concerned that we were accomplishing very little. I wondered about his level of trust in me and the degree of our engagement as a therapy team. Then I decided to tell him the following story. "It's a very real problem that you're talking about," I said, "and I should know. Several years ago, I was told that I would be dismissed from an academic position four months from the date of receipt of a termination letter. I was angry and bitter initially, much as you were. Then, I became saddened and began to doubt myself. I could not then look for another job. Friends and colleagues rallied, initially, to what they saw as unjust treatment. Then a curious thing happened. People began crossing the street when I came walking down. I believed they were saying that I was part of the past and, although they sympathized, they wanted to be part of the future. The four months of working but not being really a part of the system were very difficult for me. I gather that you've felt just that for months now. It was a great relief to finally get out of there. The bigger relief for me, though, was to separate what had happened to me from the meanings I had given to it. When you're ready to, I hope I can guide you through the disengagement process."

This acutely depressed man nodded and smiled gently through my short monologue. He then cried, grew angry, and then began to test some of the self-assumptions he had earlier outlined. A point of contact had been established, and an approach to his problem had begun.

In addition to relating my own experience, I tell some stories, as they say, on my wife, but I'm convinced that the most engaging interventions concern the problem-solving pitfalls and pratfalls of my two, now adult children. A carefully told story of a child can be surprisingly applicable to the life situation and meanings of an adult.

Another powerful tool, which must be thoughtfully applied to succeed in shifting the set, involves the *use of humor*. Some cautions

have been discussed by Beck and colleagues (1979). For humor to be effective, it must fit the therapist's style. It must be presented with spontaneity. If you do this with difficulty in social situations among friends, this technique is not for you. The goal is to illustrate the unreasonableness (distortion) in the patient's thinking.

Humor must challenge a key element in the patient's belief system. Be aware that, particularly by the depressed patient, it may not be heard as intended. It must avoid ridicule. Often, it helps if it's self-deprecating, although some depressed patients will immediately see themselves as the remark's victim. Once the joke or witty remark is made, the procedure is identical to that outlined for the use of analogy or self-disclosure. The patient must abstract the relevant element and apply it to him or herself. The form of the remark may be a quip, a rapid-fire response to a question, or a short story.

WORKING WITH
AUTOMATIC THOUGHTS

We've now come to the cusp between cognitive therapy's second and third phases. The following work with automatic thoughts is aimed at breaking the set and then at initiating the process of generating alternative meanings. It provides one answer to the question: "What do you do after you've identified relevant automatic thoughts?" Along with our triple column technique (situation, feeling, automatic thought), we now focus on a fourth category, *cognitive error*. Similar errors made in high frequency are identified and general alternative conceptualizations may be offered to personalization, polarization, and overgeneralization.

Evidence may be collected for and against the patient's chosen meaning. An experiment may be proposed to test the validity of a key assumption. The patient may be urged to compare his or her view with those of significant others or friends (*polling*). Often a belief is tested by continually questioning its consequences. This is referred to as the *so-what question* or the *downward arrow technique* (Burns, 1980).

An anxious physician patient described an incident of becoming aware of testicular pain while showering. He had become suddenly flushed and felt faint; he remained preoccupied with the meaning of

the pain for days. He had decided not to consult a urologist about it, rather to discuss it with me. "After I felt this pain," he said, "I gingerly touched the area that hurt and felt something hard, like a lump. I thought, 'This is a tumor. Most tumors of the testicle are malignant. Maybe I will die. At best, I'll need surgery and be out of commission for a long time. How will my family survive without my income? I should have bought that disability insurance. There is no way that this story can have a benign ending. Even if the tumor is benign, it will, at least, have to be biopsied. Then I'll be laid up for a long time and out of work. Maybe if I forget about it, it will go away.'"

His assumptions were outlined on the blackboard, with arrows linking one to the next. I asked him to subject his logic to reality testing. He had left no room for a benign outcome. With prodding, he found one. "Years ago, I had a vasectomy," he said, "and maybe, somehow this lump is related to it. Moreover, if I wait and it's malignant, I may be signing a death warrant. I don't want to stop working, but, I guess, that would be preferable to killing myself by trying to avoid this."

A consultation that afternoon with a urologist confirmed the most benign outcome. It was a thickened spermatic cord, a direct result of the vasectomy he had 13 years earlier which had escaped notice over the ensuing years.

In summary, the middle stage of cognitive therapy is occupied with the task of breaking the frozen cognitive set encountered in many emotional disorders. Analogy, self-disclosure, and humor, as well as various techniques to challenge automatic thoughts, prepare the patient for the psychotherapy's final stage: the generation of alternative meanings.

GENERATING ALTERNATIVES

To this point cognitive therapy, although not identical to psychodynamic psychotherapy, has followed a parallel path. Distortions have been identified as such, and the meanings that have served as obstacles have largely been removed from the road leading to change. The relationship has served to provide a trusting, accepting, and genuine context, within which learning can be facilitated. At this point, however, the path of cognitive therapy diverges sharply from that of tra-

ditional therapy. Insight-oriented treatment usually ends here, anticipating that the patient will cover the distance from making connections and removing obstacles to changing by him or herself. Paradoxically, it is the *short*-term therapy that moves into a final phase, guiding the patient to achieve the change he has sought.

In order to change, one must specify some options to *change to*. I don't believe that the source of these alternatives is significant. It may be the patient him or herself. It may be the therapist (a collaborating partner). It may be the suggestion of a significant other. It may be the result of reading a book.

The only source for alternatives that may require a bit of elaboration is the therapist. Some patients will invest a therapist's suggestions with the authority of law. They may comply, with little attention paid to their own thoughts and feelings. If the therapist's suggestions prove to be of little value, they may be reluctant to say so. They may, conversely, blame, and derogate the therapist or the therapy. It is important, therefore, to clarify the rules of the model, so that the therapist can contribute freely to the generation of alternatives. I often reemphasize to the patient at this point that, if I am to feel free to toss out ideas, he or she must give my contributions to this portion of therapy the same consideration given to contributions from other sources—no more and no less.

One generic label for this final therapeutic task is reattribution or reframing techniques. To each situation, event, or relationship, a person applies a meaning or *makes an attribution*. When this meaning has outlived its usefulness, an attempt is made to reattribute or to view the circumstance in a different frame or context.

Techniques to generate alternatives may be understood with regard to the cognitive error made in reaching the initial conclusion. If the error is personalization, the task is to *decenter* (Beck, 1976). I might use the metaphor of a television screen to explain the task to the patient. "When you reached the [distorted] conclusion, you placed yourself in the center of the screen. The outcome was expressed with you as its focus. Now, try to remove yourself from the screen, refocus, and tell me what else you see."

If the error is polarization, the task is to generate *grays* or *middle-ground alternatives*. Most judgments need not be black or white.

"You may not achieve 100% on your exam, but neither may you fail utterly. What would represent a 90% response? An 80% response?"

If the patient is so enmeshed or absorbed in the immediacy of a situation that the meaning is distorted, sometimes *perspective training* (Beck, 1976) will lead to the identification of alternatives. Consider a man in his mid-twenties who has lost a prized relationship. In its wake, he may see himself as having failed. He may expect to "never love again." He may believe that he lacks an essential element to be loved. I ask the patient to add 40 years to his age, for a moment. "Picture yourself as 65 years old, looking back upon this event as though it happened 40 years ago. Do you think that Susan will be the main topic of your book of life? Will she make up one chapter? Will she be relegated, perhaps, to a mere footnote? Will she be cited in the index?" Sometimes, this shift of set to *capture the wisdom of aging* helps the patient to regain some lost perspective.

When the cognitive error is overgeneralization, an attempt is made to make the patient account for his conclusion by specifying the data that support it. Since we learn by making (accurate) generalizations, this process is not discouraged. Rather, the illogic of accepting a related but unsupportable conclusion (overgeneralization) is challenged. If you have loved and lost (for example) because of a need or action of someone else, that event has little power to predict the outcome of your subsequent relationships with others. If you have lost due to a need or action of your own, perhaps an inquiry is indicated that will identify this pattern and suggest alternatives to you. Successful self-change can alter or remove the power of a negative prediction of the future.

Visual confrontation techniques (e.g., the triple column) have their usefulness, once again, in this phase of therapy. Now the focus turns to the fifth column (i.e., alternative responses), with the other four designations (i.e., situation, feelings, automatic thoughts, cognitive errors) serving as a context and as prompts. Once again, the work may be done during the session or assigned as homework.

Homework assignments might take a variety of forms. The patient or therapist may propose an experiment designed to develop alternative approaches to a problem. I once treated a young woman who was capable and competent in a variety of ways, despite her chronic

suffering with depression. Her mother's weekly telephone call was a time of unparalleled stress for her and usually led to a torrent of negative self-appraisals. She was told that she was "a bad wife, a horrible mother, an unskilled homemaker." It became clear that these assessments formed the basis for her own negative overgeneralizations, which could be seen as maintaining her depression. The task was to help her view the situation of *the phone call* more objectively. She had become part of a dyadic event with her mother that had serious negative consequences for herself.

"I have a little experiment I'd like you to try as homework," I told her. "It may seem silly at first, but I wonder if you'd be willing to do it? The next time mother calls, I want you to say 'hello' and then make that the last word you utter, until it's time to say goodbye. You may listen to mother, twirl the phone on its cord, or even lay it down briefly and come back." Reluctantly (the request made little sense to her), she promised me that she would try it. When she returned in a week, I asked her if she had done the experiment (she had) and what she had learned. "I want you to know," she said, "that it seemed like a dumb idea to me. Well, mother called and I said 'Hi' and then said nothing more. She talked on and on, for 20 minutes! I have always thought that she was responding to me, but this time she didn't seem to need my help. She posed questions and answered them. It felt like I was really listening to her for the first time. Some of what she said was ridiculous, but some of it made sense. I was tempted to argue back, but I said nothing. I felt an odd sense of mastery afterwards that I don't usually feel when we are together. I began to consider this phone call business as *her act* being done to meet *her need*. I'm not as sure that *my traits* play a real part in it after all."

Some time later, mother came for a visit. On the patient's instruction, her husband joined her in trying harder to observe mother more and to participate less, within the bounds of courtesy and caring. The patient found herself, on several occasions, suppressing a giggle at statements mother made that used to trouble her greatly. It seemed that she had managed to reframe the meaning of some of mother's talk. She reported feeling far more relaxed with mother and capable of "enjoying her" at home for the first time.

Another technique for generating alternatives is particularly useful in sensitizing an indecisive patient to the factors affecting his or her

decision-making. This is variously referred to as a *cost-benefit analysis* (Burns, 1980) or a *balance sheet*. Simply put, the therapist lists on a blackboard the assets and liabilities, the pluses and minuses, or the costs and benefits inherent in opting for a particular alternative. I have worked with several couples on issues relevant to infertility using this technique.

The prototype is a recently married couple in their middle to late thirties. They want to have a family and have been trying to conceive for three years. He has endured the psychologically difficult procedure of having his sperm tested for number, motility, and endurance by ejaculating into a test tube. She has endured a lengthy and fruitless workup to uncover which part of her reproductive anatomy is failing the task of providing an egg at the proper time for fertilization. Each feels more like an experimental subject than like a deserving parent.

The next phase of this mentally torturous process involves the prescription of drugs for the woman to enhance her fertility. She has suffered for a year with the disabling side effects. As a couple, they are frustrated and "at the end of their rope." Sexual relations, initially an anticipated pleasure and a source of comfort, have been converted to a means of conception that require planning and measurement. Always, now, sex is associated with a sense of failure and inadequacy. "Anyone can have a child, but we cannot," they each tell themselves. The alternative of adoption is presented to them by her gynecologist. Because neither is comfortable with this option, they consult me for help.

After the history is taken, they make it clear that neither, at this point, is interested in exploratory psychotherapy. They want me to help them make a decision about adoption and then they will go on their way. Together, we form a balance sheet and write the various pros and cons on the blackboard. If they were to adopt a child, they could be parents and start a family. They could terminate this frustrating attempt to conceive naturally. They could return to what was for them normal sexual functioning. They could end this preoccupation with conception and move on to other life concerns. They might be able, once again, to enjoy one another. They could "be in the same room with couples who talk incessantly about their own children," without feeling uncomfortable.

But, adopting a child would mean that the biological parents would be someone other than themselves. The baby's genetic traits would

have their origin elsewhere. She would forfeit the experience of carrying and delivering a child. The child might have a serious medical problem. It might be cold and distant from each of them. It would resemble neither of them. There might be trouble instigated by the child's biological mother. She cannot be certain that she could ever feel that an adopted child was *hers*.

We isolate, together, those statements that represent clear distortions of reality (e.g., that the adopted child had a greater chance of having a birth defect than would a naturally born child). They dispute with each other, and with me, the validity and importance of the various pros and cons. Over about a six week period, they make the decision to adopt. They investigate and discuss with me the various options for finding a baby and qualifying for adoption.

We terminate therapy and they keep me informed of their progress. In several cases, I have the pleasure of receiving an announcement of the baby's arrival. In each case, some ambivalence about the procedure has persisted. Each couple who has chosen to adopt, however, has seemed to be pleased overall by the outcome. Several couples have commented about how they grew together during the decision-making process.

Bibliotherapy is the formal term for recommending a book. Since risk taking is a common issue dealt with in my office, I frequently suggest that my patients read Viscott's book, *Risking* (1977). To expose a new patient painlessly to the cognitive method, I frequently recommend Burns's book, *Feeling Good* (1980). When the concept of choice is a difficult one to teach, I have given patients a copy of *Illusions: Confessions of a Reluctant Messiah* (1979) by Bach. An excellent source to teach problem-solving is Johnson's best selling *Who Moved My Cheese?* (1998).

A TYPICAL COGNITIVE
THERAPY HOUR

Now that we have reviewed the three stages in a cognitive therapy (providing structure and mastery, breaking the set, and generating alternatives), let's look at an individual session. Some time (just a few minutes) at the beginning of the hour is set aside for socialization. This is kibbitz time-time to make the transition from the anticipation of the patient in the parking lot prior to the hour to the therapeutic

work to be done in the office. If homework has been assigned, it is critical to go over it. Forgetting it will markedly diminish compliance with future assignments. The approach to homework undone is similar to that with any problem or situation. First, identify the cognitions relevant to the task. Then note the cognitive errors involved and develop alternatives.

The next agenda item is to develop the problem focus for the session. A patient may say, "You do the therapy today." At times, it is profitable to explore the meaning of this statement. Has the treatment no clear direction? Is the patient disengaged? Is control an issue being negotiated? At other times, I may suggest some unfinished business from our last meeting, taking the request at face value. After checking to make sure that the patient in fact has no particular plan for the session, I may suggest one. Most often, however, the patient specifies the problem focus. The cognitive work may entail gathering background details, identifying automatic thoughts and cognitive errors, proposing experiments, challenging cognitions or schemas, or generating alternative ways to view a problem.

As the cognitive work draws to a close, homework may be assigned, and often a summary is made of the hour's content. Periodically, progress is assessed with regard to the goals set at the outset and the time elapsed since we began. When an agenda is successfully completed, a new one may be agreed upon. At the end of a successful short-term therapy, sometimes a contract is made for long-term work, dealing largely with the identification and modification of schemas.

Termination considers whether and how change occurred and lays the groundwork for future sessions and the availability of the therapist. When there has been a mismatch between therapist and patient, an early session may consider referral options. When no (or insufficient) progress has been made, termination and referral to a different therapist and/or a different model are considered.

SOME FAMILIAR
ALTERNATIVE RESPONSES

I will close this chapter on technique by quoting some punch lines from a noted psychotherapist, philosopher, and author, Sheldon Kopp (1979). These are offered as rational (or alternative) responses to frequently distorted automatic thoughts. See if you can identify the auto-

matic thought and the related cognitive error while you enjoy some thoughtful statements about life situations:

1. Often things *are* as bad as they seem.
2. Why grieve, when nothing helps? We cry *because* nothing helps.
3. What's a person to do about feeling helpless? For a while, there's just no way to see what's funny about being stuck.
4. You can so stand it.
5. I have never begun an important venture for which I felt adequately prepared.
6. Not everything worth doing is worth doing well.
7. There's just no way to get it all straight. Mistakes are inevitable.
8. If we allow pain more of our attention than it requires, we miss some opportunities for joy.
9. Escape is not a dirty word. None of us can face what is happening head-on, all of the time.
10. It's all right to pretend sometimes. The only danger lies in pretending you are not pretending.
11. There is nothing to figure out. Life is not about anything.
12. Remember, we are all in this alone. It helps to know that everyone is in the same situation. It helps, but not a whole lot.
13. We insist that our situation is special. It's so hard to accept how ordinary we all are.
14. By now, I'm no longer interested in whether or not someone really loves me. I'll settle for being treated well.
15. We must be willing to go on caring, even when we are helpless to change things.
16. Our best may not turn out to be good enough. Still, it will have to do.
17. I'm not O.K. You're not O.K. . . . and, that's O.K.

III
Applying
the Model

6

In Love–Out of Love

The loss of a loved person is a frequently cited precipitant for acute emotional disorders, particularly depression. In this chapter, we will discuss the state of *being in love*, using a cognitive theoretical model as a guide. Then, utilizing this framework, we will consider its impact and the reparative work necessary to help the patient who is *out of love*.

IN LOVE

Most of us have experienced the state of *being in love* either personally or through the vehicle of a vivid description by another. Typically, it begins when one person encounters another in a particular situation, often recorded in memory in great detail. A series of contacts ensues in which there may take place the sharing of information about oneself and the learning of the history of another. Or, this may not occur. Common interests are identified and often pursued. This may not occur either. Feelings may be discussed and shared. This, too, seems optional.

And then, *it* happens, either with troublesome suddenness or gradual awareness. An affective state supervenes that I will call *being in love*. For some, this emotional state is so powerful that it seems to determine its cognitive and behavioral accompaniments. The objective capacity to view one's behavior and, more significant here, to test the validity of one's thinking may be lost. Instead, the behavioral and cognitive apparatuses are recruited to support the affective state.

Before moving on to understand better the cognitive aspects and changes, let me pause and emphasize the power of this affective state. It may totally envelop one's thoughts and feelings, and thus pave the way for some most unusual behavior. It may become the single most important determinant of how one thinks and acts. The critical capacity to judge someone else's behavior as well as one's own may be

dominated by the central assumption: "I am in love and nothing can change that. Nothing else matters to me."

The potential for cognitive distortion is significant, particularly in one's view of the loved person. Negative attributes may be discounted or attributed to a cause that leaves the object of love unblemished. It may become (inordinately) important to find out what the object of your love thinks (and feels) about you. Contact with the loved person becomes unreasonably valued. Some search for the person everywhere, hoping for the surprise of a chance encounter, setting themselves up for the disappointment felt when no such encounter occurs. Understanding the behavior of the loved person tends to be personalized favorably toward the self. In sum, the cognitive system is programmed to perpetuate the affective state.

Culturally, we support the cognitive distortions and sometimes the unusual behavior of the individual in love. We say, "Love is blind," and "Lovers know no reason," to excuse the cognitive errors made. Often the loved person is made a part of one's system of gratification or system of self-worth. Some people have a history of doing this with multiple relationships in sequence. For others, it may happen only once.

OUT OF LOVE

If you have followed the development of the argument so far or, better still, if you have a referent in your life or that of another to make the discussion more meaningful, you should now be prepared for the denouement. In a variety of possible ways, the loved person makes it clear to you that he (or she) does not share your love (anymore?).

Often, this acknowledgment is greeted by one's belief system as a lie, perpetrated for a purpose. With repetition and/or behavior to support it, the statement cries out to be believed. And now, the losses begin to multiply. The space occupied by the loved person is vacated. The meaning attributed to that person's loving is lost. To the extent that the loved person was made part of some judgment of the self, this self-appraisal may be in danger of sudden devaluation. Common affects experienced include sadness at the loss of love and anger directed either at the loved one (for spurning the love offered) or at the self (for having made a mistaken interpretation of another's feel-

ings). For some, a more significant loss is the termination of the state of being in love.

The lover's cognitive set may range in any of several directions. With the persistence of the highly valued status of the loved one, despite his or her withdrawal, the self may be devalued. In the face of anger directed at the loved one who has left, he or she may also be devalued. Various expectations are raised, considered in the light of the lover's own beliefs, and often go unmet. Disappointment and anger may be potentiated in this way, with no further input from the loved one. The power of the state of being may be such that the belief is raised that, "I shall never feel this way about anyone again." Or, "Nothing works out well for me." The lover mourns for the loss of the loved one, often for the loss of a part of the self, and for the lost state of extreme well-being.

Deliberate changes in behavior or attempts to manipulate the affects are of little use. My thesis is that the bereaved state of the forsaken lover is maintained by his or her beliefs. The need is for cognitive restructuring, whether undertaken by oneself or with the help of a psychotherapist. Attention is profitably paid to several areas: the lover's view of him or herself, the achievement of a more rational view of the significant other, and an examination of the consequences of the love relationship and its termination.

The lover may be plagued by a constant media (e.g., radio, magazine) barrage about being in love or losing a love. One patient told me that he could not listen to the radio station in my waiting room, since he felt it emphasized songs on these themes. (Was he being selectively attentive to these themes?) Paradoxically, for the person more distant from feelings, the mourning process may be aided by exposure to material evoking anger or sadness related to loving.

The state of being in love may form a delicious memory to keep (which no one can ever take away). Being in love and losing a love may provide a framework for growth and substantial self awareness. The resolution of the state of bereavement and its preoccupation (parallel to the preoccupation of being in love) may bring great relief and the gift of time and freedom. However, if it is permitted to wash constantly over the self, it may erode self worth, lead to social withdrawal, and diminish trust and the willingness to risk.

THE COGNITIVE WORK

The treatment of this problem begins with the provision of a framework within which the patient can view him or herself and the situation. I have found the concept of forming an illusion or icon to be a simple, useful, and vivid way to approach the problem of a patient who has lost a lover.

I discuss with the patient how the process of failing in love results in the production of an icon (much like the little box on a computer screen), which represents the sum total of his beliefs about his beloved. This icon is elaborated over time as new *positive* data are admitted uncritically and negative data are routinely blocked from gaining access. It becomes a growing hymn to the beauty, the wonder, and the value of the loved person. Negative input, whether from friends or from appraisals generated by the lover him or herself is discounted, denied, or explained away. When the rejection occurs, the starting point for the grieving process that follows is rarely the reality of the person or opportunity that has been lost. Rather it is the icon, that collection of positively biased beliefs, that must be contested before an eventual meaning can be given to the relationship and a place can be found for it that is compatible with the resumption of life's tasks and pleasures. And so, the cognitive work divides into three phases:

1. Challenge the icon.
2. Dismantle the icon.
3. Reformulate a self-view that incorporates the relationship experience but permits the formation of new links and the experiencing of pleasure.

Initially, the patient and I often discuss the acquisition of beliefs and expectations about the loved person. Then, inconsistencies are identified between what the icon predicts and what the patient has observed. This process may go on for a lengthy period of time as the patient (who claims that he or she ought to know better) continues to apply the expectancies of the icon to drive thinking, feelings, and behavior. Once freed of this framework, the patient has the task of returning to a cognitive set that existed prior to the relationship or

of growing from the experience and reformulating a self-view that is wiser for having known the loved person. If the outcome fits a pattern of lost relationships, the identification of the distorted meanings involved can pave the way for meaningful changes that may affect the outcome of future relationships.

Whether the pairing is heterosexual or homosexual, the task and process seem to be the same. A middle-aged man consulted me after the loss of a younger male lover. Faced with clues to the impending end of the relationship, my patient "tried to be the person his lover wanted him to be." He shifted his values to accept the infidelities of his partner. He emphasized their age difference as a major reason for his lover's leaving. He became preoccupied with the importance of somehow saving the relationship and with the impossibility of accepting its demise.

He believed that he would never love again, citing the claim that, in homosexual society especially, the premium placed upon youth would severely limit his attractiveness and the opportunity to meet someone else. He feared sexual impotence. He anticipated additional rejections. He wanted to "surgically remove" his grief so that he could begin living again. Simultaneously, he felt that he would grieve forever. He began to demand constant reassurance from friends and from me. He talked about a loss of pride. He had begun to drink while alone.

We adopted several strategies. First, he was to initiate no further contact with his lover. Second, he was to orient himself to involvement with friends, work, and personal tasks. Third, he was to keep a triple column log, detailing feelings, situations, and automatic thoughts. Fourth, he was continually to relate his positive urgings for his lover to the illusion (icon) and check their basis in reality before acting on them. Fifth, our cognitive work in sessions would focus on the log that he maintained for homework.

Typically a "stay-at-home" and intensely private individual, he found the shift toward taking more social initiative and engaging in more goal-directed activity difficult. Initially, there was a flood of negative overgeneralizations about the future. By the two-month mark, there was some adaptive behavior that enabled a more optimistic prediction about the future. He began to detach the relationship from other life decisions, like where to live and work. He bought a car and

took a vacation. A letter from his old lover sparked a brief downturn, but his uncharacteristically assertive response limited the reaction to a short time. He became more and more capable of going out alone and more socially involved with a large group of friends.

The holiday season proved to be another stressor for him. He recognized that the "icon was still speaking to him," despite its having been quiet now for several months. Many of his anticipations for Christmas had been linked with places, thoughts, and feelings of his lost love. It took nearly 10 months for him to feel comfortable living alone in his new place. By then, the preoccupation was gone and he could see that others "have as many problems as I do." The last six months of therapy focused on the issue of liking himself and the relevant schemas. This had been a lifelong problem, whose resolution now had a new urgency. At termination, he felt that he had indeed utilized the event of a lost love as a springboard for growth.

In this case, a relationship had developed over years, accommodations had been made to the wants and habits of each partner, and multiple common interests were pursued together. Arbitrary inferences and overgeneralizations were the orders of the day, as my patient accepted uncritically his negative self-prognosis and was certain that he would never love again. Furthermore, all that a relationship can bring would be forever foreclosed to him. He was angry at having to surrender life as a couple to return to living as a single man. Finally, he blamed himself for the outcome, confirming a lifelong self-view of inadequacy. Because he shared a community of friends with his lover, he would now be confronted with "his failure" wherever he went. He could anticipate the difficulty of seeing his partner with future lovers. Some have experienced this phenomenon in a relationship between coworkers. When the relationship ends, all must coexist "within the same, small space" or someone must leave. Certainly, the task of grieving a lost love still alive and open to new partners is more difficult than mourning the death of a loving partner.

Or is it? The next example will challenge the logic of the claim that "loss by death is always easier to overcome than rejection in life." An older woman was referred to me because she could not accept the death of her husband of 30 years, which had occurred 10 years earlier. In her view, his love and acceptance of her maintained her self-worth. Without him, she felt worthless. She traveled, knew many

people, had multiple opportunities, but she enjoyed nothing and was frequently suicidal and continuously depressed. She felt rejected by her three grown sons and one daughter, rootless in her life, and "always alone."

It seemed that the icon she had constructed for her husband was virtually impregnable. The therapeutic work consisted, therefore, of challenging the choice of continuing to see herself in terms of her husband, instead of formulating a separate self-view. By the ninth session (four months after therapy had begun), she was able to consider the choices she had instead of perseverating on the tragic consequences of her loss. She was able to see her role in making her children's time with her difficult for them. She opened the door, ever so slightly, to the possibility of a new relationship. "It could never replace my marriage," she said, supporting the validity of the icon, "but it would be nice to have someone in my life again."

As luck sometimes will have it, she was introduced to a man just as she seemed to be preparing herself to look forward instead of backward. She was ready to present herself to him in a positive and optimistic fashion. Major changes in her thinking about herself, her family, and the future were evident. Ten months had elapsed from the onset of therapy and nearly 11 years from her husband's death.

Yet another pattern involves the long-term, committed relationship that ends with one partner's leaving the other. Heterosexual society identifies this as a marital breakup after many years together. Among homosexuals, once again, the issues are little different. A man in his mid-forties came to see me because his relationship of 20 years was breaking up, and he was depressed and in crisis. Each partner had been involved in extra-marital relationships, but each time the marriage had survived. Now his mate was citing a lack of support for a burgeoning career. My patient's symptoms included sleep difficulty, crying spells, overeating, withdrawal, extreme fatigue, and an exaggerated tendency to self-blame. He felt hurt, angry, and sad.

A collateral session with his marital partner, a man five years younger than the patient, was consistent with the patient's view of the relationship terminating. The patient felt deserted. He would now have to live alone. How could he explain the loss to their friends? Possessions would have to be divided. He would "grow old alone." In sessions, he would suddenly burst out crying. However, he had begun

to redecorate his lover's room in the house. The anger gave way to depression and a search for meaning.

He dealt first with the task of confronting friends. By formulating a meaning he could convey to others, he felt that his own acceptance would be facilitated. He began to speak out at professional meetings and in social gatherings. He avoided, for now, even casual contact with his former lover. He acknowledged how important it was for him to be a nurturer.

In our sessions together, I explored with him the various facets of his identity. He was a skilled attorney, in considerable demand by clients. He had a love for history, and read (especially books on European history) voraciously. He was a capable tennis player and had a group of "tennis friends." He loved to travel and had traveled extensively. In all four areas, there were social contacts and all the elements for a rich existence. It was important to help him detach the loss of a relationship from his sense of who he was and what he could do. Gradually, he reclaimed those parts of his identity that had little bearing on his partner and their separation. With this accomplished, he had more confidence entering into social situations and meeting new people.

After three months (14 sessions), he mentioned his concern that it would be difficult for him eventually to separate from me. The therapeutic focus was kept on his adaptational issues. The issue of our relationship was not pursued at this point. As he generated, and we tested, beliefs about himself and the consequences of the lost relationship, he centered upon his need for belonging. He was reformulating an identity from the status of *married* to one of *single*. He thought about moving, a job change, and buying a vacation home.

Six months into therapy, he began a new relationship. There was a return of "nostalgic feelings" for his old lover. There was a need to validate the many years he had invested in the relationship. He had begun, at last, to let go. He talked about the vulnerability inherent in aging as a single man. He felt that he had to "clean up his inner court" before making a commitment to someone new.

He gave a large party eight months after the loss, and it went well. He felt that he had related easily to many different kinds of people. Finally, we discussed termination and dwelt upon our relationship— but also on what had changed in him, and how he felt that change

had occurred. He saw me as a guide, consistent with his interest in history. I was his teacher, a source of support, sharing, and acceptance. He hoped that we could remain friends. He wanted to know more about my professional interests, and we spoke of them. I hear from him still, from time to time. His life, relationships, and career continue to bring him satisfaction.

Young people usually confront the beginnings and endings of relationships at a high frequency. Some learn to see the sorting process as one of multiple guesses and only occasional matches. They often grow with the endings (even though they are painful) and sharpen their notion of the person who would make a good mate. Others view each relationship as an opportunity to succeed or fail, a referendum on whether or not they are worthwhile. Seeing each ending as a rejection and a failure, they sometimes lose the motivation to continue the search. Occasionally they conclude, tragically, that life without a significant other is no longer worth living.

A woman in her mid-twenties consulted me after three months of psychoanalytic psychotherapy, saying that she "needed interaction now." Ten months earlier, a man with whom she had lived for a year, and from whom she had a promise of marriage, left rather abruptly. Four months earlier, she had swallowed a significant number of pills in an attempted suicide. Now, she was having suicidal thoughts again, and a concerned friend had suggested that she seek further help.

She felt that she had never fit in with the other kids at school. There were cliques of smart, attractive, and athletic girls. She saw herself as none of these. In the years that followed school, she had found neither a mate nor a career. What she wanted most now was a return of the "extreme state of happiness" she experienced when she and her lover were together. This is similar to the state of being in love referred to earlier in this chapter. In addition, she still "really loved him" and "could not let him go." She felt the loss was "unfair." She felt sorry for herself and spoke about how she had fashioned a whole life plan around the anchor of their relationship. She articulated well how her loss had consisted of "much more than him."

We began to work with her icon. In time, she achieved a more realistic view of her lover, but she could not redirect her attention from the magnitude of her loss and its irreversibility. She had little motivation to pursue either another relationship or a career. In con-

trast to the first person discussed in this chapter, she found it useful to contact her ex and to continually reappraise his responses to her. He confirmed for her the fear of commitment that led him to break off a relationship as it approached marriage. He confirmed as well that little change was likely for him. This, for her, made for a clear attribution to "his needs" of the reason the relationship ended. After a three-month period in therapy, she affirmed that her involvement with him was now over.

She turned next to tackle a variety of identity issues that had surfaced in the wake of the end of the relationship. What did she want for herself? Who was she really? And, what would suit her in a career? These concerns ushered in a year of psychotherapy, with the original focus bubbling up occasionally. For the most part, it appeared to be resolved satisfactorily.

$\overline{\qquad\qquad}^{7}$
Separated

As if a lost love wasn't trouble enough, marital separation often complicates the situation by adding problems and multiplying the losses. Separation from a spouse may mean a loss of security, a loss of status, a loss of income, a lost role, lost stability, increased responsibility, as well as the need to function in a singles' environment, for some joyfully abandoned years ago. Particularly when one's self-definition has become centered upon the role of *spouse*, marital separation may be an event that threatens self-worth. Feelings of sadness, anxiety, anger, helplessness, and loneliness may become constant companions. These feelings (and the thoughts that are associated with them) may erode the initiative, assertiveness, and self-confidence necessary to form new relationships.

Separation may present itself in other guises, as well. The British (more often than the Americans) speak of "being separated from" (rather than "losing") a job. Here, too, the fundamental loss is often magnified by lost income, status, security, role, and stability. In addition, responsibility to provide for others may be an added burden at this time. The return to functioning in a job-seeking mode is clearly similar to the task of returning to problems of dating and meeting people.

Even when marriage and job are enduring, that stage when grown children leave home may inflict a loss similar to marital and job separation. The so-called empty nest may be accompanied by a lost role and lost status, a confrontation between husband and wife as solitary partners again, and a need to redefine purpose and direction in life, particularly when one's self-definition has become centered upon the role of *parent*.

COGNITIVE PROBLEMS
IN SEPARATION

When one has walked with a partner by one's side for a variable period of time, the end of a marriage poses the prospect of "facing life alone." A separated woman, married for 20 years and now 40

years old told me, "I can't see surviving as a single person. I have no
status alone. I'm not smart enough. I am afraid without him. I haven't
thought of myself in 20 years." A separated woman in her mid-thirties
with two small children said, "I feel like I was thrown off a ship in
mid-ocean. If he doesn't love me, how can anybody love me?" A separated woman in her mid-thirties was concerned with loneliness, dating again, and financial worries. "His leaving was my fault," she said,
"The separation is my failure."

A man in his early thirties, left by his wife, told me, "Her leaving
is my fault. I don't really like myself. I feel out of place in a singles'
atmosphere." A separated man in his mid-forties said, "I'll never find
another woman who will love me. I feel like a boat going in circles
because I don't know how to steer. If I become sick, who will take
care of me?"

Several men and women focused on the new behaviors they would
now need to learn: risk-taking, assertiveness, interpersonal skills, decision-making, independence, learning to find pleasure in being alone.
Several men and women feared or experienced a return to old "pain-
relieving" habits of substance abuse.

For many, there was the concern that "dating now" was nothing
like the behavioral repertoire they had practiced earlier in their lives.
Sexual mores had changed, I was told. The risk of sexually transmit-
ted disease had risen dramatically. The specter of AIDS affected the
prospect of acquiring new sexual partners. The need for contraceptive
protection "changed the process." What was appropriate at 18 surely
wasn't possible at 38. For some who married childhood sweethearts,
there had never been a dating phase to serve as a model. Some would
be living alone again; for a few, it would be the first time they had
ever lived alone (they had moved from parents to roommates to spouse).

When there has been deception, sometimes when a next relationship awaits the leaving spouse, or when animosity dictates an unbal-
anced financial settlement, the sense of helplessness and anger are
doubled. When a sensitive individual has chosen to leave a draining
relationship, guilt and fear for the safety of the left spouse may be a
reason for seeking therapy.

Complicating the idiosyncratic individual burdens that often accompany separation, society imposes problems and expectations upon
the individual, too. These are often presented to me as statements of

fact, or at least as consensually validated opinions. "Everyone knows that . . . " is a refrain I often hear. Moreover, we live in a paired society. Individuals are rarely invited to dinner unless the occasion is in their honor. Couples are invited by couples. It is less enjoyable to do a wide variety of leisure activities alone. One needs a partner to share the joy. The burdens of life can be nearly intolerable when they are borne alone. Two can divide the chores and lessen the load on each other. It helps to have someone to talk to. It helps to have someone available who cares about you, without your having to make a special arrangement (a date, a telephone call) to secure that person's attention.

"Besides," I am also told, "everyone I know is happily married. Why not me?" Treating people in distress, I am in a logical position to hear these arguments. I would guess, however, that most of my readers have heard them as well.

Losing a job can strike similar chords. A man in his late forties was forced out of a job after 20 years of employment. Despite widespread contacts and an admirable reputation as a worker, he felt he lacked the self-confidence to conduct a successful job search. He was highly sensitive to negative appraisals of his work. He regarded his age as an "impossible hurdle" for reentry into the job market. He discounted the encouragement of friends and colleagues as "temporary and well-meaning" and expected that he would have to "face the dragons" alone now. He procrastinated over many of the steps he needed to take for reemployment. He dawdled over the preparation of a resume; he postponed interviews. Despite a generous settlement that would allow for a substantial period without salary, he expected to be penniless and unemployed. He appraised himself as a "loser." He emphasized the stigma associated with being out of work. He saw himself as a failure.

The *empty nest syndrome* has been written about in detail. A woman in her late fifties came to see me just after she drove the youngest of her four children to college in North Carolina. She had dreaded this occasion "for years," as she wasn't sure the relationship with her husband "provided any real nourishment for her." Out of the job market for 30 years, she felt "hopelessly underskilled to function as a nurse" and unable, at her age, to start anew in another field. Her interests centered around her home and her children. Her husband defined himself largely by means of his occupation, from

which she felt quite excluded. Facing the future, she felt sad, alone, and overwhelmed.

COGNITIVE WORK

Short-term treatment for problems with separation focuses first on the *personal meaning* of the situation encountered, whether marriage, job, or child-related. Then, options are generated by collaborative dialogue, polling relevant others, and supplementary reading. Options are defined as *choices*, with the lever for self-control located within the patient's grasp. When self-worth is eroded by fallout from the interpretation of the event, lengthier psychotherapy is generally prescribed. When symptoms of depression meet diagnostic criteria for major depression, an antidepressant drug is often prescribed to complement the psychotherapy. When anxiety generated in reaction to the assigned meanings of the situation impairs functioning, a trial of a minor tranquilizer or effexor (venlafaxine) may supplement cognitive therapy.

There is some immediate gain in sharing with a therapist one's reaction to a marital separation. Conveying to the patient that you have treated this problem before diminishes (somewhat) the sense of aloneness that is experienced. A separated woman in her mid-forties presented for psychotherapy saying, "We have been apart for two years, yet I still feel addicted to him. I have not lost the image of what I thought he was, although I know it's not real." She had steadfastly opposed his attempts to reconcile; however, she maintained that she continued to feel "horribly rejected by him." The legal aspects of their separation were mired in a lengthy court battle, prolonging the process of detachment from him.

The analogy of a relationship to a drug implied by the concept of *addiction* is commonly encountered. The icon discussed in the last chapter is equally relevant here as a mechanism for dealing with separation. The need to achieve a realistic view of an ex-spouse is paramount before one can begin the work of retooling one's own self-image. Arrangements made for custody and visitation of children or legal disputes about division of property or finances frequently complicate the patient's attempt to let go of the relationship and move on.

With my separating patient, we formed a problem list:

1. Detach from spouse.
2. Change your mode of relating to him.
3. Deal with the icon.
4. Develop a court strategy.
5. Learn to like yourself enough to not need someone else.

For each issue, relevant cognitions were identified and tested. She was encouraged to challenge some. I actively confronted others. For example, she thought of the court battle as an all-or-nothing fight "for her life." Worse, she was convinced that her powerful husband could not lose it. The intensity of her sense of rejection was seen as related to the image that had persisted of her spouse as kind, gentle, and caring. As her view of him became more realistic, the impact of being rejected lessened.

The final (self-image) issue took the most work and ranged across considerations of her new career and her skill as a parent, as well as the feedback she received from new friends she had met. These appraisals were juxtaposed with her self-attitudes, reinforced by her husband's statements and actions over their 20-year marriage. She was encouraged to *update* her self-view to account for the newer data.

Another woman had been separated for almost four years when she presented for psychotherapy. She was managing a career along with three small children when she became aware of persistent anxiety and depression. Consistent cognitive errors of polarization, personalization, and overgeneralization dominated her thinking. A tendency to infer rejection quickly in relationships with men had brought her a great deal of emotional pain. Her conclusions, "I am destined to be alone. Being alone means I have failed. If I am not loved, I have no value. I need other people. To tell a man how I feel is to drive him away," were defined as maintaining her anxiety and depression.

After five sessions in which I helped her identify, challenge, and reframe her thinking about various significant relationships, she reported "feeling good for the first time in years. I am thinking slightly differently about things." Over the next five sessions, her view of herself as a victim emerged as a prominent theme. Once again, cogni-

tions relevant to specific situations were identified, errors were noted, and alternatives were discussed. She felt she was now "spending less time occupied with her own misery."

Toward therapy's termination, sessions were dominated by developing a willingness to take reasonable social risks-to "allow herself to be vulnerable again." Meanwhile, she had left a job that demanded little of her (and returned little to her) for one that "acknowledged her strengths and surrounded her with decent people." Since the job provided tuition benefits, she was encouraged to return to school and to pursue a desired career, earlier abandoned.

In all, the psychotherapy lasted nine months. It initially considered her thinking about men and relationships. Then the therapy focused on her relationship with her husband. Finally it centered upon her view of herself, her own potential, and ways of realizing it.

Some people seek therapeutic help when their sense of self has become dependent upon another in several key areas of functioning, and then separation occurs. Others consult a therapist when a spouse has assumed a representation in their life that can't be easily replaced, and then separation occurs. Less frequently, the person perpetrating the separation cannot deal alone with its consequences for his or her spouse. This was the situation when a man in his early thirties called me after he had decided to leave his wife of 10 years. She had not accepted his leaving, and his responses to her varied from support and caring (seen by her as indicators of imminent reconciliation) to repeated statements of his unwavering plan to separate (seen by her as rejection and cruelty). His thinking was organized around a sense of his responsibility for her reactions. He had made little attempt to focus on life as a single person and to adapt to his new surroundings. He was withdrawn, depressed, and afraid when the phone rang that it would bring awful news from or about his wife.

Encouraged to focus more on his adaptation, he gradually established a place for himself in his new community. This place combined his work, his preferred form of recreation, and the shaping of an apartment to reflect his tastes and pleasures. He began to meet people, both men and women, and defined some avoidant behaviors, which he was able to change. He then focused on the legal requirements necessary for a separation agreement. He became more aware of "who he was," separate from who he and his ex-wife had become as a couple. As his perspective shifted from short-term to longitudi-

nal, he began to like himself more and to rediscover his spirit of adventure.

There were 20 psychotherapy sessions over an eight-month period, with one year of follow-up sessions. Initially, therapy was devoted to defining which tasks of separation logically were his and which belonged to his spouse. He could not provide a new life for her, although he had often functioned in the role of *responsible party* in their marriage. Her misinterpretation of support as an interest to reconcile put him in a "no win" situation. His focus on her needs had eroded his time and enthusiasm for making his own transition to a single life. Once he had worked out the issue of responsibility, he began to accept his wife's choices as her own. Then he was able to confront the identity issues of who he wanted to be and what he wanted to do. He demonstrated competence in applying the cognitive method on his own to a series of interim situations that had arisen. A follow-up letter many years later conveyed the many gains he attributed to his time in therapy. This man was one of those patients who worked well in therapy, but accomplished more on his own once regular sessions had ended by applying what he had learned.

In late twentieth-century America, the concept of a person's *being married to his or her job* is well established. Some spend a large share of each 24-hour day at work, six or seven days a week. For this subgroup, the self-esteem pie usually has a large slice representing work achievement. Success in relationships, parenting, or a leisure-time hobby may not be able to overcome a perceived failure on the job. The office culture may demand or reinforce this over-allocation of time to work. I remember being most unpopular in my residency program when I told the chief that having a new baby daughter would preclude my joining him on Saturday for an optional discussion of interesting clinical problems. I felt that she would only be an infant for a short while and I wasn't going to miss out on this stage of her life to demonstrate my enthusiasm for work. Surely, I could demonstrate this in some other way.

Typical of the "separated from job" presentations is a man in midlife who consulted me because he was aware that he was being systematically excluded from the lines of decision at a job he had held for many years. For the previous five years he had suffered with the consequences. To explain his endurance, he cited his passivity and a fear of unemployment. He had developed signs of depression and

had begun to withdraw from family responsibilities. In an initial session, he spoke with feeling about his need to leave the job. Although they were allowing him to "twist in the wind," he felt incapable of taking any action. He expressed his anger at the leadership of his firm for its failure to utilize what he did well and for discriminatory treatment of a "veteran worker." He had received an evaluation that he considered biased and inaccurate. An initial homework assignment involved reviewing the appraisal, identifying its conclusions, and listing data that confirmed or refuted the statements made.

He appeared for the next session without having done the homework. I decided against framing this as a noncompliance issue or a sign of his passivity. Instead, we did the homework together in the office. Subsequently, he took the first positive step toward leaving, exploring with relevant sources the range of options for a settlement agreement, should he leave. His cognitions (e.g., "No one will hire me") were identified, and he was challenged to support or abandon them. His self-appraisal as a "loser" was reframed by him into one who had "done a good job under exceedingly difficult circumstances." He cited a collection of positive assessments he had been given by the many colleagues who had worked with him over his lengthy career.

We discussed his view of the future with regard to its uncertainties, his sense of insecurity and the need for appropriate risk-taking. By the seventh session he had left work and had started his job search with reasonable optimism. He saw himself as "marketable" and was beginning to consider situations suitable for his next employment. He took pride in his assertive leave-taking, especially as he looked back on the lengthy period of distress when he was unable to act.

He began actively to process the positive feedback he had received and to consider some reasons that were neither personal nor specific to him for his mistreatment at the hands of newer and younger leadership. He considered this interim time as one of some advantages, as opposed to a period of pure peril. He spent more time with his wife, and it was a happy time. He attended daytime events at his children's school, an option he normally saw as closed to him. We spaced our sessions now to once monthly.

By the eleventh meeting (over a six-month period), he was satisfied that he had found a suitable job, had grown in the process of leaving, and had made good use of a short-term cognitive psychotherapy.

8

Older People
Never Change

It is hard to argue with the premise that much of an individual's behavior, emotion, and thought is influenced by learning. Some of this learning takes place in the earliest years through a combination of role modeling, feedback, cultural factors, and experience. One's repertoire is enlarged in the negotiation of the various life stages of childhood, adolescence, and adulthood.

It is only logical that what we refer to as habits—whether they be behaviors, emotional reactions, or cognitive patterns—become more ingrained as they are repeated over time. With repetition, the individual becomes defined, to a degree, by his or her characteristic pattern of behaving, reacting, and thinking. The longer this process goes on, the more set in his ways an individual can be expected to become. One consequence of this prevalent process is that we often view older persons as rigid, habituated, and unlikely to change.

Consequently, older people have been seen as poor candidates for psychotherapy, even though they may possess many of the characteristics that make change likely. They may be greatly distressed, highly motivated to work hard, and blessed with the psychological mindedness that usually predicts a successful outcome. But, by subscribing to the cultural meaning given to chronological age, we cancel out their advantageous traits. The chapter title is meant to capture this societal belief; it is not to be taken literally.

As a new psychotherapist, I eagerly sought patients who were young, verbal, and well-educated. When I was referred an older person, I assumed that the psychotherapeutic work would involve identifying the patient's strengths and supporting them, rather than encouraging new learning.

My attitude changed when I met a 65-year-old man (Mr. R), self-referred for cognitive therapy. He had read about it in *Life* magazine. One exchange in our opening session went like this:

R.: I have been depressed for most of my life—this despite a satisfactory work life as the head of my own insurance firm. I have had two courses of psychoanalytic therapy—10 years of each. I believe I know most of what I can learn about depression.

D.S.: All right, then, I'll bite. If you've learned most of what there is to know about depression, what brings you to see me?

R.: After 20 years of psychoanalysis, I'm just as depressed now as I was then. I am hoping that a different approach might enable me to feel better.

I was skeptical about what he could accomplish in a cognitive mode after 20 years of psychotherapy had brought little change. But Mr. R was a thoughtful, intelligent, introspective man, with a delightful sense of humor that emerged as his depression cleared. He worked hard, sustained a high level of motivation, and seemed to prepare specifically for each session.

When I met Mr. R, he was married, a father and grandfather, and he had multiple, but not disabling, medical problems: peptic ulcer, arthritis, and a substantial hearing deficit. He met diagnotistic criteria for dysthymic disorder.

Mr. R was abandoned by his father at an early age; then his mother was hospitalized for a chronic illness during his early adolescence and died in the hospital. This led to a period of time living with relatives, in foster homes, and finally with cousins while he attended college. He had met his wife-to-be while a teenager and after college graduation they married. They had several children, and he started his business.

In our early sessions, we identified eight basic schemas relevant to his depression:

1. He constantly expected abandonment and rejection.
2. He constantly expected to be cheated or frustrated, especially if he was not in complete control.
3. He had developed a need to be "seen and not heard" to avoid others' disapproval.

4. He expected his firm to lose its clients and go bankrupt.
5. He had minimal trust of others, including his wife of 40 years.
6. He was reluctant to spend money, believing that any "loss" of money meant an increase in vulnerability.
7. He described his persistent pessimism as "always looking for the mold in the bread."
8. He continually expected to be punished for unspecified misdeeds.

These basic beliefs led to a persistent sad mood, an unwillingness to risk, multiple avoidance behaviors, and little perception of choice. In once weekly cognitive therapy, he has learned:

1. To use mood shifts and feelings of anxiety and sadness as cues to do cognitive work: identifying automatic thoughts associated with his basic underlying beliefs, challenging them, and generating alternatives.
2. To pay more attention to current feedback (i.e., update the résumé) and to challenge attitudes rooted in the past.
3. To take reasonable risks.
4. To relax; to enjoy sex.
5. To see choices more often; to generate options.
6. To develop a trusting relationship with his wife.
7. To be comfortable when alone.
8. To be comfortable attending parties, even with people he is meeting for the first time.
9. To discount things less often.
10. To like himself more. (This has led to an easier time spending money on himself.)
11. To use a fine sense of humor effectively. (He once told me, "I'm so private a person, I even keep things from myself.")
12. To maintain his new weight, achieved via a 30-pound weight loss, and initiate an exercise regimen to keep in shape.

The usual qualifiers apply. There was no control group, so attributing changes to therapy is a hypothesis. Some other approach might have worked as well (however, his long exposure to apparently "good" analytic therapy with minimal change belies this). The relationship

factors were not insignificant. I have a great deal of love and respect for him.

My experience with Mr. R has led to more psychotherapeutic work with older people and less hesitance to contract for long-term work (see Chapter 9). In brief cognitive therapy, I have found that some older depressed and anxious patients are as motivated for change as their younger counterparts. They identify specific agendas and work with me in a way indistinguishable from that used by my younger patients. Many, having had prior experience with non-directive psychotherapy, find the cognitive dialogue stimulating and a welcome change. The cognitive model is easy to learn. With some older patients, I find myself utilizing more structure (e.g., blackboard, triple column, specific homework assignments); however, with others a cognitive *framework* seems to suffice. Again, this is no different from the treatment of younger persons.

Here is a typical referral. A woman (Mrs. H) in her early seventies was referred to me by her family doctor. Her husband (of 50 years) had sustained a disabling illness almost two years earlier. She was now suffering fairly constant anxiety, concerned that he would (for example) set a fire while smoking, fall due to his impaired vision, or fail due to unaccustomed memory problems. She missed the bright, attentive, stimulating partner she had known. Mrs. H saw herself as a "screaming witch." Her husband needed help to dress himself, could no longer read, and had a poor sense of balance. She could not predict when he would be *able* and when he would be impaired.

She described to me their life together, their children, and his work as well as her own. There were many sources of contentment. "Mainly," Mrs. H said, "I feel trapped by the way his illness has changed our lives."

Cognitive principles were presented to her in brief. Her overconcern with what others might think when they saw her husband was noted. Mrs. H's error in personalizing his actions, inferring that they were somehow "meant for her," was discussed. The withdrawal of her friends was seen as a logical consequence of *her* reaction to her husband's disability. Initiative on her part could result in reconnection with her social network. The need to accept the changes in her spouse without overgeneralizing, as well as the concurrent need to pursue the stimulation she required alone, was discussed with her.

In the third and fourth sessions, she reported feeling a lot better. She told me that she had "more perspective and more awareness of what I do to limit myself." She was now more willing to compromise, while asserting herself to have more of her needs met. We parted after this brief time together, after I expressed my availability to her for further sessions at her initiative.

Some themes are more common to the life experience of an older person than to that of someone younger. With aging, physical illness more often intrudes into daily life. The phenomenon of losing significant others to death is more frequent. Some capacities central to maintaining control over the environment may diminish, with anxiety and depression accompanying an awareness of one's vulnerability. The culture treats an older person differently, often assigning expectations and restrictions based upon chronological age rather than capability. One's place in the family may change. Mandatory retirement may separate an older person from a key aspect of his or her identity. An awareness of not having reached a life goal may become a central concern, if the individual believes that the goal is no longer within reach.

As I began to treat older persons more frequently, I grew to expect these themes. Periodically, I was surprised to hear about a problem that had little connection to the age of the person. Such was the case when a man in his early eighties (Mr. V) was referred by his internist because of a conflict he was having with his brother. He described his (younger) brother as rigid, authoritarian, and demanding. His response to a confrontation was always to back down, with the result that he felt "lousy," couldn't sleep, and became preoccupied with the issue. He described his life path in brief, with emphasis on the development of his relationship with his brother. Mr. V believed that expressing himself would result in his brother's getting angry, and he didn't want that to happen. He told of a similar series of interactions he had with a neighbor. She had taken advantage of him and he could not tell her so. He had spent days brooding about this as well.

Mr. V was instructed in the cognitive model, with blackboard illustration of situations, feelings, and automatic thoughts. The cognitive error of personalization and the technique of decentering were each discussed with him. We generated several different options for dealing with anger. The cognitive error of catastrophizing was described, and he laughed at an elaborate analogy relevant to someone else's

life. He immediately focused on the link to his problem and talked in detail about his plan to speak with his brother.

Over the next two sessions, he described conversations he had with his brother (and his neighbor) on several occasions. He reported feeling relieved and was pleasantly surprised by each of their reactions. After four weeks, he said that he had "learned his lesson" and "would not be bashful to call again, if necessary."

Of a man in his sixties, I once asked, "Given your age, what explains how hard you have been working to change? How many years of life could you have to enjoy the relief or benefits of feeling better?" Mr. S indignantly replied, "No one knows how long they're going to live—not even you. You might be hit by a car and killed in your own parking lot. I've felt depressed for more than 50 years. However many years are left to me, I'd rather feel good than continue on as I have been." I felt no need to ever inquire about this again!

This patient (Mr. S) was given my name by a longtime friend. He had worked for many years in psychotherapy to combat chronic symptoms of depression and anxiety. He had tried several new forms of treatment, as well as years of group therapy. He had tried on his own to gain understanding that might affect his mood state as well. As a last resort, he agreed to consult a cognitive therapist.

His life had been an interesting one, with travel far and wide and multiple involvements in helping less fortunate others. Mr. S related poorly to authority figures (frequently seeing them as "enemies"). He was a perfectionist by nature who rarely reached his own elevated standards. He easily lost perspective in situations, retreating to concrete (literal) positions that told others he "didn't understand them" and that he "took himself too seriously." Mr. S suffered from social anxiety and would deliberately place himself on the periphery of office groups. He constantly anticipated rejection. He spoke in a rambling, discursive fashion. I wondered initially about organic mental changes, but more contact revealed a man who could focus, concentrate, retain, and recall. The working diagnosis was dysthmic disorder.

This bright and thoughtful man was concerned about what would be the legacy of his time on earth. Mr. S felt he had not distinguished himself in his chosen field. His marriage had not worked out well. His children had confronted several serious life problems. He had few friends. It was hard for him to accept responsibility, especially in

the context of a relationship. He felt that he was overly concerned with the approval of others.

We worked on establishing a reasonable self-appraisal. After about 20 sessions, Mr. S reported some "good days" when things were "clearer" and that he was less mired in detail. He was less afraid, others noticed a "glow" in him, and he felt that a "process" had begun. We had developed an easy, nonthreatening, often joking rapport. Our work together was clearly going to take a longer time than the traditional cognitive therapy model I was used to. Neither Mr. S nor I felt constrained by expectations of rapid change.

He talked about his chronic difficulty dealing with the "emotions of love." There were real ambiguities in his sense of identity. It was hard for him to surrender control. As his time in therapy neared one year, there were further gains. Clearly feeling better about himself, he began taking some social initiative. Other people were "becoming more real" to him. Mr. S was beginning to evolve a definition of who he was and to set some priorities for his life. He met a woman who was attractive to him.

A particularly difficult issue arose when he saw his son "developing, in some ways, just like me" and felt powerless to help. A second crisis came when his new female friend ended their relationship. Mr. S's initial reaction was to blame himself on both accounts. Decentering helped him to regain perspective. An earlier problem with confrontation became relevant again. Each time, we stressed the meanings he found in events and situations, identified cognitive errors (e.g., chiefly personalization and polarization), and proposed alternative strategies. He became aware that he had established his friend as the repository of his newfound self-worth. When she left him, he felt that much of his gain had left with her.

His response was to return to the notion of legacy and the building of a dream. It was here that my ill-conceived remark was made about his age and prospects. Our relationship survived even this extreme instance of insensitivity. Mr. S moved successfully to a new home. He had always defined himself in terms of the needs of others. That would now change.

At the two-year mark, we assessed progress. He felt "more flexible" in his thinking. He more often "felt normal." However, he continued to feel "vulnerable to depressed moods and pessimistic modes

of thinking" in times of crisis. Over the holiday period, he demonstrated to himself some of his newly acquired social skills. He was taking things "less seriously" and functioning far better at work.

After three years of once-weekly therapy, Mr. S reported "liking himself more" and experiencing feelings that had been "absent" during most of his life. We began discussing risk-taking and the concept of choice in great detail. He reported feeling "relaxed" for the first time "in years." We had already begun spacing visits every two, then every three weeks. He commented that the depression "had attenuated." He was making decisions now, more definitely and more quickly.

Mr. S had a brief depressive reaction to a job transfer, but regained perspective quickly. He felt he could now "evaluate people" better. He was able to "look people in the eye." He could see things, at times, from the other person's vantage point. He was less interpersonally domineering, more willing to listen.

Cognitive therapy lasted for more than four years, with sessions held monthly for the final 15 months. There appeared to be demonstrable characterological changes. He was now rarely depressed and generally interpersonally involved and skilled, with a clearer self-definition and some optimism for the future.

His age proved to be no obstacle to achieving change. The characterological elements required lengthy repetition and continued confrontation before they succumbed. However, Mr. S was a worthwhile investment of therapeutic time and effort.

It is clear to me that older people do indeed change. Little distinguishes this group from the younger cohort, except that issues of changing self-definition, retirement, and the death of significant others occur with increased frequency. As a group, older people are no more or less motivated, no more or less hardworking, no more or less creative or clever. Thanks to a societal expectation of less likelihood of achieving change, they are (if anything) more appreciative of the opportunity to experience change in psychotherapy.

To gain the stimulation of hearing about the psychotherapeutic work of clinicians who treat solely older persons, I accepted an invitation to address the Continuing Medical Education Geriatric Congress in June 2000. Over a three-year period, it has been gratifying to see how many geriatricians tell me they have found the cognitive model useful for their older patients.

E̲x̲t̲e̲n̲d̲i̲n̲g̲ the Model — IV

9
Long-Term
Cognitive Therapy

For years, I was skeptical that long-term therapy worked for anyone, whether patient or therapist. I attributed success, when it occurred, to a high level of personal motivation in the patient, combined with the benefits of the nonspecific (relationship) aspects of the psychotherapy transaction. Yet it was claimed that intensive psychoanalytic psychotherapy helped people make changes in *character or personality*. The dictionary definition of personality is, "the organization of the individual's distinguishing character traits, attitudes or habits . . . the totality of an individual's behavioral and emotional tendencies." It is noteworthy that the definition does not specify (for example) "a set of dynamics based upon the impact of unconscious conflicts, best understood considering the interplay of forces of id, ego, and superego, and best approached by an introspective review of early childhood development." Nevertheless, most clinicians seem to accept that personality change can be achieved only through psychoanalytic methods aimed at achieving insight into unconscious processes. I know of no evidence attesting to the accuracy of this judgment.

I asked myself, if the model is a vehicle that provides the language in which the person and problems are conceptualized, what benefit does a psychodynamic language have over a cognitive language? I could see none. The psychoanalytic approach to change appeared to me to present its active process ingredients in a rather obscure and inefficient fashion. The cognitive model appeared to approach reframing quite directly and to avoid the necessity of spending undue time in a study of the patient's past. Finally, if basic rules (or schemas) could actually be changed over time, it seemed logical that affect and behavior would change to be consistent with them.

How, then, could the short-term model that involved identifying automatic thoughts and cognitive errors and then generating and test-

ing alternatives be adapted to facilitate *character* or *personality change*? The obvious candidate for a cognitive focus would be the basic rules or principles (schemas) that governed the individual's thinking. These schemas are the building blocks of a person's thinking and give rise to the moment-to-moment beliefs Beck has called automatic thoughts.

In a short-term model, the relevant schemas were not usually hard to identify. In a long-term approach, these rules would be the focus of the psychotherapy. What would it take to effect the character change that long-term psychoanalytic therapy claims as its target? Would higher order cognitive change suffice?

I accepted a few patients with the stated goal of character change. I expected the work to be longer, harder, and more repetitious than its brief counterpart. It made intuitive sense that schemas, like habits practiced over many years, would be resistant to change. Dislodging a central or defining belief would leave the patient feeling vulnerable and dependent upon the relationship with the therapist. Therefore, relationship factors would be even more important here than they are in short-term work.

PRINCIPLES OF LONG-TERM
COGNITIVE THERAPY

I have treated a number of patients utilizing a modification of the cognitive model as a framework for long-term psychotherapy. Sessions are usually limited to once weekly. Duration of therapy is measured in years, rather than in weeks. Several patients have achieved major gains. Some principles have evolved to guide this long-term work. Special attention must be paid to harnessing the *nonspecific aspects* (see Chapter 1) of successful psychotherapy. Engagement is highlighted, including the match between therapist and patient, and a clear statement of goals, roles, and expectations is made at the outset. When the match is a poor one, referral is encouraged.

Central to the therapeutic work is the *identification of schemas*. Initially, a collection of automatic thoughts is made in a variety of situations, with an eye toward spotting the basic rule from which the cognitions derive. Once a schema is found, the range of automatic thoughts to which it gives rise is noted. When several schemas can be agreed upon with some certainty, a cognitive definition of the

individual may be specified. Emotional reactions and typical behaviors in certain situations define patterns that form an outline of the patient's cognitive structure. Usually, it is not difficult for the patient to locate the schemas he or she believes to be responsible for distress.

At some point, I acknowledge to the patient that a person's *basic rules may have been adaptive in earlier life circumstances*. The operative questions are: Are they adaptive now or have they been retained, unquestioned, out of habit? Do they take into account what the patient has learned since childhood? Has the résumé been updated?

Once a schema has been chosen as a focus, an experiment may be proposed to test its validity or to generate alternate strategies. Input may come from the patient's reading, his or her awareness of another's approach to the same situation, or the advice of a friend or significant other. The tedious part involves constant observation and testing of both the schema and the proposed alternatives, over a wide range of situations. Often, a log is kept and discussed at each session. Its format is yet another modification of the triple column, now consisting of: situations, feelings, automatic thoughts, schema, and alternative rule. With situation piling atop situation, and time passing in the process, change (when it occurs) is usually gradual. There is frequent backsliding and return of old forms of thinking. At these times, the support and encouragement of a committed therapist are crucial. Often the process is facilitated by engaging a significant other to rally some support among the patient's other close relations.

Frequently, the patient and I examine together the meaning of *risk* in a variety of contexts. At times, the nature of the risk is quantified and a graded schedule of risk-taking is established. Cognitions generated in anticipation of risk, as well as during performance, are studied in detail. One desired endpoint is a change in the patient's willingness to take risks. Another is the establishment of a rational process of risk assessment that leads to a balance between assertion and caution acceptable to the patient.

I work extensively with long-term patients on the concept of *choice* and on evaluating the consequences of various choices. Attributions for actions or beliefs are too frequently assigned to external events, to the patient's view of *consensus*, or to a sense of moral obligation. Examples of *external attributions* are: "Because my father was an alcoholic, I am often depressed." "Because the teacher doesn't teach,

I failed the course." "Because of my handicap, I couldn't accomplish the task." While the response to an overwhelming event may be uniform, most situations permit a wide range of interpretations.

I have learned to be wary of statements that begin with: "Everyone knows that . . . " or "All other women have . . . " or "No one I know would even consider. . . . " Clearly, *comparison with others* is one guideline we use to establish the boundaries around some of our choices. This policy is abused, however, when it is used to squelch creativity or force conformity to a perceived norm.

Ellis (1962) elaborated the idea that people often make attributions to their sense of *what should be done*. I often ask my patients: "Who is the authority, to which the *should* can be traced? Is it possible to evaluate the *should statement* much as one would any other choice? Or must it be followed blindly to avoid the guilt attendant upon questioning it?" These discussions may range into a review of a patient's religious beliefs, cultural expectations, or parental proscriptions. I stress not rejecting these ideas, but rather subjecting them to the same appraisal given other alternatives.

Whatever the personality style of the long-term patient, I have found that psychotherapy frequently considers the generic issues of *expressivity*, *independence*, and *assertiveness*, within the context of choosing adaptive interpersonal strategies. Many with an obsessive-compulsive style are aware of feelings they have, but sharing them with others has not been a frequent choice for them. The advantages and disadvantages of this approach are considered. Clues to recognizing so-called hidden feelings are discussed.

For the hitherto dependent individual, the traits necessary to overcome reliance on others are pointed out. Experiments may be proposed to try out action options that would permit an individual to function more independently. The benefits of dependency (in some situations), as well as the concept that most of us rely upon others some of the time, are brought into the transaction at some point.

For the more passive individual, psychotherapy incorporates the teaching of assertiveness. This often dovetails with the segment on risk assessment. The goal is to teach and model behaviors that allow the patient to advocate for him or herself in a variety of situations. As with dependency, the virtues of at times listening and waiting, as opposed to taking action, are stressed. An attempt is made to encour-

age a spectrum of responses, with assertion at one end and passivity at the other.

When an ongoing style or a chronic problem is the focus of the treatment, special attention must be paid to the arrangement of *mastery experiences*. Whether through experiments designed to teach mastery or via taking advantage of natural life opportunities, one can pursue opportunities to succeed, which can be powerfully reinforcing in their own right. Success may lead to a willingness to take further risks and pave the way for more success.

When change occurs in schemas, an early and sensitive indicator is often a *change in automatic thoughts*. Most patients are sensitive to this, reporting, "I approached the same situation I've encountered before, but in a different way this time. When I compared my log with an earlier one, it was evident that my reflex thoughts were not the same as before." These changes often correlate with a decrease in anxiety and depression, as reported by the patient.

To illustrate the principles of long-term cognitive therapy, let me introduce you to Mrs. T. When she came to therapy, she was 50 years old and had been married (for the second time) for seven years. Her problems with alcohol could be traced to her move to Washington from the midwest eight years earlier. She was guilty about leaving her elderly father and somewhat relieved when he died two years after she came east. Meanwhile, she met and married her second husband, amid great expectations. She gained nearly 60 pounds (to a weight of 200 lbs.) over a period of five years. Her husband apparently spent long hours at work and little time at home. She felt that in the past year he had withdrawn from her, and their sexual relationship had stopped. On several occasions, he told her that he didn't love her anymore.

Mrs. T. tended to internalize feelings and build anger which she didn't express openly. She was extremely sensitive to what others said and did, frequently personalizing the actions of others. She believed that she was difficult to get along with. She suspected that her alcohol habit, although she hid it, might be a disruptive factor in her marriage.

She had held a responsible corporate job until she left the midwest. During her second marriage she had not worked. Mrs. T maintained a close relationship with an internist and used some of their

time together to discuss her concerns. The internist was skeptical about the usefulness of her consulting a psychiatrist.

Over the six months prior to her consultation with me, she became progressively depressed. She overate, drank to excess, and had a hard time falling back to sleep after waking up in the middle of the night. She withdrew from friends and activity. She continued to gain weight, had a negative view of herself, and became quite pessimistic about the future. She blamed herself for the deterioration of her marriage and felt helpless to do anything about it.

Her father was a corporate executive who died of heart disease. Her mother had died earlier of cancer. She had a sister several years older who managed a store in Texas. There was no family history of emotional illness.

Mrs. T. graduated from Ohio State University with a degree in economics. She interrupted her college education to work and put her first husband through school. He got a good job, but his first company went bankrupt. She worked for a corporation, doing accounting for almost 12 years. She saw the downhill course of her first marriage as "strikingly similar" to what she was going through with Mr. T. today.

My initial impressions included: (1) major depressive disorder, as well as dysthymic disorder; (2) alcoholism; (3) exogenous obesity; (4) marital discord. An antidepressant drug trial seemed indicated. I received her permission to talk with her internist. Mrs. T. and I formed a contract for cognitive therapy. I agreed to see her husband collaterally and perhaps to do couples therapy, if it seemed warranted. Her priorities were: (1) her marriage; (2) her depression; (3) her alcoholism; (4) her weight gain.

A low dose of an antidepressant drug brought immediate side effects and was discontinued. Further chemotherapy was tabled for the moment. In the initial discussions, the problem focus was her marriage. She felt that her husband's work, not the relationship, was his first priority. She felt "trapped" in the relationship, as she depended upon her husband but had "little life" with him. She felt that her needs were ignored. Her husband was initially unwilling to come in for an evaluative visit with me. She blamed herself for the lack of success in her marriage, validating her low self-worth. In addition,

she avoided confrontations, seeking to please Mr. T., while her anger at the course of events continued to build.

After five sessions, Mr. T. came to my office. He told me that he saw his wife and himself as "different types." He stressed his commitment to the marriage and his willingness to attend joint sessions if that might help. He indicated that he no longer felt "any real love" for his wife. He liked being alone.

Five joint sessions followed. I explored with each of them how they assigned meanings to the behavior of the other. They each saw their styles as "incompatible." She was overly sensitive. He was passive, would not initiate or take risks. She felt continually taken advantage of. She expected him to "figure out what she needed him to do."

During this time, an issue emerged that engaged their commitment to work together. His daughter (by a previous marriage) had a problem requiring their help. Seeing Mr. T.'s initially negative response, Mrs. T. felt comfortable for the first time discussing with him their marital incompatibility. This discussion led to Mr. T.'s confronting the possibility of the end of his marriage. His behavior changed suddenly and markedly toward his wife. Mrs. T., meanwhile, was assertive and sensitive in her response to her stepdaughter. This sequence drew the couple closer and cooled the separation issue for the moment.

Because Mrs. T. needed to do considerable work, individual sessions with her were resumed. We focused on her self-worth and how she processed data, her expressivity and what she expected from others. She no longer felt that her marriage was "necessary" for her to feel good. Over the next few weeks, she noticed that her husband was staying late at work. She considered several meanings: rejection of her? another woman? workaholism? She began a diet and found a weight loss program to which she considered making a commitment.

She defined her problem with self-assertion as one of polarized thinking. She could be a "bitch" or a "pushover." We identified some midground alternatives. Unfortunately, there seemed to be no grays regarding her marriage. She consulted an attorney and began again to consider separation. She noted that, when depression enveloped her (Mrs. T.'s concept), she blamed herself exclusively for "two failed marriages." She felt that she was finally confronting her marital prob-

lem honestly, and some sadness followed. Now she started to focus
on her alcoholism and reviewed her substance abuse history with me
in detail. She also began attending Alcoholics Anonymous meetings.

Six months after therapy began, Mr. and Mrs. T. had agreed to
separate. She had lost 15 pounds in anticipation of beginning the diet
program. Her alcohol habit was coming under control, and she regularly attended AA.

In the next six weeks she lost twenty-five pounds, made a number of
good friends in the program and continued to reformulate her self-view.
She began to focus in therapy on Mr. T.'s passivity regarding carrying
out the separation, and developed several possible explanations:

1. There was still a chance for their marriage.
2. He was proceeding "by his own timetable."
3. He was concerned about her ability to "survive without him."

We discussed these alternatives and she accepted the notion that Mr.
T. was probably doing what was best for him.

Mrs. T. began to update her cognitive résumé by searching for a
job that would provide an important building block in reworking her
life. She was riddled with self-doubt. We now concentrated for several months on her view of herself as a worker. She feared failure
and had little self-confidence. She had been "out of the market" for
too long. She acknowledged that she felt "as good as she had seven
years ago," save for continuing to blame herself for the "marriage
failure." She saw a future of "interpersonal aloneness." By now, she had
lost 60 pounds and was becoming quite satisfied with how she looked
at age 51.

There were several "dates" with Mr. T., each ending with a depressed mood and a view of herself as "defective." She believed that
she was a "poor judge of men" and would "always be alone." The
errors of selective abstraction and arbitrary inference were frequent
in her self-assessment after she spent time with Mr. T. She identified
the "finality of her separation" from Mr. T. as the factor undermining
her self-worth. She had assigned too large a slice of her self-esteem
pie to the status of being married.

We discussed the uncontrollability of outcomes. She described a
sense of perfectionism that lay at the root of her "return to work"

fears. She had now been in therapy for one year and abstinent from alcohol for six months. She thought that she had achieved a more rational view of Mr. T. and of herself over the past six months of therapy. Mostly, she now liked what she saw in herself, except for the schema of self-blame still attached to her marriage. She believed that "depression and alcoholism permitted her to remain in a relationship that was bad for her." Was she avoiding the stress and challenge of once again being single? Mr. T.'s lack of sensitivity, his passivity, and his incapacity for intimacy made him a poor choice for a mate. Her error, therefore, was in *choosing* him, not in failing to make the marriage work. "You can, with difficulty, make changes in yourself," she said, "but you can't change someone else."

She was pleased that she had been able to lose weight and then stay at an acceptable level. She was proud of "no longer being involved with alcohol," but believed that she would have to maintain her vigilance to maintain sobriety. She planned to continue frequent attendance at AA meetings. Two big issues were conquered, and two remained. Her self-view was not yet where it needed to be, and she remained apprehensive about her upcoming return to the work world.

We reviewed the predictors—pro and con—available from the past relevant to her current work performance. A balance sheet on the blackboard listed the positive and negative factors. As she went over them, we discussed what it would take to convince her of her "work worth." Only performance on the job would be persuasive to her. And that, she was aware, would be subject to the meanings she applied to events. Acute depression was no longer a problem; rather, the ongoing ways in which she made attributions seemed responsible for determining her mood over time.

Our sessions accompanied her through the interviews, the deliberations, and the final decision to accept a job offer. She identified automatic thoughts relevant to anticipatory anxiety that was her companion during her initial months at work.

I continued to see Mrs. T. weekly for three more months. Her initial adjustment at work was excellent, as she was extremely well received by coworkers and supervisors. She developed a small cadre of friends, largely through AA meeting attendance. We decided to shift into a follow-up phase of monthly visits and await developments.

Over time, she received several work promotions. The first time she had to fire an employee was difficult for her, but sensitively managed. At the one-year anniversary of her sobriety, she gave a party and invited 20 guests.

When she was promoted to a position of "real responsibility," there was a brief "fear of failure." We discussed the need, once again, to update her (psychological) résumé regarding work performance and potential. The long period out of the work force had now been superseded by a one-year period of employment. The past year provided sufficient predictors of work success to counter her earlier anxieties.

Events like the Christmas holiday evoked a sense of aloneness, reawakening cognitions of relationship failure. We discussed her various social choices and some of their consequences. After one year of monthly visits, we began to meet quarterly. She signed a separation agreement. Her husband moved out of the area. She defined her goal now as a "search for a life structure." Much of her *self* was defined in terms of work, where rave reviews had resulted in leaps up the corporate ladder. Periodic personalization continued, but often she caught these now and developed alternative approaches.

We decreased visits to a frequency of once every six months. She was light years away from the depressed, overweight, alcoholic woman I had first encountered. She was aware of discomfort with intimacy and continued to shy away from taking social risks and initiative. Questioned about this, she maintained that she was not interested in exploring these areas further in psychotherapy.

Clearly, I had become a continuing figure in her life. Our contact, however, was now limited to planned reviews every six months. I rarely heard from her between follow-up visits. She was delighted by her success at work and change in personal habits. The impact of her marriage upon her sense of self-worth had diminished markedly with time. She continued to retool her self-view despite only infrequent therapeutic contact. Total time in psychotherapy was about one year, with five years of follow-up that continues, infrequently, to the present time.

For further reading about the application of the cognitive model to a range of personality disorders, please consult a book by Beck, Freeman, and associates (1990).

10
Reparenting

The lay view of psychotherapy, especially of long-term psychotherapy, is often that of one adult (the therapist) assigning blame for the problems of a child (the patient) to another set of adults (the parents). This so-called bashing of mom and dad apparently shifts the responsibility for the patient's outcome from him or herself (often manifested as depression) to one or both parents (sometimes thought of as *healthy anger*). Allowing for a considerable degree of distortion (the therapist rarely interviews the parents at any length), a case is built to indict the parents in absentia.

A cognitive therapist would accomplish little with this approach. It is central to the achievement of change, in my view, that the patient accept responsibility for his or her own thoughts, feelings, and behavior. We are each taught many things by our parents' example, their words to us, and their reactions to our behavior. Often our parents (and people in general) act in ways expected to gratify their own needs. Frequently, their actions result from an active consideration of our best interests as children. Sometimes we must conclude that they do the best they can. Sometimes other influences have formative effects on the development of the child.

In addition, the impact of parental teaching might not yet be obvious by the time of adolescence. What may be evident in the "child" is the lack of a structure on which to base the formation of an identity. Additionally, the child may be unable to achieve an effective separation from the parent(s). There may be inadequate self-definition to allow the pursuit of a career. Clinically, this picture may produce depression and/or the characteristics subsumed in the amorphous label of borderline personality.

Most of my patients are in the age range of 30 to 50 years old. My growing interest in geriatrics accounts for a small peak at age 70. I accept few teenagers as patients, believing that adolescent specialists are better equipped to deal with this turbulent age group than I am.

I have, however, treated a small number of adolescents using a model I call *reparenting*. Typical of the younger person I have treated is a 17 to 27 year old, more often female than male, usually chronically depressed kid, often in the midst of a crisis. He or she typically has no one to turn to, despite having access to a loving, interested parent (or parents). There is usually a special reason for accepting the referral. Either it is the child of a person with whom I have some connection or an adolescent specifically referred for cognitive therapy who has had little benefit from other forms of psychotherapy.

A review of the past history reveals academic failure (typically in high school), relationship failure (poor choices and bad outcomes), and often some form of substance abuse. Typically, the adolescent has many friends (one of his or her strengths), is at least of average intelligence (another plus), has siblings and parents who have achieved success, and is not living up to anyone's expectations. The symptoms these adolescents present include depressed mood, pessimistic outlook and low self-esteem; generalized anxiety and often specific phobic avoidances, along with a variety of self-defeating behaviors.

Therapy is long-term (either continuous or intermittent for perhaps five years or longer). Despite the patient's having capable people as parents (who often have demonstrated effective parenting with other children), one framework for understanding these treatments is reparenting. I become accepted as an *alternative parent* and actively challenge the conceptual matrix the adolescent or young adult has formed to meet life's situations. Little by little on a succession of issues, old ideas are discussed, sometimes acted upon, reviewed, and labeled with regard to cognitive errors (where appropriate). Alternatives are sought, tried on and tried out. When the process works, change becomes evident to the patient, producing a certain momentum that facilitates further changes. For some life problems, the adolescent seems to have no preparation or an extremely inadequate (or bizarre) cognitive map. Often there is great inertia and fear of change, with withdrawal from, rather than confrontation of, a problem.

Identity formation seems always to be a therapeutic issue. Separation from family of origin is an issue as well. Low self-worth, within the context of passing school courses, finding a significant other, or furthering a career, is constantly encountered. In the borderline patients, there is often active antagonism toward the parents, and act-

ing-out is associated with risk-taking behavior and often suicidal, or homicidal acts. In the depressed adolescents, the clinical problem is more often avoidance and withdrawal than risk-taking behaviors.

An attempt is made to help the patient reformulate his or her self-view. In the process, the view of the parents is often reworked as well. This may enable the reestablishment of a supportive friendship in place of a combative clash that satisfied neither party.

The issues, while similar in content to those I encounter with adults, seem much more immediate, threatening, and central to the lives of these "teenagers" (whether the patient is in his or her teens or twenties, the problems dealt with are the typical adaptational events of adolescence). And always, there seems little of substance to fall back upon. Only after change and some achievement can the adolescent begin to rely on recent success to support optimism in the face of stress.

Let me paint a few life pictures to illustrate the range of presentations for which reparenting has seemed an appropriate description. A 26-year-old woman had endured several "near" marriages, one six-month marriage, and many unsatisfactory relationships of varying lengths. She had a strong need for approval, was highly dependent and rejection-sensitive, and frequently felt taken advantage of by men. When a relationship developed beyond the initial meetings, it invariably was labeled as a "last chance" for her.

In therapy, she began assembling the pieces of a functional identity. She defined career interests and put herself on a desired path. She established a framework for relating to her parents and became able to ignore some of their repetitive negative comments that used to prompt withdrawal. She became more willing to take social risks, and developed a more philosophical (and less catastrophizing) outlook on relationship outcomes.

Individual sessions often were oriented toward finding perspective on an ongoing situation. The result was that she frequently "felt good" after a therapy hour. When a goal was reached and therapy stopped, it often resumed around her reaction to a new stress—e.g., illness in a family member or an unsatisfactory turn in a relationship.

Over a three-year period, she became noticeably more assertive, expressive, and self-confident and less demanding of others. She had defined a place for herself to be on a variety of life issues.

Another woman in her mid-twenties presented with a raft of anxiety symptoms, a tendency to ruminate, and dependency on, but alienation from, her family. She could not find a satisfactory job or form a satisfying relationship. She, too, was rejection-sensitive and, even more so, highly attuned to the approval of others.

She was phobic of driving, about being out after dark, and in general, about confronting novel places and situations. She continually made (negative) arbitrary inferences and overgeneralizations.

We worked at generating options, countering her negativity and identifying the ultimate consequences in many of her feared situations. She persevered through a series of unhappy job situations. She married a man who offered her some of what she wanted in life, while necessitating some real compromises by her as well. She achieved some acceptance of those traits in her parents that were unlikely ever to change. Meanwhile, she "became" an identifiable individual—far from a parental reprint—who exemplified some qualities of her mother and father but was specifically dissimilar in many important ways. Psychotherapy continued for five years.

A 22-year-old man was referred by a close friend of his when he expressed dissatisfaction with the pace and benefit of psychoanalytic individual and group treatment over several years. A precipitant was his depressive reaction to the loss of a relationship with a woman. He described continual relationship problems, alienation from his family, and little self-definition. His religion formed a major part of the identity he possessed, but he felt that more self-development was necessary and he "didn't seem to be doing it." His love and talent resided in art, but he had committed himself to manual labor so that he could make a living wage.

Early in our sessions, he spoke of "needing a blueprint" for how to proceed with several major problems. He also brought in a recent painting. He talked about his art as a necessary channel for self-expression, more difficult for him when it was verbal and face-to-face. We talked about his beliefs and expectations relevant to various relationships. He described a bragging, somewhat manipulative interpersonal style as a means of keeping control. We talked about the meaning of control, other means of achieving it, and the need to develop the capacity to do without it some of the time.

Over a six-month period, he began liking himself more and proved able to generate some optimism. He dated, but wished for a meaningful relationship. Then an opportunity came to leave the area and join an art cooperative; he took it. He stayed for two months and then returned to Washington, resuming his labor job and psychotherapy.

Over the next six months, he continued to paint and work and date. He began to achieve his first real separation from home. A career as an artist seemed like a real possibility. Therapy again stopped, and I heard little from him for 18 months.

He returned with real concern about the absence of a committed relationship in his life. He noted how most of his peers (at 26) were married or living with someone. He put his art work on a back burner and took a job working for a relative. Psychotherapy was focused now on meanings relevant to relationship. His anger and his difficulty with trust came to the fore. After three more months of therapy, he decided to terminate.

Eighteen months later, he called to tell me about some major life changes. We scheduled a follow-up session. He had met, developed a relationship with, and would soon be engaged to marry a woman with whom he could talk. They were "a lot like each other." He had a number of career possibilities but had not yet made a commitment.

Six months later, he brought his fiancé with him for a "premarital interview." Eighteen months later, he wrote to say that marriage was going well and that they were in the midst of discussing a move out of the area. Two years later, I received a card announcing the birth of their first child. Although some (mostly career) identity questions remained, this was now a man who knew himself better, liked himself, and had taken a number of positive steps forward into life.

THE COGNITIVE WORK

In each of these cases, the relationship between therapist and patient seemed crucial. An attitude of warmth and caring, combined with a noncritical acceptance of, as we say, where the adolescent was at, permitted the therapist to be accepted as a friend. One critical difference between the parent and the therapist seemed to be the lack of real life consequence to the therapist of the patient's successes

or failures. It was evident to the patients that I hoped for their success and that I tried to be comforting and encouraging when there were setbacks. However, I would not be measured in terms of their outcome.

I found that, through analogy, I talked with these patients a great deal about my own children. I felt that, if they had ever met, the appropriate greeting might be: "It's good to meet you. I have heard so much about you!" I could role model, in this way, a kind of acceptance of disappointment, a "rolling with the punches of life," as well as a pride in achievement.

By continually approaching their situations in terms of thinking (as opposed to behavior), we kept the emphasis on what they could do to affect their environment. This was meant to counter the orientation to blaming external events and listening to influential others instead of taking responsibility for themselves.

By identifying cognitive errors and thinking up alternatives, we focused on *choices* as opposed to *right and wrong*. Over time, I believe that this helped the adolescent build a repertoire that would become him or her *self*. Dwelling on displeasing outcomes was discouraged; instead, we would return to goals ("What did you want to accomplish?") and means ("How can you get there?").

Each psychotherapy had a prominent section on risk assessment, as the adolescents were encouraged to take prudent risks. This encouragement was aimed at countering the restrictions built upon the foundation of multiple avoidances over time. I would often refer to risks my children had taken in areas relevant to the issue of the moment in therapy.

At times, "talking it out with your parents" was promoted. At other times, support for the patient's growing autonomy took the path of suggesting that they keep their own counsel. I usually made it clear that I was available to them to chat at any time. Limits were set so that weekend telephone chats at home were not opportunities for hour-long sessions.

The bulwark of the therapy focused on the use of the triple column. Homework was more uniform with this group than with my patients in general. It seemed to provide the additional structure that this group required. Frequently, that homework entailed the keeping

of a log that formed the basis for therapeutic work in the office. That log usually catalogued situations, feelings, and automatic thoughts. This work progressed to the identification of schemas and then to the design of experiments to test the usefulness of basic rules.

I was flexible in terms of scheduling appointments with parent or parents, boy- or girlfriends—in fact, any significant other who the collaborating pair felt would help illuminate an issue or problem. Often, my patient and I would spend a session preparing for a future collateral visit.

Now, let me discuss one attempt at reparenting in detail to illustrate the principles. When I met Sarah she was 21 years old, living at home and being treated for depression with antidepressant medication. She was working in a bookstore, after, as she said, "barely graduating" from high school. She had tried a community college but left, feeling scared and overwhelmed. She had not had a date in two years. She described her orientation to life as: "I sit around waiting for things to happen." She had experienced severe social anxiety in a variety of situations. She had had three years of psychotherapy, with little change.

Initially, we discussed common everyday problems and possible alternative approaches to them. She learned the cognitive terminology quickly and was working in the format of the triple column. Atypically, the interaction between us became an early focus for therapy because of several missed appointments, followed by a "you're mad at me" letter that she sent to me. When the relationship is explored in cognitive therapy, it is not understood in terms of transference. Rather, it is treated as any other situation or relationship would be. What are your feelings? And what are the associated thoughts? This approach quickly and concretely distinguished our contact and task from those between Sarah and other adults.

When she began a dating relationship with a negative and manipulative young man, this became the next agenda item for therapy. Shortly thereafter, she took the first trip alone that she had taken in several years, and it went well. Earlier, she had avoided travel because of vague apprehensions about being alone. This represented a growth step, therefore, and we studied it in detail to identify both her thinking and her successful actions.

Her fear of vomiting and then of a dental procedure occupied us next. In each case, she emphasized the need to maintain conscious control or else feel the fear associated with losing control.

She moved out of her parents' home and got an apartment with a friend. She began to consider leaving the bookstore for a better job. She thought about how she might gradually return to college. After six months of therapy, she was less depressed, most of the time. There was, however, little sense of who she was and little effective separation from family, with continued unsatisfactory relationship experiences with men.

Sarah registered for two courses and got a job in a clinical setting working with the elderly. Often, she refused to acknowledge her gains, fearing they would, somehow, be taken away. Her progress was sawtoothed, with real jumps forward balanced by frequent falls backward. At several points that required a decision, suicidal ideas emerged. She understood this to mean an incapacity to cope with the consequences of choice by avoiding the decision entirely.

By the one-year anniversary of weekly psychotherapy, we began decreasing her antidepressant drug, upon which she had become psychologically dependent. In her thinking, a common cognitive error was overgeneralization. I tried to point it out whenever it came up. For example, at times she would focus on aspects of her appearance (she was extremely attractive) and find specific fault, generalizing to the belief that she was ugly.

Sarah dropped one of her two classes because it involved others scrutinizing her work and she was unwilling to permit that. In another class, she was maintaining a "B" average when she missed several classes and suddenly dropped out. Predictably, she generalized and lost the confidence for a time that she could do college-level work. Over a period of several weeks, she thought through the school experience and reached some more specific conclusions about the outcome of her "trial of school." She wanted to return to school, but was unclear as to the best strategy for doing it. Meanwhile, she began a rocky relationship with a man, adopting the posture of trying to please him and finding it difficult to express to him how she felt.

We scheduled a meeting for her parents, Sarah, and me. I told them about her gains in therapy in terms of identity, work, and to some extent, self-worth. They were proud of her but somewhat taken

aback when I suggested that she was ready to try full-time school-work. They agreed to support her if she was motivated to follow this course. She was, and their support was an important boost for Sarah. By now, she no longer took any medication.

She registered for a full schedule of classes. She handled the interview and made the adaptation to college classes surprisingly easily. She was astonished that she could now express herself in a classroom setting. She moved back home to save some money.

A long-term relationship ended. Her school term also ended, with a "B" average. She registered for another full term. Sarah liked her clinic job, but was envious of others with credentials to work with the older residents and oriented her thinking toward a mental health job. She was now comfortable in many social settings, permitting her to identify some specific phobias, for example, one of air travel. We worked on this by identifying and testing her automatic thoughts, then considering alternatives.

When she became ill with a respiratory problem, a lengthy hospitalization raised anew some issues (e.g., dependency, separation, fear of losing her gains) which seemingly had been put behind her. There were several telephone sessions during her hospital stay, aimed at reestablishing perspective.

At the same time, she had met and begun to date a young man quite dissimilar from previous choices. It was pointed out that she, too, was hardly the same as she was five years earlier, when psychotherapy had begun. Visits were now more sporadic, usually monthly. Over time, she and her boyfriend overcame some obstacles to their relationship and deepened their commitment. She worried that "something would happen" to affect this area of happiness she had found. We traced this belief to a schema in which she told herself that she was unworthy of success in any life area. Considering this, it made little sense to her in light of the changes she had been able to make over recent years. We discussed self-confidence, and what might form a rational basis for possessing it.

She talked about school and her concern with the outcome of a particular class. Meanwhile, she acknowledged doing well in all her other classes. This particular subject required intensive work and she wondered aloud whether she was motivated to do it. We reviewed her goals in school and what she expected to gain from her degree. I

asked her if in fact she felt that she was *incapable* of doing the work required or whether the issue was truly whether she *wanted* to do it. I stressed the limited time she would have to work hard to master this subject and how important it was for her that she knew she could achieve in this class if she chose to.

She saw a future issue in the need to learn to accept those aspects of the style of her boyfriend that were different from hers. She talked of career issues involved in finding a first "definitive" job. Another area that required continued work was her tendency to make arbitrary inferences about low probability events, and then to take them personally.

In the months that followed, appointments were less frequent. The young couple planned their wedding, and Sarah started her last school term. There were multiple occasions upon which she "spoke her mind," previously a difficult challenge for her. She overreacted to a class exercise by personalizing it, and then loosened its grip on her by discussing it with a variety of people. Now that she was truly "somebody," it was okay to share even the rough edges of herself with significant others. We worked to differentiate what belonged to the "old Sarah" and might occasionally recur from those areas that would require continued vigilance and work for her to feel good. I remarked, on many occasions, how rewarding it was for me to see the person she had become. She felt not quite like a daughter, not quite like an adult peer. I always looked forward to our now infrequent sessions.

Five years had passed and Sarah had achieved some self-definition. She had completed her schooling and had begun to actively look for a job. She had met and married a man who fit her concept of a "mate for life." She was a functioning member of a loving family, but was busy now establishing a family of her own. She had a real feeling of having successfully negotiated a difficult life passage. She seemed ready to confront the challenges and uncertainties of life that lay ahead. Those adaptive qualities of sensitivity, hard work, and loyalty that she had been taught by her family early in life were now evident, unobstructed by the obstacles of depression and anxiety.

11
Couples Therapy

I don't deliberately treat couples very often. Sometimes, though, I commit myself to a person who has clear communication problems with a spouse. The *couples therapy*, therefore, evolves as a second stage of an individual treatment. I also see significant others as part of an evaluation often enough so that I have gotten to know (at least a little bit) some husbands and wives of my patients.

More is involved when a second party is introduced into the therapy than merely providing another chair in the room. When the initial treatment was individual, the entering spouse may logically consider the therapy pair as bonded in some way. At the least, the therapist has had contact with and learned about one person in detail. He or she has formed an impression of that person and likely identified some admirable qualities. They may have achieved some success together, paving the way for an attempt to work with the marital pair.

The spouse may believe that he or she has already been represented in the therapy, perhaps unfairly. The view of the spouse has been presented (distorted?) within the context of another's needs, beliefs, and meanings. How can the therapist now be unbiased and helpful to the couple? Won't he or she support the views of his patient against those of the spouse? These considerations make the success of a venture proceeding from individual to couples therapy less likely. And, to be fair, at times this procedure does not work well. A new therapist, meeting the couple afresh, may have real advantages.

However, at times the good relationship with the initial patient is not seen as an obstacle, but rather as a benefit. The patient may have shared with the spouse much of the content of the therapy sessions. The therapist may have been presented to the spouse as a source of support, rather than as an adversary. He or she may be seen as a family friend. Several patients have told me that their spouses were not motivated to "start with someone new," but that they were willing

to see me because they believed that they would be comfortable and "familiar with how I operate."

Aside from considering the meanings to each person of events in the therapy, applying the cognitive model to work with couples appears to offer few additional problems. Once again, the model provides a language within which to understand the interpersonal difficulties of two people. Often, I have found, the hard work of one member seems to spur the other to work hard as well.

One couple I encountered years ago is particularly memorable. Rather than meeting and treating one first, with the couples therapy following, I shifted back and forth between individual and couples work. In prospect this would seem to offer maximal opportunity for disruption and discontinuity, with little chance for success. In practice, I believe it worked optimally for each partner, as well as for the partnership.

Rebecca came with her husband for an initial evaluation. She told me that she and Robert had problems talking about things, but more urgently, that she had, as she said, "stopped functioning" in her usual manner. Robert was an attorney in the small town in which they lived. For many years, Rebecca had organized and managed his office. They had raised three "smart, good children."

Twelve years earlier, he had changed the focus of his practice and she did what today would be called paralegal work. Eight years earlier, they consulted their family doctor because of their communication problem and had 10 joint sessions with him over a three-month period. Three years earlier, Robert's practice decreased in volume, Rebecca got a job as a secretary to someone else, and he felt abandoned. She felt pretty good. Only later did her depression manifest. For the past six months, they had tried to deal with the consequences of her leaving the practice, with little success.

She described herself as a 50-year-old woman who seeks approval, avoids anger, needs autonomy, is generally passive, and makes considerable demands on herself. She felt that she had not accomplished much in life thus far and often seemed to have little time for herself.

Over, the past six months, she had experienced disrupted sleep, awakening in the middle of the night, and again earlier than necessary in the morning. She felt a tightness in her throat, a loss of appetite, a decrease in energy, constant fatigue, and poor concentration. She

had sustained a 20-pound weight loss. In sum, she described dysthymia, with symptoms of major depression becoming prominent over the past six months.

She had not led a sheltered life. Born in Maine, she left home to attend nursing school in Texas. She became a nurse in a small town, then joined the Navy and was abroad for five years. She met her husband abroad, married, and then moved to a small town in Virginia. They had three children and, as they all grew older, she worked in her husband's practice.

Robert was 49 years old. His father, too, had been an attorney. Born in a small town in Ohio, he attended college in the midwest and law school in Boston. He met his wife while in the Army in Germany. He was attracted to her physically, and stressed that he liked her independence.

He saw the marriage as bringing each of them some fun and the chance to travel together, as well as three fine children and untold hours spent together. They had worked in the same space for years and now he knew that she needed more distance. The marriage, despite its many positive aspects, had provided little feedback for him, little real "contact." He knew she didn't easily tell him how she felt and that often she felt "inferior."

Robert was action-oriented and extroverted. His relationship with Rebecca was very important to him and he found that he missed terribly her physical presence at work. At the initial evaluation, his major problem seemed to be an interpersonal (relationship) one, while Rebecca had a depression that required immediate attention. I decided to treat her individually first.

She began the initial session by describing her identity as "totally wrapped up in Robert and the practice." She desperately wanted to be herself, "whatever that was." She wanted to do something "all her own." In subsequent meetings, she described a life filled with "shoulds." We discussed rational parameters for her self-worth, how she assessed risk before acting, what were her choices, and whether there was any benefit in her expressing "minority opinions."

She became aware, over time, of some anger at Robert. I took this as a cue to invite her husband into the therapy and began to identify with them an agenda for the couple. In the first joint session, they demonstrated to each other how each of their concepts of *spouse* was

seriously flawed. Also, their temperaments and styles were substantially different. She was, by now (two months into therapy) becoming less depressed. I assured Robert that she could tolerate his anger and disappointment with her and encouraged him to express it. Likewise, she permitted herself to get angry with him.

He found it difficult to "take risks" with her, hard to allow himself to become vulnerable. His overriding expressed concern was a fear of hurting her with his words. As she became more open, he was able to take more risks. By the fourth joint meeting, they reported less tension at home and more "cross-talk." Now, a dominant issue was determining what Rebecca wanted out of life and facilitating her achievement of that goal.

Toward that end, I scheduled several individual sessions with Rebecca. She identified some negative automatic thoughts:

1. "I do it differently, and I'm wrong."
2. "When he feels sad, I feel responsible."
3. "I expect him to do as I do."

The cognitions were challenged, and I told Rebecca that she needed a better guide to understand Robert than she would find by her own example. She reported continuing recovery from depression and was now ready to decide whether she wanted to return to Robert's office or to continue at her present job. She worried about not having any autonomy if she returned, but acknowledged that she was now better able to express her wishes to Robert. She, too, missed the "special time" their work together had provided.

Six months after therapy began, she decided to rejoin the law practice. They brought me a gift, a blackboard, which I have since used on a daily basis. ("Every cognitive therapist needs a blackboard," Rebecca said.) We discussed two levels of communicating: a focus on content and a focus on process. At any point, either Rebecca or Robert could make a comment to the other on either level.

They worked hard, separately and together, between sessions. Rebecca described a trap that she set for herself. "If I do what I want to do," she said, "I may get what I want, risk provoking Robert's anger and then feel guilty. If I don't do what I want, I won't get what I

want and then will put myself down for it. The way I see it, I lose either way," she said.

"I, too, have a trap:" Robert said. "I avoid telling her what I think because she may do what I want in order to get my approval. Or, she won't do what I want in order to assert her independence. I lose either way," he said.

Each could see in listening to the other how one's cognitive set paved the way to the trap. The solution involved first challenging the expectation and then faithfully representing to each other their real needs. Once again, Rebecca was confronting her sense of responsibility for her husband's happiness. And Robert needed to learn to accept his wife as a person in her own right. By the next joint session, they each expressed an awareness of movement. He began to think of her statements as "trial balloons." She saw her main issue as choosing between freedom and responsibility.

With Rebecca scheduled for minor surgery, I planned my first individual session with Robert. He reported feeling "more understood" by her. He felt she was "gaining inner strength." As a group of three, there was a growing friendship among Robert, Rebecca, and me.

A decidedly more optimistic Rebecca turned up for the next few individual sessions, but now she thought that Robert was becoming depressed. She attributed his mood change to his "seeing her slipping away" and fearing that she would leave him. He had expressed to her a need for a few "private lessons with me."

I scheduled a few individual sessions with Robert. He described the phenomenon as "twinning;" his expectation was that Rebecca would be like him. I compared their style difference (each effective, parallel roads to Rome) to the differing color of their eyes. We discussed in detail the consequences of accepting one's spouse despite (or because of) the differences.

Rebecca and I then met individually. She discussed two important issues that she felt she was dealing with effectively: conveying her sexual needs to Robert and dealing with a daughter's college choice. When next the spouses came together, they jointly lamented how they seemed to be moving in opposite directions. He was looking to leave the practice of law to move on to something else. She was looking to find a career to form part of a new identity. Over a short time,

she came to the conclusion that work wasn't *necessary* for her to have an identity, and wouldn't suffice for one, either.

They spent a fun vacation together, the first in many years. She reported "liking him again" and no longer fearing that she would imminently become depressed. Robert, who enjoyed sailing as a hobby, quoted Seneca: "For the man who has no harbor, no wind is a good wind:" He was focusing now on a career change that threatened his self-worth equation. Rebecca noted how multiple options presented themselves to her in most situations now, where there used to be only *shoulds*.

Now, one year after therapy began, the couple came in and each told of a return of depressive feelings. "I am nothing, feel phony, empty and weak," she said. She had found an old diary and relived her past negative thinking. She had been "fooling" me and her husband into believing things were now different. Nothing had really changed. Robert told of having few friends. His self-confidence was diminished because his "children were leaving, his wife no longer needed him, his practice was disappearing, and he was faced with the loss of Rebecca as a partner."

I talked with them about being "stuck in the same old x–y axis." It was time to shift their focus to the rules (the process) rather than battling with the content. In response, they each reframed their dominant view as a "crisis of confidence;" as opposed to "their plight." Each acknowledged that they had distorted their appraisal of the gains achieved in the past year to fit a reaction of the moment. Robert emphasized his need to look inside himself for guidance to life's next stage. Rebecca pointed to how important it was for her that she and her husband have a "common identity" in addition to her own. One unexpected consequence of Rebecca's return to the practice for both of them was an insight into how working together now was not the same as it was before. Neither found it as satisfying as was anticipated.

Eighteen months after therapy began, Rebecca no longer had signs of depression. She had quit her job and "returned home" to an uncertain future in the practice. She felt it was the right thing to do for herself. Robert had learned to have input without exercising total control, He told of "getting a glimpse 25 years later of 'the girl' I married."

In the last session, we reviewed formally what each of us saw as having transpired in therapy. They stressed the "unique relationship" we three had shared. She saw major changes in herself, having been put in touch with her resources. Robert described a loosening and relaxation of an essentially obsessive-compulsive style. He could more easily relinquish control and relax now, in a new way. He remained unclear about his career direction, but felt confident he would find a "rewarding port in which to drop anchor."

I am not suggesting that, for any individual psychotherapy, the patient's spouse can easily be shuttled into and out of the treatment room. Most clinical cautions have some sound reasoning as their basis. I have found, however, that there are potential advantages as well as potential disadvantages to this clinical *sequencing*. While issues of maintaining confidentiality and siding with one of a pair may defeat this arrangement, the good will generated with one family member may present dividends in the engagement of another. With gains for each of two individuals added to the growth of the couple, the outcome validated an attempt at therapeutic flexibility.

For those clinicians with a special interest in marital therapy, a book by Beck, *Love is Never Enough* (1988), presents cognitive strategies and interventions that may augment your clinical repertoire.

12
Follow-up

The mission of the University of Pennsylvania's psychiatry residency program was to train academicians. Their graduates would teach and do research, treating enough patients to maintain living contact with their subject of inquiry. We were taught that every patient was an *n of one* research study, worthy of considerable thought and likely to contribute ideas to the treatment of subsequent patients.

This approach led naturally to keeping detailed records, to noting hypotheses whether or not they proved to be correct, and to using rating scales for more quantitative measurement of significant variables. While a resident in training, I was encouraged to terminate a psychotherapy treatment properly by considering what had happened in the therapy, why change had occurred when it did, and what the nuances were of ending the relationship between therapist and patient.

It was evident to me that most therapists never again see their patients after psychotherapy is over, unless there is a call for more treatment and the patient chooses to resume with the same therapist. However, I had been taught that this leads to a lack of understanding by the therapist of where the treatment fit in the context of the patient's life. Surely, a patient who subsequently found another therapist, may have received medication, may have required inpatient treatment, or may have found success in another modality of therapy had reached a different outcome from one who applied what he had learned over a period of months or years, with success and without further consultation. Similarly, someone who had a few booster sessions (*reminders*) of the therapy approach at key times in the future was in a different outcome category from one who had several lengthy periods of therapeutic contact. It seems obvious that there is no way to know this at the time therapy ends.

In this framework, my commitment to follow-up was nurtured. I would suggest to my patient, after all but the briefest of contacts, that we meet again one month after termination. In a flexible program, a

subsequent meeting would usually be set for three months later and then for three or six months after that. I was told many times that a follow-up program facilitated the patient's initiative in calling me at a time of future need. It implied continuing interest. In addition, for most people having problems subsequent to a period of psychotherapy, a short course recalling the cognitive approach, one session in the office or one chat on the telephone, led to successful problem-solving. My commitment to follow-up visits antedated managed care regulations being imposed on psychotherapy. Intriguingly, as justification was more regularly required to schedule sessions, my request for follow-up visits was never denied. I believe this was because they were *seen* as cost-effective.

Early in my psychotherapy experience, a depressed man successfully completed about 20 sessions and resolved his midlife problem. For follow-up, I saw him three times over the following year, in what would become my standard paradigm. Toward the end of what we described as our "final, final session," he asked why we needed to stop. He had found these periodic life and coping reviews to be useful. He made the analogy to car care, "If I am willing to bring my automobile to the dealer every 10,000 miles for routine maintenance," he said, "why shouldn't I take similar care of myself?" In this way, the concept of follow-up as an "oil and lube" for the cognitive apparatus was born. We made a contract to meet every six months, until he decided that it served no further useful purpose. We met six times over a three-year period.

A significant number of people I have treated return, at some point, for more therapeutic work. Several have recalled to me my standard departing statement: "Remember, if you run into an obstacle you cannot deal with alone, you now have an account at Chase Manhattan. Call me, and we will determine together what will meet your needs."

Colleagues have told me that few clients or patients would be willing to pay for therapy when they are functioning well. I have found just the opposite to be true. The follow-up program is often seen as an insurance policy against the possibility of future incapacitating problems,

For the therapist, the gains in follow-up are potentially enormous. I have been able to differentiate those who have learned and applied

the cognitive model successfully from those who feel better at the end of therapy but have *learned* little of lasting value. I have identified a group of relapsing depressives (for example) whose problem seems to be biologically based and whose course seems impervious to psychological learning. Especially in these patients, and in some less seriously ill as well, there are characteristics inherent in learning that occur in one state (e.g., *well*) that do not transfer to another state (e.g., *ill*). This state-dependent learning can defeat the patient's attempt to apply gains in psychotherapy to abort subsequent depressive reactions. A final benefit for the therapist comes from intermixing, in a single day, a few follow-up sessions with relatively well individuals with those draining hours spent with the acutely ill.

The structure for these follow-up hours is fairly well established in my practice. Following the initial greeting, "It's good to see you again" (and if it isn't good to be together again, the patient usually won't come!), we review events and circumstances over the elapsed period. We note emotional symptoms and recurrent problems. The format most commonly employed utilizes a triple column structure. I remind the patient of the cognitive therapy approach and together we apply it to situations and reactions. Even if there have been several emergent problems, a detailed application in therapy to one of them often permits the patient to take on additional issues by him- or herself. The session ends with a plan for further contact at my initiative at a specified time, or at the patient's calling as needed.

REVIEW OF FINDINGS
AT FOLLOW-UP

Joan, a 25-year-old, unmarried woman, consulted me after becoming depressed while on a vacation trip. Her first episode of depression had occurred five years earlier, accompanied by a serious suicide attempt. She was not now suicidal, but did score 18 (of a maximum 39) on a short form of the Beck Depression Inventory (BDI; Beck, 1967), a score consistent with severe depression. I treated her with an antidepressant drug (Desipramine, 150 mg per day) and cognitive therapy.

Psychotherapy consisted of 10 sessions over a 10-week period. The focus was on a recent relationship that had gone awry. We considered her need to grieve the loss, her continuing need for his approval, her

anger at how he treated her, and her negative self-view. As her depression cleared, she was able to learn to be more assertive with her wants and expressive of her feelings. She gradually reoriented her self-view, detaching it from the input of her recent boyfriend.

When I saw her two weeks after the course of therapy was complete, she talked about pressure from her old boyfriend to resume their relationship. She told him that she "still cared for him" but was not interested in a reconciliation. She was dieting and had managed to lose seven pounds over a three-week period.

When I saw her one month later, she felt "good to be alive" and remarked that she was now "letting people know how she felt on a regular basis." Three months later, she had sustained her gains and her BDI score was zero. A new relationship had begun and "blossomed." She was sleeping well and was energetic, taking now a maintenance dose of the medication.

Three months still later, her relationship, job, and self-esteem were all doing well. We discontinued the medication. A telephone call one year later revealed no recurrence of depression. The follow-up program permitted some conclusions to be stated with confidence. I believe that her depression responded to a course of antidepressant medication and that she had made good use of a short-term cognitive therapy to make some adjustments in her thinking about relationships.

Dave, a 35-year-old man, married with two small children, presented with complaints about the rigidity of his obsessive-compulsive style. He had a history of alcoholism, and he and his wife had once had couples therapy after he had disclosed an extramarital affair. Their therapist suggested that he find some individual treatment to complement the couples work.

We discussed the disparity between his expectations for himself and his achievements, his difficulty with openness and intimacy, and his problems acknowledging dependency and feelings. This was accomplished within the context of a cognitive approach based upon the triple column technique.

He became better able to enjoy a social occasion without alcohol. He found it easier to talk in therapy about what angered him. During one part of the almost nine-month course of treatment, he noted real difficulty in handling feelings of which, in the past, he had been unaware. He began to cultivate interests outside of work. At another

point, he emphasized that he found the "repetitiveness" of therapy hard to tolerate.

Late in our time together, his son expressed anger at "not seeing enough of daddy." Dave supported the observation and made significant schedule changes in response to it. He saw himself as "much more flexible" and "much less uptight." He saw workaholism as a danger to avoid.

Two weeks after our what we then considered our last session, he noted that, for the first time in memory, he was pleased with himself. He reviewed how he was dealing with the major areas of his life.

One month later, he described a "new willingness to share himself with others." He was now able to "have some fun." He told me how difficult it had been for him to accept the suggestion of individual psychotherapy and how glad be was that he had come. He would miss the "social aspect" of our work together.

Dave called 18 months later to set up an appointment. The stimulus of a job offer had led to a return of "old thinking." On a blackboard, we outlined in detail his thinking concerning the meanings inherent in his accepting a new position. One session proved sufficient for him to reestablish perspective.

Three years later, he called during a period of self-appraisal, triggered by some new work opportunities. He was so attuned to the needs of those around him that, he felt, his own needs were getting lost. He was considering marital separation. We agreed to a brief course of cognitive therapy focusing on his marital decision. Over a six-week period, Dave successfully resolved his doubts and recommitted himself to the relationship with his wife. I believe that our relationship, nurtured through follow-up, facilitated a successful brief therapy years later for a man otherwise unlikely to have sought consultation.

Phil, a man in his mid-thirties, consulted me 10 weeks after his wife had left him. He blamed himself for her departure and stated, "Right now, I don't like myself very much." He had many obsessive traits and found it hard to express anger.

By our second session, his wife had decided that he should have custody of their daughter Annie, age 4. He talked about how angry he was at his wife and how anxious he was about assuming the burdens of single parenthood.

By the seventh session, he felt confused by his wife's behavior and by her decisions. Soon he was made aware of her relationship with

another man, and of her plan to leave the area and settle elsewhere. By session 15, he had recovered the bases for his self-worth, accepted his expanded parental role, and resumed many of his prior behaviors.

We made an appointment for one month later, after a discussion of issues relevant to termination. At that time, he had begun a new relationship and deepened his tie (and time) with his daughter. We had several follow-up sessions at monthly intervals. Relationships came and went. He was alternately irritated by and delighted with the demands and antics of his daughter. During a time when everything appeared to be changing, the follow-up sessions were a useful anchor for him.

A meeting after the passage of six months revealed an obsessive man who had weathered a challenging situation after an initial adjustment problem and was now attacking life with his previous verve. He was more aware of and expressive with his feelings, and his young daughter remained the first priority of his life. For him, follow-up provided a useful bridge to a life of difficult and novel circumstances.

Susan, a woman in her late thirties, was referred to me by an old friend and colleague when she became acutely depressed. A perfectionist by nature, she viewed most problems through a polarized (black and white) lens. She desperately sought the approval of a rejecting parent who had led a radically different life from that chosen by her daughter. She didn't know how to relax or how to spend free time.

Psychotherapy centered around the concept of choices and consequences. Cognitive errors (chiefly personalization and polarization) were consistently identified, and alternative strategies were developed for approaching situations. She recovered from the acute depression and made significant gains at work and at home over a five-month period. The follow-up sessions reemphasized the cognitive method for her.

Over a six-month period, she called twice for sessions aimed at helping her cope with brief absences of her husband related to his job. Her problems concerned feelings and beliefs of dependency and a host of *what-if*'s that were generating anxiety.

One year after termination, she returned for a second course of psychotherapy, precipitated by the birth of a child and her transition from full-time work to full-time parenting. She felt "trapped" and overwhelmed. Her self-view, previously tied to work success, was tak-

ing a beating as she tried to establish herself at home. This therapy, lasting three months, facilitated a life stage transition for her.

Monthly phone calls charted a continuing good adaptation, until a proposed job transfer for her husband precipitated a third course of therapy. Three sessions were devoted to helping her establish an acceptable meaning for what had transpired. Having been born in the midwest and having moved to Washington, she would now reside in Massachusetts. In this short contact, real impediments to the couple's communication were revealed. I believe that my continuing contact with her over this two-and-one-half-year period facilitated the scheduling of several very helpful joint sessions at this time.

Susan's husband, Stephen (with whom I had had only brief telephone conversation), joined the therapy with surprising ease (see Chapter 11). He revealed that he felt he "had known me for a long time" before we finally had the opportunity to meet. There were no preliminaries, and we set right to the task of pinpointing their communication problem. Susan seemed proud of Stephen's "ease" in therapy, and pleased that the two of us could finally meet. She felt confident that, reasoning together, we would soon find a solution. Stephen knew the cognitive method from some preparatory reading he had done, as well as from conversations with his wife. She expressed her anger to him about feeling excluded from his decision-making process. He asked her how he could atone for the regrettable error he had made in not involving her from the outset in the process of relocation.

The family moved to Massachusetts and several lengthy, warm letters followed. About one year later, Susan called requesting a "telephone appointment." She was having a "crisis of confidence" and the option of starting psychotherapy with someone new was not attractive to her. Besides, she "only needed a brushup" to regain some lost perspective.

A letter one year later described a functional family, two satisfying jobs, and two growing children. Their adaptation to New England was proceeding "on course." The therapist in Washington was granted "honorary family membership" and offered a place to stay while visiting the region.

V

The Model
in Practice

13

Case Examples

This is a time of change and uncertainty for psychotherapists in general and psychiatrists in particular. Over thirty years ago, I was taught, both formally and informally, a series of rules and expectations to guide my future work. Several of the conditions upon which these expectations were based have changed. The future promises still more changes. Before I describe a range of patients who have benefitted from cognitive therapy, let me consider some of today's realities that affect the model in practice.

GENERAL CONSIDERATIONS

The traditional roles of and definitions for *psychiatrist, psychologist, social worker*, and *counselor* have changed and to some degree blurred. The correct answer to a recent exam question I posed to my College of Charleston abnormal psychology class ("Who does psychotherapy?") was: "All four." Many trainees in the Medical University of South Carolina (MUSC) psychiatry program have been highly motivated to learn cognitive therapy. Several of the cases featured in the following section are theirs, not mine. At the same time, the list of places hiring psychiatrists and yet prohibiting them from doing psychotherapy grows. The prospect of spending four years of psychiatric training so one can only prescribe a range of medications and treat four patients each hour would not have been attractive to me when I entered the field of psychiatry. It is an unattractive prospect to many of MUSC's psychiatrists in training.

THE NON-HUMAN ENVIRONMENT

To aid the reader's transition from considering the cognitive model to doing cognitive therapy, let me paint a picture of the process of attending a psychotherapy session in Charleston.

After parking in a large visitor's lot, the patient crosses the street to enter the Institute of Psychiatry, a five-story building with two wings. Passing a large Information Desk, the patient proceeds to take the South elevator to the fifth floor. There, a secretary greets the patient, and registers him or her for our clinic. A phone call tells me that my patient has arrived.

My office is small, but fitted out with a desk, a file cabinet, a bookcase, and a couch. Sunlight streams in through two windows. College and medical school diplomas, a board certification in psychiatry, and a certificate acknowledging me as a Founding Fellow in the Academy of Cognitive Therapy display my credentials. Paintings represent a range of personal interests: jazz, running, basketball, and a Charles Bragg rendering of "Psychiatrist," complete with straggly beard, fingers crossed, horseshoe, rabbit's foot, and sand clock!

The bookcase is laden with memorabilia from places I've visited and things I've done. It is a treasure trove of conversation pieces, or "background noise," suggesting that a real person, with real interests resides within. My desk has a computer, a clock, and a tile plaque that reads: "Aqui vive un profesor" (A professor lives here). The books reflect my interest in cognitive therapy and depression. Papers and journals are kept in stacks.

ON DOING SUPERVISION

With the passage of time, I have grown increasingly dissatisfied with "just doing therapy" and have sought ways to broaden my work experience. This mindset led directly to my decision to leave Washington, DC, and move to Charleston. At MUSC, my job description provides time for treating outpatients with cognitive therapy. In addition, I spend ten hours a week supervising the cognitive work of our third year psychiatry residents.

A wonderful opportunity open to a clinician cognitive therapist is the chance to have an impact upon the thinking of trainees learning to do psychotherapy. Five years after beginning as a supervisor, and over fifty resident therapists later, I have formulated some ideas about the process. Engagement, the initial task in treating a patient, is also the first step in supervising a trainee. When this relationship is warm, caring, and interested, useful learning is likely to follow.

When either the supervisor or supervisee is cold, distant, and unmotivated to learn, the training is largely a waste of time.

I typically begin a supervisory relationship by inquiring about the ideas about psychotherapy the trainee brings to our venture. I then briefly present the essence of the cognitive model, emphasizing the need to "think cognitively" as well as to utilize cognitive techniques. As the trainee presents his or her patient, I teach "listening for the cognitive elements." A dynamic formulation is of no use in this process. What does help is a cognitive map of those beliefs that initially seem related to the patient's distress.

At times, a trainee will state: "I don't have a good patient for the cognitive model." My response to such a statement may be that, had I reviewed the same intake evaluation, I might have actually found several reasons to use the cognitive model! Sometimes what the clinician *listens for* (his or her mindset) may determine the recommendation of a therapy model. Once a patient (or two) has been chosen, we work at helping the trainee to identify relevant automatic thoughts. The teaching of disputation emphasizes a range of approaches. At the more unstructured end of the methodological spectrum, the conversational therapist–patient dialogue is framed in a cognitive context: lots of therapist questions, a focus on present-day meanings, and the use of stories and analogies to *shift the set* so as to illustrate or evoke alternatives.

Supervisor–supervisee interaction moves smoothly from a patient context, with the supervisor modeling potential responses, to a personal context with the supervisor utilizing self-disclosure or focusing on an issue in the trainee's domain. This will work best when interpersonal engagement is well established, along with trust and motivation to learn. When done well, it makes the sessions unpredictable, stimulating, and, often, fun for both parties.

The reward for a successfully treated case in the form of a case study published in a journal has served as an important incentive for trainees to work hard. Later, once the trainee organizes the case materials, it assists him or her in learning to write a case report while respecting confidentiality in the therapeutic context. My selection of assigned readings begins with the initial four chapters of this book. Further reading typically awaits a relevant case, or is done on the trainee's initiative, with questions provoked by the supplementary reading brought to the supervisory hour. Additional readings are cho-

sen individually, to support the interest of the trainee. Cognitive therapy cases—those published by residents as well as my own—are distributed as examples of the model in practice, as well as guides to case writing.

I have found that telling "appropriate" stories to the resident in supervision often represents the best illustration of how to shift set in order to teach the patient. I have been paged by several trainees to tell me that they have "told their first story" in therapy.

In summary, cognitive therapy is best taught by an apprenticeship experience in which the trainee works with an individual supervisor over a period of six months to one year. A motivated supervisor paired with a motivated trainee provides the highest likelihood of success.

ON BEING A CONSULTANT

The offer of a job in Charleston consisted of 50% salary for work in psychiatry, and 50% salary for work in internal medicine. Over the past five years, budgetary considerations have reduced my consultative work to one day per week.

One of the trends evident over the past decade is the redistribution of responsibility for the treatment of the emotional disorders. Once the exclusive domain of psychiatrists, psychologists, and social workers, the depressions and the anxiety disorders commonly present in the offices of family doctors and internists. Typically, the providers of care are not yet well enough trained to recognize them, and so they often go untreated. Presenting with an emphasis on physical complaints, the search for a cause may exhaust the professional medical training of staffs, involve costly medical tests, and often result in overtreatment.

These developments provide an interesting opportunity for the provider of mental health care. An *attached psychiatrist* may now work alongside a multi-disciplinary group of health care providers in a primary care clinic.

Not surprisingly, the initial challenge for the psychiatrist working in a medical setting is engagement. Similar to the first stage of successful psychotherapy and the initial task in supervision, the psychiatrist must form working relationships with the various members of the health care team. Demonstrating an interest in the personal con-

cerns of team members (e.g., families, children, community, sports) is a key first step. Defining a clinic teaching role is step two. Finding a way to be informed about patients to whose care you can contribute, is step three. That no patient comes to the clinic specifically to see you validates the need for performing steps one and two.

When I arrived at the Adult Primary Care Clinic, I quickly became familiar with the interests of the staff. As a result of an early retreat for clinic staff members, I was asked to organize and teach a didactic hour each week, covering the range of emotional disorders encountered in the medical clinic. Students (e.g., medical, physician assistant, and pharmacy) typically spend one month in this ambulatory medical setting. Two Wednesday mornings a month, I present cases treated in the clinic that involved depression or one of the anxiety disorders. The third session covers general cases, which range from schizophrenia through obsessive-compulsive disorder (OCD), dementia, eating disorders, and alcoholism. When management of any of these cases is discussed, the relevance of psychotherapeutic treatment is stressed, in addition to drug therapy approaches.

It quickly became evident that psychotherapy was not adequately taught in the three training programs. Therefore, the fourth monthly session is devoted to this topic. It begins with a discussion of preconceptions about psychotherapy and ends with a brief presentation of the cognitive model. Several case presentations are always included.

In a neat connection of two of my roles, cases requiring brief psychotherapy are often referred to the psychiatry resident's clinic, where I supervise the trainee's work and can follow the progress of the case. I challenged the procedure of "referral to a list," by calling the resident psychiatrist personally (as I would in private practice) and asking if he or she would be interested in the referral. They nearly always said "yes," and often made arrangements to meet and evaluate the patient in a timelier fashion than their intake schedule would allow.

In an article published in a major medical journal (Schuyler & Davis, 1999), my internist coauthor and I described in detail the process of becoming a successful attached psychiatrist. In a second article submitted for publication, an internist colleague and I describe setting up the didactic program on emotional disorders in a primary care clinic (Schuyler & Clyburn, 2003). I wrote a brief paper discuss-

ing psychotherapy in terms familiar to general medicine (Schuyler, 2000). Its publication in the *Primary Care Companion to the Journal of Clinical Psychiatry* led to a request that I submit an article on brief cognitive therapy for each issue. This led directly to a feature called: "Psychotherapy Casebook," which has enabled some of my cases, as well as a significant number of resident cases, to be published over the ensuing years.

In the reworking of the road map that will describe the opportunities available to the psychiatrist of the future, be mindful of the rewards of working in a medical setting. I am grateful for having the chance.

A WEEK AT THE OFFICE

For twenty-five years, I had an office practice of adult psychotherapy. Although some patients were treated with medication when I thought it was indicated, *all* were treated with cognitive therapy. Although some patients were seen for lengthy periods of time with character change as the goal, most received brief cognitive therapy aimed at relieving distress.

At MUSC, the pattern that earlier defined my outpatient practice in Rockville, Maryland, has continued. The ingredients that have been added to my professional life at MUSC have been discussed in the previous two sections on clinical supervision and psychiatric consultation. Significantly, my work with psychiatric residents (more properly their work with me) has produced a broad range of successfully treated cognitive therapy cases.

I will present a combination of cases drawn from my patients and their patients as if they were "yours." My goal is to simulate a week in the life of a cognitive therapist working in an office practice, twenty-five hours a week. My hope is that, after "seeing" these patients through the eyes of several clinicians, the reader will have a clearer idea of how to do cognitive therapy.

Monday Morning, 9:00 A.M.

In Chapter Six, I presented a cognitive view of falling in love. In this process an icon is formed which represents the idealized beliefs about a loved one. When the relationship ends, grieving the actual

loss may not be the hardest part. A bigger challenge may involve dealing with the loss of the hopes, the dreams, and even some mis-representations—the dismantling of the icon. Failure to deal with the icon may delay the individual's capability to move on with life, and grief may evolve into depression.

Your first patient is Alice*, a thirty-year-old, caucasian woman whose chief complaint is: "I'm having a hard time adapting to being a sepa-rated, single parent." She had moved to Charleston, South Carolina, from Nashville six months after Peter, her husband of six years, left her. Their daughter was then two years old. Peter claimed he was "unhappy being married and didn't want to be a father." After Alice related her story during a visit to her primary care doctor for a routine physical exam, he referred her to me.

Alice knew Peter from the time they were each thirteen years old (in middle school). Her parents divorced when she was twelve, and her fa-ther (to whom she had remained very close) died of a heart attack he suffered at work when she was twenty. She dated one boy throughout high school and he died in a motorcycle accident when they were se-niors. At this point, Peter became a close friend and looked after her. They married when they were each twenty-four, and she worked to sup-port them as he began a law career. Alice described herself as someone who "takes responsibility for, and tries to fix, people." She was her mother and father's only child. After graduating from high school, Alice took college classes for five years while working. She had worked in Charleston for the past few months as the office manager for an ac-counting firm. Periodically in the prior year, she had "shut down" be-cause of stress. She would stay to herself, sleep fitfully, overeat, get exhausted, and be unable to concentrate at work. She was unhappy about being alone and did not really understand how Peter could have loved her for so long, and then left her and their daughter.

Her goal for therapy was to learn "what she needed to know to move on without falling apart." She had no history of alcohol or drug abuse. The diagnosis was major depression. She wanted a problem-solving therapy, and specified that she wanted to take no medication.

I explained the cognitive therapy model to her, with its focus on meanings, beliefs, and options. She defined her problems as: 1) dealing with separation, 2) dealing with being a single parent, and 3) formulat-ing a life plan.

---

* This case is adapted with the permission of *Primary Care Companion to the Journal of Clinical Psychiatry*. The case originally appeared in D. Schuyler (2002). Being left. *Primary Care Companion to the Journal of Clinical Psychiatry*, 4(2), 76–77.

We worked first on establishing an explanation for the separation. We examined how she understood her situation and her ideas about Peter's thinking. I used some analogies and self-disclosure early on to help her focus when she could not look profitably at her own situation. The material came from the lives of friends of mine, as well as from my own life. Sometimes people can see a concept more easily in the context of a life other than their own. She rapidly engaged in the therapy process, forming a genuine connection to me as a helping agent.

When Peter arrived for a one week visit "with his daughter," we discussed her expectations. Only afterward did Alice reveal her hope that he would decide to "stay and reconcile." She was angry with him when he left after the brief visit. She blamed Peter for "ruining the life of his wife and daughter, and taking no responsibility for it." I encouraged her to keep a log of her strong reactions in the form of a triple column table: situations, feelings, and thoughts. Each of the next several sessions began with an examination of this assignment.

In session five, she began to think about a life plan by crafting an elaborate agenda for herself. The plan included imperatives for her to get out more, work out, make some new friendships, take time to play the piano, and also to "get over Peter." We discussed strategies for achieving her goals, referring back constantly to the meanings she assigned to events.

By session six (three months into therapy), she reported sleeping and eating better, having more energy, and enjoying a markedly better mood. We discussed her view of dating and some parenting options for her little daughter. Using a format of choices and consequences, she related her plan to move to a new house in one month. She had gone house-shopping with a girlfriend, found a suitable place, and had made an offer that was accepted. She discussed potential relationships with men, her reinvigorated view of herself, and her pride in her daughter's milestones.

At session ten, she told me she had decided that Peter was really not good for her. She had also embarked on a weight loss program and shed ten pounds in just three weeks. Session eleven occurred after her move, which she viewed as a real accomplishment and a herald of a new beginning. We reviewed the changes she had made over the prior five months. Over the next two sessions, she demonstrated real initiative in social and work situations (previously lacking) and expressed surprise at her own success, but felt really good about herself.

At the end of six months and thirteen sessions, we terminated therapy. At that time we discussed her view of what she attributed to herself, to me, and to the therapy process. She wrote to me one month later to describe her application to a program to earn a degree in accounting. Two months later, a second letter told of her acceptance. Three months later, amid talk of success in her classes, a letter described her reaction

to Peter's initiation of divorce proceedings. The most recent letter arrived almost one year after our last visit. In it, Alice wrote in detail about school grades, her daughter's school successes, her stipulations for the divorce, a new job, new friends, and an active social life. Alice seemed ready now to go on with her life.

Monday Morning, 10:00 A.M.

People who are somewhat shy, self-conscious, and introverted, typically fall within that portion of the bell-shaped curve that we consider to represent the "normal personality." They minimize social interaction, and often devote themselves to successful solitary pursuits. It seems clear, however, that for some people a similar group of personality traits result in substantial restriction. As children, they may have been fearful of being called on in class. They may experience great discomfort eating in a restaurant with others. Typically, they don't date much. At work they may refuse to make public presentations. They may even be unable to use a public restroom.

This picture defines a less familiar component of the anxiety disorder spectrum known today as *social anxiety disorder* (SAD). Once the disorder was conceptualized so that cases could be tabulated, it was found to be the third most common psychiatric disorder in the United States (after major depression and alcoholism).

Fortunately, SAD is often treatable with selective serotonin reuptake inhibitor (SSRI) antidepressant medications (even in the absence of depression), as well as with brief cognitive therapy. Cognitive distortions are a common feature of the syndrome, making this form of psychotherapy particularly applicable. Sufferers anticipate social rejection, fear uncontrollable anxiety, and often desire social approval. They "validate" their negative expectations by avoiding social situations.

Your second patient, Tom*, is a 30-year-old, married, radio broadcaster who consulted his primary care physician for chronic problems

---

* This case is adapted with the permission of *Primary Care Companion to the Journal of Clinical Psychiatry*. The case originally appeared in D. Schuyler (2002). Fear in the presence of others. *Primary Care Companion to the Journal of Clinical Psychiatry*, 3(2), 80–81.

with diarrhea. The doctor's determination attributed the problem to irritable bowel syndrome (IBS). She recommended dietary discipline and suggested that Tom consult a psychiatrist to shed some light on emotional factors that might be contributory to his complaints. She referred Tom to me for further evaluation.

The patient described himself as "nervous talking to people, avoiding social opportunities, and periodically finding job-related interviewing difficult to do." He had always been shy and introverted, but did not begin actively avoiding social contact until one year prior to our initial meeting. He compiled a fine academic record in high school and college. He had, however, no close friends. He was aware of being extremely uncomfortable at public functions, and typically tried to "get out of going." He was at ease only in the presence of his wife. Married for four years, he and Lisa had no children. He frequently felt anxious but never had experienced a panic attack. There was no evidence of posttraumatic stress disorder (PTSD), no depression, and no specific phobia.

His parents had divorced when Tom was five years old, and he, his brother, and his sister were raised by their mother. His brother was three years younger and, by Tom's account, emotionally stable. His younger sister had received treatment for a bout of depression. There was no other family history of emotional disorder.

My diagnosis was SAD. I suggested to Tom that a brief course of cognitive therapy might be helpful. I told him that medication is sometimes useful for this problem, but that I would recommend a brief therapy approach to start. If we were successful, medication would not be needed. He agreed to the plan I outlined. I sent a note to his primary care physician detailing my diagnosis and plan.

In our second session, I taught Tom the cognitive model for identifying meanings in the context of a situation that might explain the anxiety he felt or the avoidant behavior he had chosen. We utilized examples from his history to stress the relevance of the model to his situation. In describing a stressful encounter with his boss, Tom identified the relevant automatic thought as: "He sees me as lazy." We examined his logic and considered alternative explanations. His first homework assignment was to keep a triple column table (listing *situations*, *feelings*, and *thoughts*) to catalog events associated with distress.

Key automatic thoughts identified in the third session included: "Other people often notice me" and "I worry that people won't like me." I asked Tom to support his predictions, and, when he had no data, to consider alternate possibilities. In the subsequent session, he noted strong anticipatory anxiety prior to meeting a new group of people. Once again, we identified (similar) meanings and worked to find reasonable alternatives. He noted that he was "beginning to see results from using the cognitive approach."

My case notes documented a high frequency of black-and-white

thinking. When, in session five, he provided another example of this polarization, I asked Tom about it. He told me that he "rarely saw grays." We worked to expand his thinking to include a range of options rather than only the two extreme categories. He noted that "as a side effect of therapy" he was becoming "more assertive" in his interactions with people. This was of interest because we had never discussed assertiveness or passivity. This observation was a testimony to Tom's tendency to think about psychotherapy issues between sessions.

Session six led us to the consideration of the pros and cons of a potential work promotion that would alter some of Tom's job duties. We defined the choices he saw and their likely consquences. He also told me about a social evening spent among his wife's friends that "would have been impossible before." He noted that he felt surprisingly at ease with people he didn't know well. His wife later commented to him about "a major change in his social ease."

In our seventh and final session, Tom said that therapy had "helped overcome years of shyness and avoidance." When patients successfully conquer a social anxiety problem, they frequently view their new adaptation as a major change in their life to date. Tom's life had become "much busier." He now saw little, if any, self-imposed restriction. He told me that he was spending much less time ruminating about himself. Once again, he had never previously mentioned rumination. We discussed the changes he had made, and how he understood them. We agreed to end psychotherapy for now, with the promise of availability in the future at his initiative. A year then passed since he and I began our work together, and a follow-up phone call found Tom maintaining his gains.

Monday Morning, 11:00 A.M.

An adjustment disorder represents a reaction to an identifiable stressor and in which the reaction occurs within three months of the onset of the stressor. The patient's distress is either in excess of the norm or is attended by a clear impairment in social or occupational functioning. The syndrome does not meet criteria for an axis I disorder (e.g., major depression or generalized anxiety disorder [GAD]), does not represent the worsening of a preexisting disorder, and is not related to bereavement. Once a successful adaptation has been accomplished, or the stressor has ended, the symptoms generally disappear over a short period of time. The treatment of choice is psychotherapy, not medication.

Your third patient is Rosalie, a 43-year-old woman married for twenty-one years, with a fifteen-year-old son. Her recent move (two months prior to the first session) to Charleston was the sixth recent relocation due to her husband's frequent reassignments at work. Upon arriving from Philadelphia, she found herself crying constantly. She had disturbed sleep and disrupted concentration.

The family lived in a small rented townhouse, quite different from their home in Philadelphia. Her son, initially unhappy with his new school, had recently transferred and "was doing better." Her husband received a raise related to the move, found this job less stressful, and was nearer to his family. She wished the family could return to Philadelphia. A concern for Rosalie was the neighbors, who were decidedly younger than she.

Rosalie doesn't drink, smoke cigarettes, or abuse drugs. She has held various (mostly writing) jobs in the past; in Charleston she has yet to gain employment. Born in the midwest, Rosalie was raised in eleven different states as her father's construction job led to multiple family moves. She described her mother as an intelligent scientist who raised six children. Rosalie is the youngest of the children. Growing up, she had few close friends. She graduated from high school in Texas and then left home for a job in New Orleans. Three years later, she met Richard and after a year had passed, they married when she was twenty-two-years-old. She "does not like change."

My diagnosis was: adjustment disorder, with depressed mood. I explained the cognitive model to her and she agreed to a course of brief cognitive therapy. In session two we applied the model to some of her son's demands of her, as well as to meanings she related to the move. I pointed out her tendency to catastrophize events. Together we outlined a list of things she might do to "take charge of her life." I posed questions, and she generated a list of actions.

Session three occured two weeks later. She reported successfully applying the model and feeling "more settled" with her son, with school, and with herself, "now that she knew she would be staying here." She had investigated a job at the city newspaper and was planning to volunteer at her son's school. She and her husband had discussed looking for a house.

Session four took place one full month after the third session. She reported feeling "on top of the situation" now. They had found a house and would be moving "to a more permanent area" in a month's time. Her son could continue in the same school. Her husband was initiating social activities for them. She had met people during her time at her son's school.

We reviewed her move and how her thinking could be seen as having triggered the adjustment reaction she had experienced. She told me how similar her reaction was to what she had encountered with previous moves. She hoped this would mark a definitive change, because the "Charleston period" would be uncertain in duration (as usual). This fourth session was our last, until she called me two years later.

"My husband has been reassigned to Nashville, Tennessee," she said. "We move in two months, and I have noticed symptoms similar to the last time. They are milder, and I know I am anticipating the move. This time, I want to 'nip it in the bud.'"

Once we renewed the therapy, Rosalie described in detail her successful adaptation to life in Charleston. She even had become involved in a network that helps newcomers adapt! In the interim, her father had died of a stroke. She loved the beaches here, and would miss the friends she has made. Recently, she had noted periods of sadness, apathy, and procrastination; there were no crying spells, however. I asked what she expected of Nashville. We outlined her key beliefs in a conversational format: no triple column tables, no blackboard, no homework. We planned to meet in two weeks and then once again just before she left for Nashville.

In the second session in advance of the move to Nashville, we discussed farewell parties, packing, and issues her son (now seventeen years old) had raised. She talked about the contacts she had already made in Nashville: elected officials, newspaper people, a realtor, a school board member. In this session we employed a triple column table to approach some anticipated situations that she linked to distress.

At session three, Rosalie told me of their plans to leave in a week. She emphasized that she thought she had done a competent job this time, and was "prepared to leave." There had been few tears and "lots of perspective." She felt that she had helped others deal with the family's departure. She and her husband had several preparatory talks with their son. In the past two months, she had been three times to Nashville. She called cognitive therapy "a tool for life," and promised to write to me once they were settled. Two months after this last session in Charleston, a letter arrived expressing her gratitude for our therapy sessions and extolling the virtues of Nashville.

Monday Afternoon, 1:00 P.M.

Obsessive-compulsive disorder (OCD) forms a particularly paradoxical recommendation for cognitive therapy. The patient's obsessive thinking style would logically fit well with an approach focused on cognition. If part of the problem, however, is an exclusive (and often ruminative) preoccupation with thinking, what's the purpose of providing more grist for the mill? Despite the paradox, a cognitive therapy intervention has proven useful for some patients with OCD. You be the judge.

Back from lunch and ready to go, your fourth patient of the day is Robin, a 28-year-old married mother of a three-year-old daughter. Her

chief complaint centers around a variety of checking behaviors that have come to dominate her life over the past three years. Robin knew she needed to get help when her three year old said to her: "I'll check the curling iron for you, mommie."

Really, she recalled, her rituals began in childhood when she "checked things" for her mother. This is what made her daughter's remark so urgent for her. Her husband sees her as a perfectionist and has noted that her rituals are driving them apart. Six to seven times a day she checks to see if the curling iron is off, and she must count to five each time. About seven times a day she checks whether the garage door is shut. Twice each night, she gets out of bed to see if the ice machine is off. When she checks the stove (five times daily), she checks each of six notches on two knobs, and must count to twelve each time. She "supercleans" the house (e.g., vacuums, dusts, cloroxes "everything") each Monday, Wednesday, and Friday. On Thursday, she cleans "the entire house." Feedback from others starts new rituals. She has rituals before bed, upon arising, and when leaving home. Once she feels "ownership" for a place (e.g., her mother-in-law's home), she begins rituals there as well. She is angered when a ritual is interrupted.

My diagnosis was OCD. I explained the cognitive method to her in session two and, "it made sense." We identified automatic thoughts related to her various ritualistic behaviors. I asked her to test them for rationality (e.g., "Does it make sense?") and strategic worth (e.g., "Does this help get you where you want to go?"). If the belief failed either test, she was to try and identify viable alternatives. We discussed the curling iron, the garage door, and her cleaning from this perspective.

She began session three noting that she was able to "not dust" the living room table for the first time. She was able to "leave her daughter's fingerprints" on the glass top table. She "didn't wipe water" from the bathroom mirror after her husband brushed his teeth. Asked exactly how she was approaching her rituals, she told me: "After I turn the curling iron off, I say to myself, 'The curling iron is off,' and I don't seem to need to go back to it. Same with the garage door. I ask myself, 'Why is it necessary to do this?' and the answer is, 'It needs to be perfect' or 'It will feel better.' I can now dispute these thoughts successfully."

In session four, she reported doing housework more related to need than to ritual. She noted how for years she had kept "lists for everything." I suggested that she keep them for now, and eventually decide which ones she needed. She was noticing that she had time for lunch now, when it hadn't been there before. She had her first nap in over three years because, she said, "I had nothing I had to do!" She actually allowed her daughter to play with play-dough (It used to be a clean-up nightmare, and she would forbid it).

We met two weeks later, for session five. She had "gotten rid of the lists." She was doing laundry once a week, instead of daily. Her husband couldn't believe the changes, and Robin felt much more comfortable

with her daughter. She reported less checking, less cleaning, was less often anxious, angry, or overwhelmed.

Our final session was scheduled for one month later. She noted being able to "forget to do things" without consequence. A self-worth dividend appeared in that she felt "great about herself" and what she had accomplished. She could be interrupted during a task now, without a problem. She had suggested to her husband that they "date" each other so he could learn about "the new Robin." We discussed what was attributable to the patient, the therapist, and the process. Robin felt that she had overcome a major life burden. A call to her six month's later found that her gains had been maintained.

Monday Afternoon, 2:00 P.M.

During my psychiatry residency training at the University of Pennsylvania, I gravitated toward Aaron Beck because his cognitive model represented a natural application of how I tended to approach problems. I took the risk of telling my supervisor that I found his therapy approach useful because "it was what I did." Instead of responding (accurately) that, at that early stage, I didn't know how to "do" anything, he touched my shoulder and suggested that we'd likely be spending a lot of time together. I remember feeling transformed and to this day, I credit that statement with providing an important contribution to my self-worth.

I had a similar experience with one of my supervisees, Marc Dalton. When I spoke cognitively with him, it came as no surprise that he seemed to "intuitively understand." I saw myself—thirty years earlier! As Dr. Dalton told me about his work with a patient of his, Frank, it was clear to me that he was elaborating his own adaptation of the cognitive model. It was an experience I was to have several times again when I worked with a group of bright, young, creative trainees. Dr. Dalton was teaching his patient to be "thought observant," to be empowered to find a self-view unrelated to his emotional disorder.

Your last patient of the day is Frank*, a 25-year-old Asian-American man who recently completed a graduate degree in public policy. He

---

* This case is adapted with the permission of *Primary Care Companion to the Journal of Clinical Psychiatry*. The case originally appeared in M. Dalton & D. Schuyler (2001). A marriage between pharmacotherapy and psychotherapy. *Primary Care Companion to the Journal of Clinical Psychiatry*, 3(3), 140–142.

presented at the university clinic seeking management of a previously diagnosed bipolar affective disorder. He had recently been hospitalized following an episode of serious depression. Earlier, Frank reported a lengthy period of stability in which he was maintained on lithium carbonate, 600 mg. per day, and sertraline (Zoloft), 25 mg. per day, for approximately five years. Unfortunately, a new family physician recommended that he try a different and not widely prescribed mood-stabilizing agent for the management of his symptoms. During that drug trial, Frank's depressive symptoms reemerged: depressed mood, lost energy, and diminished appetite. His sleep cycle became erratic, and suicidal ideas appeared. No manic symptoms preceded the episode of depression. However, he did report having two episodes of mania in the past, neither of which resulted in a hospitalization.

At the time of Frank's intake evaluation, which was two weeks after his discharge from the hospital, he continued to report depressed mood, decreased energy, and trouble sleeping. He also felt anxious and confused, with clouded thinking. He denied current symptoms of mania, panic anxiety, obsessive thoughts, compulsions, or substance abuse. He wanted to return to his original medications.

Frank also exhibited low self-esteem. He had come to view the world in an "all or none" fashion. He had concluded that he would not ever be able to have a successful relationship with a woman, and would probably never be able to hold down a respectable job. He worried about becoming dependent on his family, feeling guilty and frustrated about having to rely on them for financial support.

My diagnosis was: bipolar affective disorder, Type I, currently depressed. A second visit was scheduled one week later to continue information gathering and to explore additional treatment options. By the end of our second visit, I decided to add Zoloft, 25 mg. per day, to his treatment regimen, and also to titrate lithium carbonate upward, while tapering and then discontinuing the new mood stabilizing agent. A Beck Depression Inventory (BDI) score of 24 was consistent with his current depressive state.

Our third meeting took place approximately three weeks later. Frank's serum lithium was in the therapeutic range. Additional tests had ruled out other possible causes of depression including thyroid abnormalities and anemia. His BDI score was now recorded as 0. His thinking was no longer clouded. He felt better, but still did not feel as if he had the confidence to proceed with his life. This loss of effectiveness commonly accompanies depression, is not generally responsive to medication, and has been called demoralization. I presented psychotherapy as an adjunctive option for Frank.

While listening to Frank's thought patterns during the second session, I became aware of cognitive distortions. I believed that these erroneous thought patterns might be contributing to his demoralized state, pre-

venting him from achieving his goals. When I introduced the idea of cognitive therapy to him, he responded that he had tried psychotherapy in the past. He went on to describe a nondirective, insight-oriented approach. I explained that dynamic therapy explored the past in the hope of recognizing symptom origins and, thereby, initiating change. I contrasted this with cognitive therapy, which focuses instead on meanings in the present, and teaches the patient to examine his thoughts and choose ways to think that facilitate achieving his goals. Frank stated that he had never thought about psychotherapy in this way, but he was willing to try.

In session three, I presented him with the triple-column model for examining problems. He understood the method after using two examples of everyday situations taken from my (the therapist's) everyday life, like not performing well on a test. We then applied the model to situations in his life, like meeting a woman he was interested in dating. Frank believed that having a mental illness would prevent him from having a meaningful relationship with her. He thought dating for him would be associated with failure.

Frank discounted the fact that his last romantic relationship had lasted approximately three years. Further, he generalized his pessimism to include an inability to maintain health in other areas of his life. He said that he "was doing nothing with his life." He ignored his recent completion of graduate school, successful control of his illness, and acquisition of a job. We prepared several triple-column tables to examine the errors in his thinking. We identified cognitive errors of discounting (an inability to accept positive feedback), over-generalizing (reaching a conclusion not supported by data), and catastrophizing (believing that the worst possible outcome was also the most likely to occur). Frank expressed surprise that he could actually "think himself" into a state of feeling depressed.

During our fourth and fifth sessions, Frank demonstrated that he had mastered the technique of identifying key meanings so well that we no longer needed the structure of the triple-column table. Instead, we just spoke. Frank defined situations, I pointed out cognitive errors, and we, together, challenged them. During the fourth hour, I learned that he had established a relationship at work with a female colleague, Sally. We discussed an episode in which he had not heard from her in about a week, and how, as a result, he had felt depressed. We identified the errors of mind-reading (jumping to conclusions) and catastrophizing. He believed that she had lost interest in him because he had discussed his illness with her. We considered that, although bad things do happen, personalizing events can result in guilt and self-blame that are often misplaced. In session five, he proclaimed that he had learned that his fears with Sally were unfounded, and that he had some data that he could use to challenge his cognitive errors.

By sessions six and seven, Frank was able to catch his own cognitive errors. He later obtained a better job working as a public relations officer for a local events management company. He acknowledged that at times he had the tendency to revert to old ways of thinking. I told him that this happens to everyone. The key was to become "thought observant" and not be trapped by our own erroneous thought patterns. During our eighth session, Frank stated that he had started a new relationship and had noticed no visible signs of an emotional disorder. His thinking was no longer catastrophic in nature. He seemed energized by the new relationship, and unencumbered by his previous beliefs.

In session eight, we decided to end the brief psychotherapy intervention and focus our future, less frequent, meetings on medication management. Our ninth appointment was set for two months later. Frank continued to manage his illness well, and he became successful in his new job. Eventually, he decided to move away to live on his own and look for a more lucrative job. Together, we recalled how this decision would have been impossible for him earlier. He said the difference for him was being able to recognize how his thoughts influenced his mood. At our last meeting, Frank was stable on his medications and eagerly anticipating the future.

Tuesday Morning, 9:00 A.M.

The symptoms of a panic attack often lead patients to seek initial evaluation at a medical clinic, making it very likely that a primary care or emergency physician will be the first to see a patient suffering from this disorder. What follows is the case of a patient who is prototypical of the patients seen frequently at the Adult Primary Care Clinic (APCC) at MUSC. Our aims with the panic disorder patient in a medical setting are: 1) To make the diagnosis, 2) To acquaint the internist or student with relevant medication options, and 3) To refer the patient to a reliable facility for brief cognitive therapy.

Phyllis had presented to the APCC complaining of episodic chest tightness and shortness of breath. Once the medical evaluation was complete, I was asked to see and evaluate her condition for a possible diagnosis of panic disorder. My consultative recommendation was that panic disorder was the likely cause of her distress. I suggested a trial of paroxetine (Paxil) to start at a dose of 10 mg. per day, and offered to refer the patient for brief psychotherapy. I thought that Jeff Cluver, a sensitive and motivated trainee, would be a good match for Phyllis. I also knew that he could "think cognitively," and do cog-

nitive therapy skillfully. I called Jeff and he seemed eager to accept the referral. Here is his report.

Your first patient this morning is Phyllis*, a 29-year-old single woman who had experienced some improvement in her symptoms of generalized anxiety, but no change in the frequency or intensity of her panic attacks, after taking Paxil (now at a dose of 40 mg. per day). She has no other medical conditions and was taking no other medications, although she had recently been tried on clonazepam with no symptom improvement.

In the intake session, Phyllis described ongoing episodes of the sudden onset of intense physical sensations as well as feelings of dread and fear. The episodes would start suddenly and last about ten to fifteen minutes, during which she would experience palpitations, chest tightness, sweating, shortness of breath, lightheadedness, and a feeling that she was becoming very sick or dying. These episodes were occurring almost every day. She was concerned about the panic attacks and their consequences—the impact that they had on her daily life. Phyllis reported that her generalized anxiety and related difficulty with sleep, concentration, irritability, and muscle tension had improved markedly with drug therapy. She was frustrated, however, that her panic attacks had continued despite taking medication.

After working for several years at a local radio station, Phyllis now found herself unemployed and living with her parents. She had had several panic attacks at work and become increasingly fearful of recurring attacks, to the point that her job performance had suffered. On two separate occasions, she had been taken, directly from work, to the emergency room after having a panic attack. She eventually quit her job despite her long-held dream of working in broadcasting. She found herself abusing alcohol for the first time in her life, and she began to use marijuana several times a week. Phyllis tried a series of low-paying clerical jobs, but had been fired on multiple occasions for being late for work. She believed that she was fired from one job because her boss had witnessed her having a panic attack. She could not point to any specific triggers for her panic attacks and did not avoid specific situations or places. Phyllis reported feeling like she could "lose control at any time" and that the panic attacks were actually starting to last longer and become more intense. She was very upset with her new living arrangements and about her seeming inability to find a good job and keep it.

---

* This case is adapted with the permission of *Primary Care Companion to the Journal of Clinical Psychiatry*. The case originally appeared in J. S. Cluver (2002). Mastering panic anxiety. *Primary Care Companion to the Journal of Clinical Psychiatry*, 4(4), 155–157.

Her recent alcohol and drug use were out of character, and her once vibrant social life was now described as "nonexistent."

At our first meeting Phyllis was dressed casually, showed herself to be very polite and cooperative, and appeared somewhat nervous. She appeared to be intelligent and did not appear intoxicated. We discussed her ongoing symptoms and the impact that her continued panic attacks were having on her daily life and overall functioning. Phyllis related feelings of despair, stating that she felt that she would never live a normal life again because of her disorder. We first contracted for her to cut down on her alcohol and marijuana use, with the understanding that psychotherapy would not be helpful to her if she continued to use alcohol and marijuana regularly.

She began the second session by telling me about the circumstances in which her panic attacks had occurred over the past week. I asked her to describe in detail her most recent panic attack in terms of her physical symptoms, which she was readily able to do. We then examined the thoughts that she had both during the attack and after the physical symptoms had resolved. She found this difficult at first, stating that she "did not think at all when she felt this way." I offered to graph her panic attack on paper, with her help. With time on one axis and intensity of physical symptoms on the other, we were able to construct a curve that shot upward over the course of one to two minutes, and then slowly returned to baseline after another five to ten minutes. Looking at the initial upward curve, I asked her what was going through her mind. She quickly replied: "Oh, no. Here we go again." Further up the curve, she told me that she thought: "Why is this happening again? What is wrong with me?" At the peak of the curve, she thought: "Am I really sick this time? Am I going to die or end up disabled?" She seemed somewhat surprised by her own thoughts as we wrote them down at the appropriate places on the graph, but was excited about the concept of *seeing* her panic attack on paper.

I explained to her the concept of automatic thoughts. We looked at possible errors in thinking that led to the thoughts she associated with her panic attacks. I assured Phyllis that panic attacks are self-limiting and not life-threatening. We worked on generating alternatives to her thoughts. I asked her to consider the probability that she would meet with death or disability during one of these attacks. Because she had not sought emergency treatment for her attacks for several months, despite worsening symptoms, we explored the reasons for this. We found that she had already started generating alternatives on her own. Specifically, Phyllis was able to tell herself that there was nothing the emergency physician could do for her. Taking it a step further, she told me that she had been told before that she could not die from these attacks, but that it had been "hard to believe it when she couldn't control her own breathing."

I then introduced the concept of the *feedback loop*, and I asked Phyllis if she thought there was any relationship between her thoughts and the symptoms she was having. I specifically asked her if she thought that her concern about the symptoms made them more intense. We talked about *short circuiting* a feedback loop by taking away one of the driving forces, and we wondered together what would happen if she were able to change the initial automatic thoughts that occurred during the onset of her physical symptoms. We were able to generate specific alternative thoughts, and she felt confident that she could exert some control over her panic attacks.

Phyllis returned for our third session looking dejected and stating that "those things that we talked about didn't work." She described having further panic attacks and felt that it was becoming more and more difficult to stay away from alcohol and marijuana. Phyllis stated that she was able to identify the onset of the symptoms and the thought, "I know what this is; I am not going to die, and everything is going to be all right." As the symptoms continued, however, she was unable to keep these thoughts in her mind. Eventually, she returned to the original thoughts that she indeed might die, and she even thought about returning to the emergency room. We reviewed the errors and challenged her thought that "this attack is different from the rest; this is the one that is going to kill me." The alternative she chose was: "This attack is no different, and I know that in ten minutes I will be fine and will be able to go back to work."

She greeted me with a smile to start our fourth meeting. She reported only one panic attack over the past two weeks. She then clarified this by saying that she thought she might have had several "mini" attacks, but they did not last very long or even feel like the typical panic attack. We examined the mini-attacks as examples of a short-circuited feedback loop. We discussed her alternative meanings. During the fifth session, she happily reported that she had experienced no panic attacks during the previous two weeks, and asked if it would be possible to make our next appointment for three weeks later. She returned stating that there had, once again, been no panic attacks. She reported that she was dating for the first time in a year, and had recently moved out of her parents' home. She had become much more aggressive in her job search, confiding that she had been "scared" to get a job due to the panic attacks. We agreed to meet one month later, at which time she continued to do well. Overall, we had seven sessions over the course of three months.

Panic disorder is a potentially disabling illness that is often refractory to initial treatment. Medications are often used in the initial treatment of this disorder and can diminish the frequency and inten-

sity of the panic attacks in some cases. Brief cognitive therapy offers another treatment option in place of, or in addition to, the use of medication. Cognitive therapy offers patients a treatment that is effective, free of side effects, and provides them with the tools to continue their treatment long after they have stopped coming to the clinic.

The major contribution of the cognitive model to the treatment of panic disorder is the concept of the *feedback loop*. This approach fixes the responsibility for the rapid escalation of panic anxiety directly in the patient's hands. Some patients, despite the burden of significant anxiety, can counter this escalation by identifying and disputing relevant automatic thoughts. Dr. Cluver's technique illustrates this approach clearly.

Tuesday Morning, 10:00 A.M.

A not uncommon "packaging" for panic disorder links it with episodes of major depression. Once again, medication might play a role in treatment, but, by itself, medication is typically not adequate to treat both syndromes. Therefore, a referral for brief cognitive therapy makes good clinical sense. Dr. Stephanie Thomas contributed this case.

Your second patient is Mary*, a 40-year-old woman, married for ten years to a computer technician. She has a ten-year-old son from a previous marriage, and she and her husband have a two-year-old daughter. Mary taught high school for several years before returning to school herself with the goal of becoming a medical researcher. Her past medical history is unremarkable and she only complained of peptic ulcer disease. Her mother is being treated for hypertension and migraine headaches. Mary knew little about her biological father except that he has been described as "an abusive alcoholic."

Mary had consulted internists five times in the past decade for complaints of intermittent shortness of breath and palpitations. These epi-

---

* This case is adapted with the permission of *Primary Care Companion to the Journal of Clinical Psychiatry*. The case originally appeared in M. Dalton & D. Schuyler (2001). A marriage between pharmacotherapy and psychotherapy. *Primary Care Companion to the Journal of Clinical Psychiatry*, 3(3), 140–142.

sodes are described as being quite severe and occasionally accompanied by chest pain. Two cardiac workups yielded results that are within normal limits. Twice, while driving on the interstate, these symptoms led to emergency room visits. Previous outpatient psychiatric treatment had always been in response to an identifiable stressor such as career change or divorce. She noted some improvement with Effexor XR (venlafaxine) and Klonopin (clonazepam). She complained of feeling "out of it" taking benzodiazepines, and did not wish to take medicines in that class again. She had no history of alcohol or illicit drug use.

Referred to our clinic by her latest internist, Mary presented in my office requesting both medication management and psychotherapy, despite not having a good experience in psychotherapy in the past because it "stirred things up." On examination, she was well groomed and somewhat anxious in appearance, frequently wringing her hands. She described her mood as "pretty bad." Her affect was constricted. There were no suicidal ideas or psychotic symptoms. Mary met DSM-IV criteria for panic disorder as well as recurrent major depressive disorder. We contracted for ten weekly psychotherapy sessions. I believed that she would be an ideal candidate for brief cognitive therapy and I also started Paxil (paroxetine), 10 mg. per day.

We began the second session discussing the principles of the cognitive model, including automatic thoughts and triple columns. She was able to give several examples of automatic thoughts without much prompting. Her first homework assignment was to use the triple-column technique with an emphasis on panic-provoking situations. She seemed comfortable with the notion of homework which was not surprising since she had spent the majority of her adult life in school. I explained that her untreated panic disorder was most likely driving her depression.

One week later, Mary returned and reported that in most cases, she thought that her panic symptoms came "out of the blue." However, when we examined (by role-playing) the situations involved we found that all three recent panic attacks had occurred when she was alone. Her automatic thoughts had centered around the notion that no one would be available to help her. She also believed she might be dying when her panic symptoms did not remit after five minutes. We explored the probability of dying from a panic attack, a process referred to as decatastrophizing. Through the use of positive self-talk and cognitive retraining, she was given tools to avert panic symptoms without requiring the assistance of others.

Through the next several weekly sessions, it became clear that one of her fundamental cognitive errors was overgeneralization. A recurrent automatic thought was that "things never worked out for her." This belief left her feeling sad and hopeless. Mary was, consequently, less likely to apply for career opportunities that she was interested in pursuing, or to try new things in general. We evaluated whether she had objective

evidence to support her belief. Further discussion involved looking at the numerous things that had indeed worked out well for her, including two graduate degrees with honors, two healthy children, a ten-year marriage, and the very real possibility of a career that would satisfy her life-long dream of doing scientific research. She believed that she would always have panic symptoms despite reassurance that effective treatments were available.

By identifying and challenging her recurrent overgeneralizations, she became able to generate alternative responses. During the next few weeks, she began to note her own anxiety-associated self-statements, such as: "My panic is beyond my control." As she became able to catch these statements, test them, and find acceptable alternatives, Mary noted that the panic symptoms of tachycardia, dyspnea, sweating, and loss of control diminished. By paying attention to thoughts associated with panic symptoms, and testing them for rationality and strategic worth, she found she could avert panic attacks.

After four months (fourteen sessions) of treatment in which an ancillary goal was empowerment, Mary decided to apply for a higher paying job in which she felt her work would be more appreciated. She was hired and given the responsibility of directing a division of research associates. She was able now to parent her children more effectively, and she reported that she was now using cognitive therapy principles with her pre-adolescent son. At a one month follow-up appointment, we reviewed her application of the cognitive method. Mary had been free of panic symptoms for the previous two months.

Recently, I saw her for a one year follow-up review. She has continued to do well on her paroxetine dosage of (now) 15 mg. per day. We discussed dose reduction and discontinuation of medication in the upcoming year. Her primary care physician told me that she has not required benzodiazepines for anxiety, and that she has had no further visits for panic-associated symptoms.

Note that, although panic disorder contributes significantly to Mary's problems, an approach to the *feedback loop* plays no part in Dr. Thomas's successful treatment. Rather, a continuing focus on identifying, labeling, and disputing cognitive errors forms the basis for Mary's good outcome. A skilled cognitive therapist has a repertoire of approaches that she matches to the patient's style as well as to the needs of the clinical situation. Even within the cognitive model, there are "many roads to Rome." While medication is likely to have helped Mary's depression, the low dose of paroxetine is unlikely to suppress panic attacks. That outcome can be reasonably attributed to Stephanie's successful cognitive work with Mary.

Tuesday Morning, 11:00 A.M.

I met the oncologist, Frank Brescia, about eighteen months ago, introduced by Marilyn Laken, a thoughtful nurse, administrator, and researcher. We began making rounds together at the Hollings Cancer Center outpatient clinic: three hours, 6 to 8 patients, every Thursday morning. Brescia had said (and I remember it exactly): "I'd give my eyeteeth to have a psychiatrist make rounds with me." An expatriate New Yorker, reveling in the beauty and peace inherent in life in Charleston, South Carolina, I felt I had known Brescia all my life after only a brief amount of time together. Brescia came to MUSC to establish a supportive care program for cancer patients. As a psychiatrist, I wondered what I could contribute to the management of the cancer patient. Eighteen months after the introduction of the program, and lots of clinical experience later, there is a funded research project and a proposed psycho-oncology fellowship program being designed. Oncology and psychiatry now function as a team, continually expanding our individual and common reach.

When cancer is diagnosed it is a traumatic and life-altering experience for the individual and his or her family. It calls for a monumental adaptation to a life now filled with life-threatening experiences: surgery, radiation and chemotherapy, diagnostic tests and the often agonizing wait for results, as well as statistics, probabilities, and life expectancies. For some, the event of diagnosis is followed some time later by a deadly prognostic statement: "Your cancer has spread. We are unable to remove or destroy it all." These patients will most likely die from their primary disease. At this point, sadly, some doctors withdraw their interest.

Supportive care encompasses relief of pain, insomnia, anorexia, fatigue, anxiety, and depression. It provides the physician with an excellent opportunity to engage in *doctoring* and, often, problem-solving. It emphasizes the third word in *doctor-patient relationship*.

After I met and interacted with a significant number of terminal cancer patients, a disturbing trend became evident. Psychologically, many patients began each day focused on how few days they had left. These patients carefully noted their "last" birthday, their "final" anniversary, the "ultimate" Mother's Day or Father's Day, or the "last" Christmas. It seemed logical that a dying patient would focus

his or her attention on milestones on the road to death. It seemed logical—but maybe it was not the best strategy. I remember thinking: "If I felt anywhere near decent, I would not want to begin my day anticipating death." That way, you stop living long before you actually begin dying. An estimate of weeks or months "remaining" seemed useful so that a patient and family could make reasonable preparations for dying. After this had been taken care of, however, I wasn't sure how useful this framework really was. Could a dying individual manage two different mindsets simultaneously? One mindset would be geared to facilitate putting his or her affairs in order, and the other mindset would be oriented to facilitate living more fully the time remaining to them.

Brief cognitive therapy had proven effective in treating depressions, as well as many of the anxiety disorders. Could it help the terminal cancer patient live out his or her life more sensibly? The question seemed worth investigating, and our success in gaining grant support showed that others concurred in this opinion. My research took the form of a six session cognitive therapy for the cancer patient with an "adjustment disorder." The case presented is a composite of the initial sample treated in our study.

Your second patient today is Paula*, a 45-year-old woman, married for twenty-four years, with two grown sons and four grandchildren. Born in Illinois, she graduated from college in Washington, D.C., and after her marriage led to multiple moves necessitated by her husband's job, she and her husband relocated to Charleston. Her mother died of a stroke in her seventies, and her father died of lung cancer in his mid-fifties. She has an older brother, who is in good health, living in California.

Paula and her husband have both been in good general health. She has no past history of depression or anxiety. Shortly after returning from a long anticipated trip to Europe, a routine laboratory screening done by her family doctor showed signs of markedly elevated liver function. Magnetic resonance imaging (MRI), part of the evaluation that followed, revealed several masses in the liver. These masses were later confirmed

---

* This case is adapted with the permission of *Primary Care Companion to the Journal of Clinical Psychiatry*. The case originally appeared in D. Schuyler & F. Brescia (2002). Psychotherapy of a patient with terminal cancer. *Primary Care Companion to the Journal of Clinical Psychiatry*, 4(3), 111–112.

to be metastatic cancer. A primary tumor was never found. Surgery and radiation were rejected as options, and chemotherapy began.

The family was devastated, but highly supportive. Paula began to dwell on the poor prognosis she was given and said she "wanted to know statistics so she could plan better." The oncologist told her there was no way to know for sure. Pressed for an answer, he replied that she might live for a period of four months to two years. Prior to and throughout her course of chemotherapy, Paula was essentially asymptomatic, except for periodic fatigue. She noticed a decided elevation in her general anxiety level, but no symptoms of depression except for occasional crying for "no apparent reason."

My diagnosis for Paula was: adjustment disorder, with anxious mood. With the intake evaluation completed, we began our six-session course of cognitive therapy which was aimed at improving her adaptation. I had met her during an oncology visit with Dr. Brescia, so no introductions were necessary. She was eager to start. She spoke of being "sad and scared." She often cried when others mentioned plans for the future. She had little religious experience, but now had multiple spiritual questions. The cognitive model, with its focus on meanings, was presented to her. We talked about how cancer typically robs people of the control they need in order to adapt. I introduced the Alcoholics Anonymous concept of "one day at a time," in an attempt to offer her a mindset that would differ from her unitary focus on cancer. We discussed how prognoses are arrived at, and how their accuracy is measured in probabilities. She seemed engaged, motivated, and eager to meet again. "I have no one I can really talk to about my cancer," she said. (This statement recurred over and over again in the ten patients in my original sample.)

In session two, Paula examined how she might explain being symptom free in the light of clear evidence of having cancer. We discussed human beings as "predictive animals" and estimated the worth of spending time predicting the future. She wondered if faith was "all-or-nothing" or if she could find a home in a church that would fit for her. When she identified her meaning for a relevant belief, I asked if it seemed "rational," and if so, was it "strategic for her"? We defined her beliefs as her choice, not dictated by cancer or by anyone else. At last, here was something Paula could control.

In session three, we tried to separate inference from fact. I asked her directly what she knew about her cancer, and what she was inferring about it. Paula had talked with her husband about burial plans, and found it easier to talk with him about dying, a topic they had been avoiding. She saw how the same things had different meanings to different people. This realization helped her to accept the notion of choices and consequences.

Our next session began with Paula relating how difficult her birthday had been for her, despite both children and their families coming to

celebrate with her. "This could be my last birthday," she said. She spoke of nightmares in which she saw herself dying. Paula felt weak in the heat, and attributed this to the chemotherapy or the cancer. In each case, we focused on her logic. Did her conclusions make sense? Were her generalizations supportable? How else might she view the situation?

Paula began the fifth visit by discussing her responsibility for her husband Jack's adjustment to her illness. "This is so unfair to him," she said, and wondered, "How will he be able to cope when I'm gone?" We discussed the concept of responsibility and associated guilt, and I asked if this would hold if her situation were reversed (i.e., husband ill and she well)? We talked about spirituality in detail, as she had had a lengthy and useful talk with a friend's minister. We agreed that this was an important time to remain "open to ideas."

In our last session, Paula spoke of having markedly increased her activity. She continued to have no symptoms that she could definitively relate to cancer. Meanwhile, a repeat MRI suggested despite chemotherapy, the continued growth of the cancer. She had driven to visit her son and his family. Company had visited her for several days. Paula continued to treasure time spent with her husband. She told me that she began each day assessing how she felt and then she made a plan for the day. Predictive thoughts about dying from cancer periodically recurred, and she would work to appraise their value for her.

Paula told me that these sessions were "extremely useful," that she was "much less often anxious" and now felt "armed to deal with negative thoughts" when they occurred. She asked if we could find a way for every cancer patient to have access to this therapy. I told her that she could call and request a booster session with me whenever she wished.

It seemed to me that, although there is little a person can do to escape dying from terminal cancer, there is much one can do to avoid a *premature death* and to live more fully in the days that remain. Especially, but not exclusively, in those cases in which the prognosis offered is not borne out, it seems a crime to be robbed of life by the mindset: "I am dying of cancer." I have asked more than one patient: "What if you were to live another ten or twenty years? Do you want to approach each day as if it might be your last? Or, would you more likely look back at that as a failed strategy?" Patients often find these questions to be a plentiful helping of food for thought.

Tuesday Afternoon, 1:00 P.M.

It is typically not difficult to arrive at a diagnosis of an emotional disorder for most people seeking help. That diagnosis commonly guides the clinician toward choosing medications that may help and often directs the psychotherapeutic focus as well. In some cases, this

sequence is not followed precisely. I have received a significant number of referrals for what the patient calls *anger management.* This case and the next will illustrate some clinical presentations of emotional disorders and a cognitive approach to controlling one's anger.

Before I treated my next patient (please see Tuesday Afternoon, 2:00 P.M.), I was fortunate to supervise Lisa Sebotnick. She described to me in detail a man named Samuel, a patient she had worked with near the beginning of her training in psychiatry. Dr. Sebotnick's successful treatment of Samuel was so sensitively and creatively done at such an early stage of her learning, that I saw her to be a superb cognitive therapist in the making, and I encouraged her to contribute this case report.

Samuel* is a 50-year-old, married man, separated from his third wife, who had been treated in primary care for a sleep difficulty, depression, an anxious mood, and ruminative negative thoughts. His diagnosis met criteria for major depression, with anxious features. He was treated with Zoloft (sertraline), titrated from an initial dose of 50 mg. per day to 150 mg. As a result, he was sleeping better, but continued to have a mood disturbance. His symptoms began shortly after he separated from his wife. An angry public outburst had preceded their separation, and they were currently living apart.

Samuel had a lengthy history of relationship difficulties. He had been married twice before, with both relationships ending abruptly. He had worked as a corporate chef and was typically on the job, 16 to 20 hours a day while managing a large kitchen. He had retired early, and this major change was a cause of stress for him. When Samuel consulted me, he was living in town with a friend and was at risk of losing his third wife. As a child, he related, he was physically abused by his father, and they continued to have a difficult relationship. He expressed the desire for help with "anger management," as Samuel believed his temper was the cause of his failed marriages, as well as his work difficulties. Some psychotherapists would have insisted on reviewing his childhood history in detail. However, following the clinical maxim of *taking the patient where he's at,* I decided that a cognitive approach rooted in the present might work best.

---

* This case is adapted with permission of *Primary Care Companion to the Journal of Clinical Psychiatry.* The case originally appeared in L. S. McLean & D. Schuyler (2001). Teaching the tools: Prolonging the benefit of psychotherapy. *Primary Care Companion to the Journal of Clinical Psychiatry,* 3(5), 222–223.

Much of the initial intake session was spent discussing the details of his marital separation and the role his anger outburst had played. It was Samuel's belief that his anger traced to his early interaction with his father. I suggested to him that this may well be true, but that our work would focus on his problems in the present time. He described himself as a very driven person, noting that his aggression had been seen as a beneficial trait in the workplace. With the decline in job status, as well as the loss of home and wife, he had become depressed. He doubted his abilities, both as a husband and a chef. We chose to focus on Samuel's impulsive actions by examining the associated thoughts, moods, and behavior. I taught him the cognitive model for identifying automatic thoughts in times of distress.

In the second session, Samuel was able to list numerous situations in which his quick temper and subsequent reaction had resulted in negative consequences, as well as feelings of depressed mood and anxiety. In session three, he told of his wife's sale of a piece of construction equipment no longer needed at home. Samuel noted that upon hearing this on the telephone he became very anxious, without knowing why. His homework assignment was to keep a record of automatic thoughts in distressing situations.

Samuel reported for session four with a typed record of automatic thoughts. In several instances, he had become very anxious when he had to interact with coworkers in the grocery store where he worked. The cognitions had a persecutory quality: "She must have done the deli display incorrectly just to get at me," and "He gave me that assignment to get at me since I had more experience than he did." We examined the relationship between his thoughts and anxiety.

By session five, Samuel had begun to question his reactions as they related to his identified thoughts. During this visit, I introduced the concept of cognitive errors. Samuel frequently personalized others' comments, leading to inaccurate interpretations of their actions. Now, he managed to find some convincing alternate explanations: "Perhaps she [his coworker] did the deli display as she had been instructed to, or it is possible that she made an innocent mistake." He concluded that his wife's selling of the equipment may not have been done to hurt him. "Perhaps the sale was simply an effort on her part to save money," he reasoned.

By session six, Samuel began questioning his reactions to work situations that led to anger. When he formulated alternatives, he noticed that the sadness and anxiety decreased. Looking back over his relationships, he stated: "You know, I think I've been doing this all along. I do a lot of personalizing and polarizing, and that's been a continuing problem." By this point, his sleep, along with his mood, were improving.

We then turned to the marital relationship, its history, the conflicts, and their effect on him. When his wife had a conversation with a male

friend at a dinner party, Samuel took this as a personal affront, and "flew off the handle." Next, we focused on his tendency toward all-or-nothing (polarized) thinking. In anticipating a reunion with his wife, Samuel predicted, "Either the birds will be singing and it will be a beautiful moment, or we'll never speak again." We role-played some *middle ground* interactions to illustrate some alternatives for him. When he began to feel nervous during this part of the session, Samuel said: "I'll need to think about what thoughts are making me nervous." The patient had actively incorporated cognitive techniques in his everyday life and was now designing his own homework assignments.

In later sessions, Samuel brought a typed list of five scenarios for the planned reunion with his wife, ranging from "ideal" to "worst case." He had written out the scripts, along with triple-column tables for each. We role-played the worst case possibility. I taught him some relaxation techniques (abdominal breathing and progressive muscle relaxation) to help reduce the anxiety so he could better examine his thoughts. Excitement about returning to his wife was replacing anxiety.

By our thirteenth session, the couple was once again living together. Samuel was very pleased with the balanced way he had handled the situation. He was once again sleeping well, with less anxiety and improved energy and mood. As with learning anything, we noted, practice and frequent use would lead to mastery. Although relapses would quite likely occur, he now had the capability to deal with them.

At our final visit, Samuel acknowledged the changes he had made in psychotherapy over a six month period. He felt some anxiety about ending therapy and leaving the area with his wife. He requested my email address "in case of emergency." Four months later, I received an email stating that things were going well. Samuel also cited an example in which he had "used the tools he had acquired." One year later, he contacted me again when he returned to the area for a brief visit. We met for one session so he could "touch base" and explain to me how our work together had benefited him and his marriage.

Later on, during this week of cognitive therapy (Thursday Afternoon, 1:00 P.M.), we can trace Dr. Sebotnick's development as a cognitive therapist. On that afternoon she contributes a case successfully treated one year after her work with Samuel.

Tuesday Afternoon, 2:00 P.M.

Supervising the resident learning to do cognitive therapy provides an opportunity for an experienced clinician to share his or her knowledge with a therapist in training. However, teachers often claim that

they learn both concepts and techniques from their students. See if you can spot my adaptations learned from Dr. Sebotnick's work with me as my student. I met Reggie shortly after our supervisory work ended.

Your last patient today is Reggie, a 50-year-old man who has been separated for six months after twenty-five years of marriage. His wife left because "she couldn't take his anger anymore." One area of conflict involved limit-setting with their three teenaged children. When limits were set by Reggie, there were multiple examples of angry outbursts. Several times, he had responded to the childrens' challenges physically. His wife was appalled.

Reggie's father was a strict disciplinarian who rarely spared the rod with him or his younger brother. Reggie drank alcohol excessively until fifteen years ago, when he stopped completely. He is college educated, and has worked at a managerial level job for each of three companies over the past nearly thirty years. He was once, at age thirty, diagnosed with irritable bowel syndrome (IBS), but has had no symptoms over the past ten years. He has no history of either major depression or generalized anxiety, and takes no medications. Reggie has had frequent periods of feeling sad, accompanied by little energy and low self-esteem.

My diagnosis was: anger management problem, in a man with dysthymic disorder. In the second session, I reviewed the cognitive model with Reggie, using examples from his history. I introduced the concept of choices and consequences. I defined various cognitive errors, focusing on arbitrary inferences (jumping to conclusions). His homework was to keep a triple-column table that would form the basis of our psychotherapy sessions.

In session three, Reggie described his wife as "constantly criticizing," and suggested that she frequently misinterpreted his behavior. He used to "walk on eggshells" at home. Our focus was now on the cognitive error of polarization. I noted that a decision on working toward reconciliation or marital separation would need to be made at some point. In either case, work would need to be done toward a rapprochment with his children.

In the next hour, Reggie presented evidence of applying cognitive tools. In the first situation, he was "run off the road by a truck." In the second, he opened a phone bill in which he found hefty charges for his daughter's lengthy calls. In the third, he was told by his wife of his youngest son's refusal to attend a church youth group. Reggie emphasized "choosing his battles" and "trying to see things from the other's perspective."

In session five, Reggie reported his wife's phone call to him expressing pessimism about reconciliation. He acknowledged having suicidal

thoughts for the first time. As he spoke, he reframed his wife's response and related his anger to low self-esteem. He could "learn to be a better man and father," but he "couldn't save his marriage" unless his wife agreed to meet him halfway.

The next hour, he discussed "widening the space" between the stimulus to anger, and his reaction. Accomplishing this would put Reggie in charge of his anger, rather than the other way around. He noted several occasions in which he used humor to defuse anger. Having had control problems watching sporting events, he was proud of watching a basketball game with his wife (she had reluctantly agreed to go) and remaining calm throughout. Over the past two weeks, there had been dramatically more contact with his wife, and several significant conversations with each child. Reggie felt he had turned an important corner. He expressed the wish to stop therapy for now, and to "see if he could make it on his own." We had worked together for six sessions over a three month period.

Six months later, a lengthy letter came from Reggie, expressing appreciation for the therapy and noting that the family was living together. One year later, another letter conveyed that his gains had been maintained. He told a story about a business contact who had been advised by his doctor to "avoid cognitive therapy." Reggie took the man aside and told him about his experience with cognitive therapy. He directed him toward a referral source for a cognitive therapist. An old medical adage stresses: "See one, do one, teach one." Reggie had done some research before calling me initially. He had worked hard in therapy to achieve some real gains, and then encouraged a friend to follow a similar path.

Wednesday Morning, 9:00 A.M.

Charleston is a peninsula, surrounded on three sides by water: to the east, the Cooper River; to the west, the Ashley River; and to the south, the sea. In Washington, D.C., with the city surrounded by a three-lane, highly-traveled beltway, the phobia-of-choice was *beltway-phobia*. (A typical inquiry by a new patient there was: "Can I reach your office without driving the beltway?") Not surprisingly, the phobia-of-choice in Charleston is *bridge-phobia*. You can't drive too far here without the necessity of crossing a bridge. Even the little traveled, not yet completed "imitation beltway" is elevated, and boasts two "serious bridges." Your first patient, today, is representative of many help seekers here who fear driving across bridges.

Roxanne is a 50-year-old, divorced African-American woman. She is the mother of three grown children, and a successful managerial level employee of her company for many years. Her chief complaint is a "fear of driving, and avoidance which is interfering with her life."

One year ago, driving on the highway Roxanne became anxious approaching the bridge over the Cooper River. Asked about her thoughts at the time, she replied: 1) "That bridge is high." 2) "Suppose something pulls me off the bridge toward the rail and the water?" 3) "When they built the bridge, my daughter told me, there were stories of defects." and 4) "I remember when they repaired a hole in the bridge, so it's not safe."

Recently, she drove to the McKinley-Washington Bridge to Edisto Island (south of Charleston), pulled over and turned around and drove back home. Roxanne was unable to cross the bridge to reach the home of relatives she wanted to visit. The Cooper River Bridge (site of the eighth largest 10 kilometer race in the world) "is too narrow," she said. She went on to tell me that she became anxious standing on the Folly Beach Pier (that juts out into the Atlantic Ocean) because, "if the pier broke, I'd be in the middle of the ocean, and I can't swim."

I defined her issues as a need for control, and a thinking pattern of making catastrophic predictions. Roxanne is a college graduate, divorced after seventeen years of marriage, and a caretaker (the youngest of eight children). Her mother died at age 80 (ten years prior to the first therapy session) and father had died earlier (age 65) of lung cancer.

My diagnosis was: specific phobic disorder (bridges, heights). In session two, I explained the cognitive model to her. We applied it to bridge crossings and anticipations. I drew a triple-column chart on the blackboard, writing a series of illustrations as we spoke. By session's end, Roxanne offered to drive across a bridge the next day, and keep an automatic thought record. I asked to see her in a week; she responded by saying that two weeks would give her more time "to practice."

Roxanne returned in two weeks to say that she had "done well." She had driven across several bridges, using cognitive tools, and noticed no anxiety. She had driven to see her Edisto relatives, and was struck for the first time by "how beautiful the bridge was! It is not a monster." I labeled this as a good example of reframing. She had allowed the phobia, she said, to erode her self worth. A return of some mastery "made her feel so much better about herself." I asked her when she'd like to return. "Six weeks sounds about right," she said. "Could I call you earlier if I needed to?" I assured her that she could.

At session four, Roxanne reported continued success. She drove across bridges with confidence and without fear. "It is unclear to me," she said, "what the problem was before. Why had I allowed it to take over my life?" We discussed her view of the change that had taken place, and terminated our sessions. A call to her six months later found that

the change had been maintained. This is, for me, a lovely example of the therapist teaching some simple principles, and a highly motivated, intelligent patient rapidly and successfully applying them.

Wednesday Morning, 10:00 A.M.

The cognitive model was conceptualized by Aaron Beck (and others), beginning in the early 1960s within the context of developing successful psychotherapy for depression. Once this was accomplished, the next logical application was to the anxiety disorders. Beck and colleagues accomplished this by the mid-1980s (Beck, Emery, & Greenberg, 1985). The extensive self-questioning (the "what-ifs") that define generalized anxiety disorder made this frequent problem a good candidate for cognitive therapy.

You meet your second patient of the day in the waiting room. Rico, a twenty-nine-year old sculptor, is accompanied by his wife. When you greet him, they both stand up. As you invite him to your office, his wife walks by his side. You think of telling her to wait, as you wish to talk with him. However, the couples' body language strongly suggests "two for the price of one," so you invite both of them to sit down. His chief complaint: "I can no longer deal with a high level of stress, plus I've had several panic attacks."

Rico describes himself as having been generally nervous and shy since childhood. He dealt with his constant high anxiety by working at home in his studio, rarely going out and otherwise avoiding situations which he anticipated would be stressful. "I maintained a controlled environment," he said. Further, he believed that taking pills for anxiety "caused anxiety." He had been given brief, unsuccessful trials of Paxil (paroxetine) and Celexa (citalopram) by his family doctor. His wife came with him today because he was scared to come alone. He has taken Ativan (lorazepam), 0.5 mg. three times a day for over a year, with little benefit.

In elementary school, he remembers having "bad test anxiety." In high school and college, he tried hard to "keep busy," never wanting to be alone in public with his thoughts. Rico moved to Charleston after college graduation and worked at an art supply shop. When the store did badly, he anticipated being blamed and fired, so he quit. He met and married his wife four years prior to coming to me. Her income as a nurse supported them for several years, while he stayed at home and sculpted.

About nine months ago, Rico's anxiety markedly increased, so he went looking for a job. With a degree in elementary education, he was

hired as a teacher. He got panicky riding to work each day in the company of a coworker who lived nearby. He had consistent difficulty falling asleep. He had horrible anxiety on Sundays, mostly in anticipation of the work week. He has become unable to go grocery shopping, feeling threatened by groups of kids who "hang out there." (He has had no interaction with them.) He had twice had to leave his purchases and dash out of line because of a panic attack.

My diagnosis was generalized anxiety disorder (GAD), and panic disorder. In light of the severity of his anxiety, and his seeming intolerance to selective serotonin reuptake inhibitor (SSRI) medications, I started him on a low dose of Effexor XR (venlafaxine), 37.5 mg. My hope was that increasing doses of Effexor along with cognitive therapy would allow the gradual discontinuation of Ativan.

One week later, both Rico and his wife returned for session two. Rico reported no drug side effects. I taught him the cognitive model, and applied it to his trips to the grocery store, as well as to his car ride to work. We discussed each situation in detail. His homework was to keep a record of anxious situations, using a triple-column format. I increased the dose of Effexor XR to 75 mg. per day.

Husband and wife returned for session three, again one week later. Rico reported using the cognitive model to "defeat anxiety" while riding to school. His success "brightened the day." He went twice to the grocery store, both times without anxiety. On his own, he decreased Ativan to "only occasional use, when he needed it." (I would have been more careful and tapered the dose gradually, but he seemed to tolerate the rapid reduction well.)

Rico came for session four, alone. When I inquired about his wife's absence, he said, "She worked a late shift last night, so I told her to sleep in. I'm comfortable here by myself now." He shifted our focus this hour from situational anxiety to more general anxiety. Any change in routine, it seemed, was accompanied by anxiety. We worked to identify automatic thoughts in a range of situations, then tested them for *rationality* and *strategic worth.* We noted his tendency to overthink. We discussed the concept of a *comfort zone*—and what comprised this for him.

One week later, again alone, Rico reported taking only one Ativan tablet all week. He had had a "great week." He noted that some situations that were formerly anxiety-provoking, now seemed exciting and interesting. The fifth grade kids at school now stayed after class to talk with him. Before, no one did. Rico visited with his parents, also without anxiety. Then he spent the weekend with his in-laws, again with no anxiety. His wife commented about his having more spontaneity and told him that his "sense of humor was back."

Rico claimed that he felt better "than he had in years." He was much more in control of his life, and no longer restricted his activity to prevent anxiety. We agreed to terminate therapy, but continue the prescription

of Effexor XR. Rico called two months later to say that his wife was pregnant, and also that he had successfully tapered and discontinued the drug on his own. He called next to tell me of the birth of their son, and his wife's plan to return gradually to work. His anxiety problem, he believed, was "solved."

Wednesday Morning, 11:00 A.M.

As cognitive therapy has moved closer and closer to a preeminent position among psychotherapy models, the applications have generally followed the path of common sense. From its origin as a model for treating depression, to an application to generalized anxiety (GAD), panic disorder, specific phobias, obsessive-compulsive disorder (OCD), and posttraumatic stress (PTSD), cognitive therapy has, with little surprise, proven efficacious. Even for eating disorders and substance abuse, it has simply taken creativity rather than wholesale revision in order to apply the cognitive model.

But when it comes to schizophrenia, I harken back to the wisdom imparted in my residency training thirty years ago: Don't try to argue against psychotic thinking. I was delighted, therefore, when in the course of supervision Chris Pelic began describing to me his successful application of the cognitive model in treating Carol, a schizophrenic patient of his. It is true that the treatment of schizophrenia has typically emphasized medication management, with "supportive psychotherapy" as an adjunct. It is Dr. Pelic's belief, however, that "Many windows of opportunity are lost that could have a dramatic impact on these patients and their problems." See if you agree.

Your third patient today is Carol*, a forty-eight-year old, divorced African-American woman who was referred to the clinic by her primary care physician for the treatment of symptoms related to an earlier diagnosis of schizo-affective disorder. Approximately twenty years earlier, Carol was diagnosed with schizophrenia, later modified to schizo-affective disorder, depressed type. She described a past history of paranoia and disordered thoughts, with occasional auditory hallucinations. Along

---

* This case is adapted with permission of *Primary Care Companion to the Journal of Clinical Psychiatry*. The case originally appeared in C. Pelic & D. Schuyler (2002). Rethinking the treatment of psychotic disorders. *Primary Care Companion to the Journal of Clinical Psychiatry*, 4(5), 198–199.

with these psychotic symptoms, she noted a predominately depressed mood for a large part of her illness. She had had at least a two-week period of psychotic symptoms in the absence of depression, which meets criteria for a DSM-IV diagnosis of schizo-affective disorder.

Carol's longtime psychiatrist, who she had been seeing for medication management, retired and her primary care physician wanted to ensure continued outpatient psychiatric care. As a result he referred Carol to me. Recently, she had spent several years in and out of psychiatric hospitals. On presentation to our clinic, Carol was taking an atypical neuroleptic (Risperdal), an antidepressant (Zoloft), and a minor tranquilizer (Librium). Medication compliance had been sporadic. Carol spoke of a depressed mood, with episodic and vague paranoid ideas. She denied current auditory or visual hallucinations, or any other psychotic symptoms. "Out of reality" is how she described her past. Personal hygiene was an indicator the patient and her physicians had used in the past to monitor how well she was doing with treatment. When her hygiene declined, hospitalization was often imminent.

In describing her history and current situation, Carol continually made cognitive errors, including over-generalization, selective abstraction (emphasizing one detail out of context), and polarization. She described being depressed in the past and therefore assuming: "I will never be happy." She made statements such as: "Everyone is cruel" and "I can never learn to function in this world." It was these *intake clues* that suggested to me the value of a cognitive approach for Carol. If she were able to examine critically the meanings she applied to situations and relationships, and replace them with more adaptive meanings, she might be able to lessen her depression, and perhaps, the burden of schizophrenia as well.

Carol has spent the past twenty years living a lonely, quiet existence. She remained in the house except for running errands, and she had few friends. Financial support came in the form of a disability check. She had been relatively free of major medical problems except for hypertension. She denied a history of substance abuse.

At the initial intake, Carol appeared slightly nervous. Her personal hygiene was fair. Her mood was sad and empty, and her affect was blunted. Her thought content revealed no suicidal or homicidal ideas, but there were some paranoid ideas. Her thought process was somewhat disordered, but overall it was comprehensible. We discussed medication management initially and agreed to substitute ziprasidone (Geodon) for risperidone (Risperdal). Zoloft and Librium were continued at the current doses. We contracted for a few medication management visits. Although I suspected that Carol might benefit from cognitive therapy, I refrained from discussing psychotherapy options initially.

By the end of the fourth session, Carol appeared considerably better (i.e., her hygiene and grooming were improved.) She reported no para-

noia, but moderate, continuing depressive symptoms. At this point, we discussed adding biweekly psychotherapy sessions to address her depressive thinking. Given her history of chronic mental illness, we did not contract for a specific number of sessions, but planned to revisit progress at the tenth visit. She identified as goals the remission of her depressed mood and an improvement in overall functioning.

During the fifth session, we focused on identifying automatic thoughts such as: "I've always been unhappy, so I can never be happy," and "I've been out of reality for so long that I can never learn to function," and "I can never learn to do things normal people do." With some collaborative work, Carol was able to generate alternatives to her depressed way of thinking.

Although I did not present the traditional triple-column format to her as homework, we incorporated these principles into each session. Carol readily presented numerous situations and thoughts to guide our discussions. Despite her tendency to dwell on the past, I continually refocused treatment to the present. Humor and analogies were used to help the patient begin to make a shift of set so that she might identify a cognitive error or find a more suitable meaning for a situation.

By the sixth session, Carol reported a significant improvement in depressive symptoms. She became adept at examining her thoughts, with little prompting from me. I continually challenged her to *reframe* her views of life situations (consider alternatives) when her beliefs did not serve a strategic purpose for her. The family validated that she was doing "somewhat better." Carol stated that she was, once again, hearing voices, and this was addressed successfully by increasing her dose of ziprasidone.

Overall, Carol's depressive symptoms nearly remitted. She was now attending church and church groups regularly. She was becoming involved in volunteer work. Throughout the next several sessions, we utilized cognitive principles to *reintroduce* Carol to reality. She told me that she was feeling a lot less lonely. Over the next two months, she continued to be functional, and her depression remained essentially in remission. Her psychotic symptoms were limited to an "occasional voice." Medication compliance had been dramatically better, and the patient remained out of the hospital. At session ten, we reviewed her progress to date and each of us concluded that the additional cognitive therapy sessions were useful.

Psychotic disorders are defined as *thought disorders* and, because of this, many clinicians do not consider psychotherapy for these patients. Ironically, especially when symptoms are well controlled with medication, these patients benefit from cognitive therapy. Those who

have improved on medications are more likely to relapse without psychotherapy to aid their adaptation to the real world in healthy ways. Medication compliance generally improves with successful psychotherapy.

Teaching Carol the cognitive model helped her to overcome depression. It supported the message that she could work effectively at solving her problems and achieve results. It seemed to result in increased compliance with a medication regimen that sought to control her psychotic symptoms. Finally, it helped prepare her to assume a more satisfying connection to the world around her.

Wednesday Afternoon, 1:00 P.M.

The diagnosis of alcoholism encompasses a broad spectrum of people from different walks of life who suffer a range of consequences varying from personal to interpersonal to occupational. The treatment of alcoholism includes medications and a broad selection of environmental interventions. Where does cognitive therapy fit on that spectrum?

Your fourth patient today is Ethel*, a 68-year-old woman, married for forty years to an electrical engineer. They have three adult children and ten grandchildren. She taught elementary school for twenty-eight years and has not worked since retiring fifteen years ago. Her mother suffered with hypertension and died of a stroke, ten years prior to this first session, at age 81. Ethel's father died after a heart attack at age fifty-five more than twenty years before her mother. She has two younger sisters, aged 63 and 60 years, who are in good health.

She sees her family doctor for control of asthma and high blood pressure. The same family doctor has treated Ethel for nearly twenty years. For much of the time he has known her, he has been aware of Ethel's drinking problem. It apparently began in the early 1970s after she was involved in a legal battle with the parent of one of her pupils. Although the school backed her and the case was eventually resolved in her favor,

---

* This case is adapted with permission of *Primary Care Companion to the Journal of Clinical Psychiatry*. The case originally appeared in D. Schuyler (2000). A case of alcohol abuse. *Primary Care Companion to the Journal of Clinical Psychiatry*, 2(3), 103–104.

Ethel remembers the period as one of constant fear and uncertainty. By this time, she had been drinking heavily for ten years. On three separate occasions over this most recent two year period, she was hospitalized for detoxification, and brief periods of sobriety ensued. The doctor inquires regularly about her alcohol habit, and believes that Ethel is mostly truthful about her bouts of drinking and times of abstinence.

One week ago, her husband and a daughter called the family physician to request time to "talk with him about mother." The husband related that Ethel had resumed daily drinking (about one pint of vodka) three months ago. At times, he noticed that she slurred her words. The daughter has become fearful of leaving the grandchildren with Ethel. When they each spoke with her, Ethel denied "heavy drinking" and thought they made "more of the problem than there was."

The doctor agreed to talk with Ethel, telling her that her husband and daughter had spoken with him, and she agreed to come for an appointment. He pointed out, skillfully, that the problem was not new, that it was having marital and family consequences for her, that she had made several unsuccessful attempts to deal with it in the past, and that he felt it was time to take a definitive step to resolve the problem. He was somewhat surprised when Ethel agreed to accept a referral to a psychiatrist for brief psychotherapy.

In the intake evaluation with me, Ethel related in detail the history of her alcohol habit. She noted several brief attempts to attend Alcoholics Anonymous meetings, until one year earlier when she stopped going "because she was bored." She described her mate as a "workaholic who is domineering and often makes her feel defensive." She acknowledged drinking daily for the past three months. She had slept poorly for six months, which she attributed to "bronchitis and a chronic cough." Her energy, appetite, and weight were all stable. She denied depressed or anxious mood.

She was kempt, cooperative, and appropriately behaved. Her mood was stable, and her affect was full in range. There were no psychotic symptoms, no suicidal ideas, no obsessions or compulsions. She qualified for no psychiatric diagnosis, save alcohol abuse. We contracted to meet every two weeks for up to ten sessions to attempt to help her resolve her alcohol problem.

In session two, Ethel's narrative history was completed. In session three, I taught her the cognitive model for understanding behavior, and suggested that this was the framework we would employ. When there was a distressing feeling or an alcohol-related behavior, we would seek to identify the relevant meanings she applied to that situation. I stressed the relationship among cognitions, feelings, and behavior. For homework, I asked her to keep a triple-column chart listing situations, feelings, and thoughts relevant to the urge to drink. In session four, we sought to identify alternative choices to drinking and examined their conse-

quences. During a one-week vacation, her drinking habit sharply declined. We discussed various meanings for this.

By session five, she reported ten days that were alcohol-free. She identified cognitions preceding earlier drinking bouts as: "to have nerve" and "to forget an insult." Many of the meanings she offered were polarized, and we discussed this error of black-and-white thinking. Together, we sought alternatives that were "grays." I suggested that she had successfully taken the first step toward change. In session six, she reported nearly a month of continuing abstinence. She believed that a key to her success lay in applying the model when she anticipated a drinking situation and working with the identified meanings. She noted her difficulty with assertion and how a conversation with her husband seemed like "an interrogation" by him.

In session seven, Ethel focused on a visit by her grandchildren, with its attendant demands and pleasures. She had remained abstinent for six weeks and noted how her mood was "more even" and that she angered less easily. We defined this phase as "successfully having stopped drinking," but noted that Ethel had achieved this much before. The harder task would be maintenance. We searched together for potentially high risk situations that we could anticipate and plan for.

In session eight, Ethel talked about two recent slip-ups. We worked to understand each situation in cognitive terms, and examined alternate meanings, their consequences, and behavioral options. In session nine, she reported believing that she had achieved control over her alcohol habit, and that she felt free for the first time in years. We arranged a follow-up visit for one month later.

In our final meeting, we separated drinking alcohol as a habit from choosing to drink, in light of the consequences to her of an alcohol addiction. We utilized *shift of set*, in which she was encouraged to advise a person in a story who had a range of alcohol-related problems. We discussed the positive value of our relationship, the work we each had done, and what she had found useful in the cognitive method. I encouraged her to call if another meeting would be helpful.

We terminated therapy after ten sessions, conducted over a five month period of time. I sent a letter summarizing the treatment to her primary care physician. A six month follow-up indicated continued abstinence. Individual psychotherapy was appropriate in this instance because AA had been initiated and had proved of little help to the patient. Group therapy might have been a reasonable alternative, depending on the group's focus.

I have often said (and written) that the patient's motivation to change and his or her willingness to take responsibility for their behavior are necessary features for a successful cognitive therapy. It

is worth pointing out that Ethel met both of these criteria. Having encountered literally hundreds of patients in the context of my work in the medical clinic for whom alcohol is a problem, I believe that the absence of these criteria will defeat even the most skilled therapist.

Wednesday Afternoon, 2:00 P.M.

MUSC participates in the national program that sets aside one day a year as National Depression Screening Day. Heavily advertised, this service offers a free evaluation to anyone requesting it and who believes he or she might have clinical depression. Peter found his way to our clinic on this day, and was lucky to have his assessment done by one of our uniquely talented trainees, Susan Douglas. She believes strongly in the value of providing structured reading materials to emphasize the psycho-educational aspect of good psychotherapy. Below, Dr. Douglas describes the outcome for her young college student patient.

Your last patient of the day, Peter*, a 20-year-old white male college student who scored in the moderately depressed range on a screening instrument. Based on this score, I suggested treatment in our university clinic. He had no prior history of depression or any other emotional disorder. His family history included a great aunt with diagnosed depression. Peter had no current medical problems and was in good health.

Peter is a college junior who is maintaining a good grade point average while he works two part-time jobs. He has a good relationship with his parents and his younger brother, all of whom live two hours away. He recalls feeling down during the summer, approximately three months prior to his presentation in my office. His sleep during that time was disrupted, his mood was sad, and he experienced no pleasure. These symptoms, however, were relieved momentarily when school began, only to return one month later. In addition, Peter felt excessive guilt, had poor concentration, suffered from a poor appetite, and experienced hopelessness. He denied suicidal thoughts. There were no symptoms of psychosis and no evidence of mania. He often felt "too embarrassed to ask questions in class." Peter thought he would "look or sound stupid,

---

* This case is adapted with permission of *Primary Care Companion to the Journal of Clinical Psychiatry*. The case originally appeared in S. Douglas (2001). Co-morbid major depression and social phobia. *Primary Care Companion to the Journal of Clinical Psychiatry*, 3(4), 179–180.

and that people might laugh at him." He acknowledged dropping two classes due to the requirement to make a presentation in front of the class. With public speaking, he has experienced anxiousness, flushing, tachycardia, shortness of breath, and near syncope. These symptoms of social anxiety are dysphoric for him, and he has tried to avoid such situations. He denies using illicit drugs, and drinks alcohol only occasionally to relax with friends.

During the initial office visit, Peter was unsure of what to expect with a psychiatrist. He kept his baseball cap on during the interview, and periodically gazed downward. He described his mood as "down" and thought that nothing would get better for him. He knew he was depressed, but expressed surprise that his screening score was high enough to lead to a referral for treatment. He believed that he should be able to "snap out of this himself."

Although he denied active suicidal thoughts, he expressed little hope for the future, and even though his symptoms of social phobia were bothersome to him, he had never spoken about them with anyone. My diagnostic impression was: major depressive disorder and social phobia. The options of medication treatment and cognitive therapy were presented to him, and Peter was open to both. Three brief handouts explaining depression, social phobia, and the cognitive model were given to him, and we agreed to meet once every two to three weeks. I asked him to read the brief, descriptive material and prescribed trazodone (Desyrel), 50 mg. at bedtime to help him sleep.

During our second session, we discussed the reading material and then reviewed the cognitive model, explaining the focus on how one's negative thoughts can affect feelings. Peter stated that he felt bad when he looked in the mirror each morning. When asked what he was thinking at that time, he replied: "I'm stupid, and I'll never get through college. I should have already graduated. I'm a loser." These thoughts represent cognitive errors (e.g., over-generalizing, should statements, catastrophizing). The depressed brain can take any situation and turn it into a negative one. When this was described to him, Peter was able to recognize this faulty, self-deprecating thought pattern. By beginning his day with negative thoughts followed by bad feelings, Peter was setting himself up for failure and continued depression. Possible rebuttals to his thoughts were discussed. His suggestions included: "Well, I guess I'm not really stupid because I do make good grades. I probably will graduate, but maybe a little later than I hoped." It is important to stress that cognitive therapy is not simply a program of self-affirmation, but rather an approach that identifies and disputes those negative thoughts that maintain and perpetuate depression. I prescribed Celexa (citalopram), 20 mg., to add a pharmacologic treatment to psychotherapy. I also provided Peter with a handout that defines and describes the various cognitive errors to reinforce our work.

During our third session, it was apparent that the Peter had started to recognize more of his cognitive distortions and their impact on his mood. He described his tendency to think in all-or-nothing terms (polarization). We discussed examples in which a person can be good but also have some undesirable qualities, leading to some "gray" areas. Peter also noticed a tendency to have negative thoughts about himself during class, preventing him from participating and asking questions. He had begun disputing these thoughts when they occurred, replacing them with more realistic alternatives, such as: "Nobody is really staring at me. People are probably thinking about themselves, not necessarily me." These thoughts led to his feeling more relaxed and allowed him to gain the courage to speak up in class.

Our fourth through seventh sessions focused on his steady progress utilizing the cognitive strategies he had learned. Peter noticed that he was less frequently jumping to conclusions. When invited to eat with friends, he no longer thought: "They're just asking me because they feel sorry for me." Another thought made more sense to him: "It's nice to have friends who want to be with me." Peter noticed significant mood elevation. His appetite had returned. He felt confident enough to quit one of his part-time jobs which he realized he did not enjoy. His sleep improved. He had excelled in his psychology course, and he felt that he had a greater understanding of it due to his real-life experience with depression and its treatment. Peter was now participating in class discussions. He reported entering a classroom fifteen minutes late, without dread. (In the past, he said, he would have skipped the class out of fear of embarrassment.)

During our eighth session, we reviewed Peter's treatment and discussed options for continued contact. He thought the psychotherapy was very useful and would be "helpful throughout life." Peter had mastered the skills necessary to utilize cognitive therapy, but asked if we could continue to meet every two to three months for follow-up. I agreed. Celexa was continued, but the hypnotic trazodone was no longer needed.

I believe that Peter obtained optimal improvement in an approach that combined medication and psychotherapy. Either strategy alone may have worked; however, in my opinion, the combination afforded him the best chance of recovery. Simply rereading the cognitive therapy handout served to "refill the prescription" for him of a model that had proven useful. Cognitive therapy provided a sense of autonomy (rather than dependency), with booster sessions available as a reminder of the model that he had used to help himself.

Thursday Morning, 9:00 A.M.

When a new model presents itself as a psychotherapy alternative, the practitioner is typically referred initially those patients who have

not been helped by traditional approaches. It reminds me of the promotion of a young, skilled hockey player from a minor league to the parent NHL team. Typically, this goal scorer (at a lower level) is placed on a defensive (checking) line, so as not to disrupt the team's chemistry. As a consequence, he often fails to demonstrate his skills and is demoted. Placing the talented player an "impossible" situation often dooms his efforts.

The opportunity to treat a patient who has been unsuccessfully treated by a psychodynamic approach offers similar perils to the cognitive therapist. Referrals to me from other therapists often follow this format. Once the cognitive therapist forms a working relationship with a physician in primary care, he or she can more easily demonstrate skills that lead to other (appropriate) referrals. Ralph came to me in the early days of my cognitive therapy work. I was motivated to help him succeed, but I knew the task would not be easy.

Your first patient today is Ralph, a 56-year-old male accountant, who has been depressed and "in psychoanalytic psychotherapy for all of his adult life." He was looking for an alternative approach, had read about cognitive therapy, and contacted me to schedule an evaluation session.

Ralph had never suffered an episode of major depression, but he had been moderately depressed continuously for "as long as he could remember." He had persistent problems with sadness and lack of motivation, concentration, fatigue, and indecision, but had never had psychomotor changes, felt worthless, or had disruption in sleep, appetite, or weight.

My diagnosis was: dysthymic disorder. It appeared that his eight years of psychoanalytic psychotherapy, once to twice a week, had had little lasting significance. In addition, several adequate antidepressant drug trials had been of no benefit.

In session two, I taught him the cognitive therapy model. He defined the problem focus as his inability to leave an ungratifying marriage. It took six hours for him to make the transition from the role requirements in a psycho-dynamic psychotherapy to those of a cognitive therapy. His monologue of past recollections dominated these sessions, despite my periodic reminders of the format (dialoguing in the present) for cognitive work. But he persevered, asking at times, "Are we doing cognitive therapy yet?" I was impressed by his commitment and hard work, despite the continued frustration of "not getting it right."

Ralph began session seven with an appropriate focus, allowed me to participate by asking questions, and remained rooted in the here-and-

now. We quickly identified sources of distress, automatic thoughts, and consistent cognitive errors. We discussed his tendency to be perfectionistic in his expectations for himself, but more understanding and lenient regarding others. His options were typically polarized, with categories established for right and wrong; there were no grays. I shifted the focus to choices and anticipated consequences. At one point, I suggested that he *update his resume.* His self-view seemed to have passed unaltered from earlier troubles through later triumphs, without modification.

Our sessions emphasized disputing the reflex meanings that he could now identify, and generating and considering alternative ways of thinking. The substance of the treatment took 36 weekly sessions. It is fair to point out that managed care was just beginning to exert impact. After session twenty-two, I requested a series of follow-up monthly sessions. These were, somewhat surprisingly, granted and led to an additional year of therapeutic work.

By therapy's end, Ralph had moved out of his house, instituted divorce proceedings, handled the life changes skillfully with his college-age son and daughter, and established a more rational (and less perfectionistic) self-view. His dysthymic symptoms were largely gone, and he demonstrated a capability to use the cognitive method when stress arose. A one year follow-up call (initiated by Ralph) showed continued well-being.

Thursday Morning, 10:00 A.M.

Charleston is a beautiful city, with mild temperatures, lovely beaches and plentiful golf courses, all surrounded on three sides by the soothing sight of water. Access to rivers and the sea are a boon to fishermen, boaters, and anyone who enjoys water sports. Boasting these ingredients, it should come as no surprise that Charleston is seen as an attractive place to retirees.

As a person progresses through life's stages—from childhood and schooling to adolescence and then young adulthood, with marriage, family and work—there seems always to be a new and potentially exciting period of life on the horizon. For many men and women in our culture, this progression ends with retirement. Leaving the workplace (an equivalent for some may be the "empty nest" when the last child leaves home), however, ushers in a life stage for which some adults have little preparation. When self-worth has been defined in large part by one's work, the transition to retirement is often accompanied by anxiety and depression.

Your third patient is John*, a 65-year-old man, married for forty years to Betty, with two sons and four grandchildren. He is a college graduate who went on to obtain a degree in business administration. He held a series of responsible administrative positions throughout his work life at several universities, a medical center, and several community organizations, all in the mid-west. John's father died at age 55 of heart disease. His mother died at age 60 after a stroke. He is an only child. He has no prior history of depression, nor of an anxiety disorder nor of substance abuse.

John retired from his last job nine months prior to our first meeting. With Betty suffering from asthma, a move south was suggested, and the couple moved to Charleston three months later. An internist referred John to me for additional treatment of his "depression." Since retiring, he has had a "negative outlook." There is little pleasure. His life is disorganized. He feels like a "fish out of water."

John has multiple awakenings from sleep at night, but does not see insomnia as a particular problem. His appetite is unchanged, and his weight is stable. He feels more generally nervous now than he did during stressful periods at work. He doesn't believe that his thinking is "sharp." His energy level is unchanged, and fatigue is not a problem. He can concentrate, but in truth, there is "little need for concentration." He has noted no memory changes; in fact, he seems to recall all too well the days he worked, the problems he faced, and the goals he set. He thinks of them daily.

John feels no sense of belonging in Charleston. He has met several people, all of whom are retired, whose lives are focused on "golf, fishing, and grandchildren." He has little interest in golf, does not fish, and seeing his grandchildren twice a year is quite sufficient for him (although Betty might disagree). He feels he has little in common with the people he has met, but acknowledges that "Charleston is a beautiful place."

John's new internist prescribed sertraline (Zoloft), and titrated the dose up to 150 mg. per day. He felt somewhat less anxious but, in truth, little better. There were two other drugs offered, but he cannot recall their names. Feeling no better, he went to the library and read about cognitive therapy. He then asked his doctor for a referral.

My diagnostic impression was: adjustment disorder, with anxious and depressed mood. There was no major depression, no dysthymia, no formal anxiety disorder. I suggested no drug prescription and agreed to a course of brief cognitive therapy. John reported for our initial therapy session with his wife and asked if she could join us. I agreed. Their mar-

---

* This case is adapted with permission of *Primary Care Companion to the Journal of Clinical Psychiatry*. The case originally appeared in D. Schuyler (2001). Retirement. *Primary Care Companion to the Journal of Clinical Psychiatry*, 3(6), 265–266.

riage was a close one, and they enjoyed each other's company, but each maintained a need for some privacy. Betty would be a *participant-observer* in the therapy. John's goal for treatment was "to be able to relax more and to accept retirement."

As he had some knowledge of the cognitive model, I began with a brief discussion of how we would work by describing my understanding of it "so we would be on the same page." He described spending an inordinate amount of time each morning ruminating about the past. He was concerned with what he "ought" to be doing. We reviewed his interests: bicycling, swimming, bridge, pottery, and "university life." I suggested that he keep a log of those occasions when he felt particularly sad or anxious, and then try to capture and write down his thoughts. We would use this log to guide our work in subsequent sessions. We agreed to meet every two weeks.

John and Betty came together for session three. His log had eleven separate situations. His thoughts ranged from: "It is hard to find affordable housing to meet our needs," to regret over a purchase he had made ("I should have thought through the process better"), to waking up anxious and thinking "I wish we had a more pleasant place to live." We patiently went over each situation, stressing the relationship of the thought to the feeling. I asked him to judge the thoughts in terms of their reasonableness and their strategic value to him. If they failed either criterion, we sought alternative possibilities. Betty was encouraged to contribute options. I emphasized that no alternative belief was "right." Rather one alternative might suit him better than another.

In session four, John once again brought in his log of situations, feelings, and thoughts. I encouraged him to add a fourth column for options or alternatives. Now, we referred to the alternatives as *choices* and considered likely consequences as we discussed each one. He reported that he was actually using the model between sessions, and his wife added that he seemed enthusiastic about it. He reported sleeping better, and that his mood was "more even" than previously.

In session five, we discussed life stages and defined retirement as the end of one stage and the *beginning of another*. I stressed that the stage ending was often better defined than the one beginning. I reminded him that the Chinese character for crisis combines a symbol for danger with one for opportunity. He had focused on the first, while ignoring the second. He noted that he "needed permission to experience pleasure."

John was more familiar with life as an obligation. We discussed a reordering of priorities. In the next session, he and his wife agreed that he was now "making real progress toward the goal of a more tolerable retirement." We focused on self-standards and setting priorities for himself. John and his wife now walked for one hour each morning. He had met with the pastor of the church they had joined and discussed a role for him involving education. John had made a friend of a man in his

community, with whom he was now speaking daily about some common interests. He and his wife were actively house-hunting, and they had defined the area in which they wished to live.

He described the cognitive approach as a "life skill" and wondered if he would be qualified to "put a group together, teach the cognitive model, and be of help to a group of retirees." We discussed John's gains over the period of three months and how they had occurred. Periods of anxious or depressed mood were now "rare" and "manageable" for him. We agreed that we would end this active phase of therapy that day. The next session would be at his initiative. Jack called six months later to say that he had been functioning and feeling well.

Thursday Morning, 11:00 A.M.

Common sense might prescribe brief therapy for the patient with an isolated, focal problem. When the presentation includes three separate diagnoses, it seems logical that the treatment will be more complex and take more time. Sometimes, however, complexity is trumped by a high level of patient motivation, as well as a tight fit between the cognitive method and the patient's style.

Your third patient of the day, Ellen,* comes with a "suitcase of problems." This combination (generalized anxiety disorder [GAD], specific phobia, and panic disorder) typically presents in a primary care setting. Dr. Nikki Brannon did a masterful job of helping the patient define her problems and then crafted a cognitive approach to treatment. Her style emphasizes cognitive thinking and utilizes less concrete structure. It is conversational, problem-solving, and present-oriented.

Ellen, a 58-year-old married woman, was referred by her primary care physician to evaluate the contribution of stress to her complaint of skin rash. He had recently started her on alprazolam (Xanax), 0.5 mg. per day. She has had no previous psychiatric treatment. Ellen's other medical problems included hypercholesterolemia, glaucoma, hypothyroidism, and leg pain. Prescribed medications were Premarin (conjugated estrogen), and Synthroid (levothroxine).

After working in the food industry, Ellen has been unemployed for several years secondary to her stated inability to remain on her feet for

---

* This case is adapted with permission of *Primary Care Companion to the Journal of Clinical Psychiatry.* The case originally appeared in N. Brannon & D. Schuyler (2000). Comorbid generalized anxiety disorder, phobia, and panic disorder. *Primary Care Companion to the Journal of Clinical Psychiatry,* 2(4), 141–142.

lengthy periods. She is in the thirty-third year of her second marriage. She dropped out of school in the ninth grade because of academic difficulties, then was married at age sixteen. She had three children from her first marriage; however, one son died at age three in a house accident. Her first marriage ended after five years, shortly after the death of her son. She has no history of alcohol or drug abuse. She does have a history of tobacco use, which she states "calms her down." Her family history is significant for alcoholism in her father and a maternal uncle.

On initial evaluation, Ellen's chief complaints were expressed as: "problems with her nerves, and an inability to deal with stress." She reported excess worry about various situations: crowds, leaving home, traveling over bridges, initiating conversations with others, and driving a car. She was particularly afraid to drive downtown, fearing that she would get lost, be in the wrong lane, or drive too slowly. Her anxiety was so great that she had not driven downtown in twenty-five years, limiting her driving to short distances around her home. She had become dependent on her husband for most of her needs and voiced frustration that "he always wanted to stay home and watch television." She had suffered from panic attacks, typically triggered in crowds or in driving situations. She had some intrusive thoughts related to her son's death, but no other symptoms of posttraumatic stress.

At our initial visit, Ellen was well-groomed and made good eye contact. Her speech was normal in rate, volume, and tone. She described her mood as okay, but her affect was anxious and, at times, tearful. She had no psychotic thinking and no suicidal ideas. My DSM-IV diagnoses were: GAD, specific phobia, and panic disorder with agoraphobia.

I described the model of cognitive therapy to her at the end of the intake session, and we agreed to meet in one week. During session two, Ellen spent much of our time emphasizing that her problems were too great to be helped. Remembering that she had told me that she enjoyed fishing, I made an analogy of a rock being thrown into a pond, with the resulting ripples getting bigger and bigger. I told her that even a small change in one area can have rippling effects in other areas. This analogy hit home, as she referred to it often during subsequent sessions.

Session three was spent challenging dysfunctional beliefs about driving downtown, talking with her neighbor, and going to the beach. She took the viewpoint that if something minor were to go wrong, the outcome would be a catastrophe. I challenged this black-and-white thinking, asking her to specify the likely consequences should something go awry. Ellen drove to my downtown office for session four. We used this as an opportunity to discuss some other places she might like to drive, such as the beach and the small town in which her son is buried. Because she felt that she was making progress, Ellen requested that our next appointment be in two weeks, and I agreed.

By session five, Ellen was driving downtown without problems (or the need for medication). She had been able to visit her neighbor on two separate occasions. Sessions six and seven were used to challenge dysfunctional beliefs about driving in unfamiliar areas. We discussed in detail specific routes she might take, attempting to anticipate potential obstacles and choices she might make to overcome them. We scheduled our next meeting for one month later.

In sessions eight through ten, Ellen reported various trips she had taken, the difficulties she had experienced, and how she had approached each one without allowing anxiety and negative thoughts to prevail. These appointments were staggered six weeks apart, and she used the time between them to practice what she had learned.

In our last meeting, we reviewed the experience of eleven sessions over an eight-month period. She had noticed a significant decrease in general anxiety and had conquered several specific fears. She had successfully driven downtown, visited her son's grave, initiated conversation with others, and enjoyed a long-awaited picnic on the beach. She felt a great deal more independent. We celebrated her accomplishments, and I told her to call if she felt that further meetings would be useful. With the increase in mastery and self-confidence (and the decrease in general anxiety), there was no recurrence of the original anxiety-related complaint of skin rash.

Thursday Afternoon, 1:00 P.M.

What predicts therapeutic success? Motivation is often one key ingredient (see Chapter One). How can the power of motivation be harnessed when external factors form obstacles to change? A second factor in successful therapy is the power inherent in the doctor-patient relationship. A third factor may be helping the patient find a way to reframe the problem, so that solutions become evident. Dr. Lisa Sebotnick integrates these three factors in a brief cognitive therapy that exemplifies the healing power of the relationship, in addition to the perseverance of a motivated patient and the value of reframing.

Your fourth patient today is Naomi*, a 27-year-old single mother of three young boys. Her presenting complaint told of a bad environment

---

* This case is adapted with permission of *Primary Care Companion to the Journal of Clinical Psychiatry*. The case originally appeared in L. S. McLean (2002). Overcoming obstacles: Therapeutic success despite external barriers. *Primary Care Companion to the Journal of Clinical Psychiatry*, 4(1), 27–29.

which she perceived as causing her a great deal of psychological distress. Her financial and situational circumstances initially limited her perceived options.

Naomi's specific presenting complaint was: "My caseworker thought I needed some help." A social service worker with whom she was involved referred Naomi to our clinic. She was very nervous during our first encounter, and had difficulty initiating conversation. She talked about crying most of the time, having no motivation, feeling constantly tired, having problems concentrating, and frequently worrying. She worried about her children, their father, and the family's financial situation. Naomi denied a history of panic attacks, obsessive-compulsive symptoms, psychosis, mania, suicidal or homicidal thoughts, or suicide attempts. She denied abuse of drugs or alcohol. However, she acknowledged smoking one to two packs of cigarettes per day.

Naomi described the most current stressor as having mixed feelings about leaving her boyfriend Jim, stating, "I'm not very strong and I can't say no." She provided me with a detailed account of their relationship. They met in their senior year of high school and began dating. From their first date, Jim would arrive drunk and without money. She financially supported the relationship. Naomi became pregnant that first year, had her first son and then graduated from high school. She and Jim have remained together, on and off, for several years. When he is away from home, it is usually because he is in jail for offenses such as drunk driving and criminal domestic violence. He has an alcohol abuse disorder and, while intoxicated a few years ago, physically attacked Naomi and her son. This incident led to the involvement of the Department of Social Services. Jim has also been unfaithful several times. Naomi believed that "he has taken everything away from her," but also "she doesn't want her children to be raised without a father."

There is no significant past medical or psychiatric history. Naomi's family history includes alcohol abuse and bipolar disorder in distant relatives. She and her two brothers were raised in a middle class family. It was not a very emotionally expressive household. Currently, her parents are very involved in helping out with the care of Naomi's sons.

My diagnosis was: major depressive disorder. Her stated goal for therapy was "to have happy kids that don't grow up to be white trash." She wanted to stop crying, to feel okay being alone, to stop feeling punished constantly, and to get a decent job. She was not interested in medications, but rather psychotherapy. We decided on a cognitive approach to address distortions regarding her relationship with Jim, and her constant feelings of being punished.

Naomi began session two by telling me that she had left some things out for fear of being judged. She reported having approximately two mixed drinks three times a week, but denied symptoms consistent with alcohol dependence. She reported occasionally getting physically ag-

gressive with her children (e.g., grabbing their arms, holding them still, but not hitting them), and she described living in a small camper on a yearly income of less than $6000. We discussed her reluctance to report these details, the associated anxiety, and how the actual outcome of these disclosures differed vastly from her fears. This provided a good transition to introducing the cognitive model. Naomi understood the theory, and noted that she could "apply this at home." She was encouraged to identify and write down automatic thoughts.

At our next visit, we applied the model to her relationship with Jim. We examined the evidence for and against her beliefs. We noted her tendency to catastrophize and its impact on her subsequent feelings and actions. She feared that if she were not with Jim, he would find another woman, fall in love, and "become the perfect father and partner that Naomi had always wanted."

Over the next three sessions, we continued to examine the reasons she was staying with Jim. It was evident that the relationship was causing significant distress. We noted Naomi's error of polarization (black-and-white thinking). Between visits, Jim had broken into their camper while drunk and become verbally abusive. Naomi was conflicted, thinking that: "Either her kids will have a father and develop into healthy, normal kids, or they won't have a father and they will miss out forever." To provide evidence to the contrary, we looked at the value of an environment with a physically abusive, alcoholic father, versus an environment with a single, supportive, non-abusive mother.

Over the next few sessions, Naomi began to spontaneously challenge her own beliefs about Jim. Her focus then shifted to questioning her ability to be independent and be a good mother. She believed that, if she could find a better job, she would make more money and be more respected. Naomi believed that this would help her self-esteem and her financial position. However, she would be away from the boys more often and, "they would lose another parent." She was able to identify the cognitive distortions in her thinking, but saw no alternative option. We labeled her stance as an "active decision not to change."

Naomi began to consider the option of moving in with her parents, and assuming a managerial position in the town where they lived. She worried that the independence she was gaining from Jim, and her progress in therapy would be jeopardized by returning to the scene of her father's overbearing, critical nature. This laid the groundwork for the next therapy focus: Naomi's self-esteem.

In discussing her automatic thoughts with regard to moving in with her parents, it became evident that Naomi feared resuming the child role. She feared this reversion despite being an adult and the mother of her own sons. She could not foresee being able to set boundaries with her parents, even though she had started doing so with Jim. I emphasized her strengths in parenting and interpersonal relationships along

with her ability to separate from Jim. I gave Naomi a chapter on a cognitive approach to self-worth as a reading assignment. At our next visit, she commented about how useful the worksheets were in the chapter. It seemed that setting limits was, for her, a central facet of self-worth. Examining her thoughts, we identified the same set of cognitive errors noted earlier: catastrophizing and polarizing. Over the span of several sessions, she began to practice limit-setting. We discussed her fears about change and how the outcomes did not always resemble her expectations. As Naomi continued to practice limit-setting, her affect brightened, the language she used to describe herself was much stronger, she was able to take note of her own needs, and she was able to refer to Jim's behavior in an appropriately negative way. Her crying diminished, as did her irritability.

The remainder of our sessions were spent discussing Naomi's frustration at feeling stuck. She recognized her progress in therapy, but also understood the financial constraints that kept her from moving forward. One higher paying job she had been offered would result in the loss of government assistance which would mean that she would, paradoxically, end up with less money if she took this job. There was no way out of the hard choice between losing time with her sons and a higher paying job.

A friend called Naomi with a lead on a job in another town. We spent our second to last visit discussing what it would be like to "start over." She addressed anxiety-provoking situations, and saw that challenging her automatic thoughts could lessen the anxiety. We set a routine follow-up appointment for two weeks later.

Naomi began the session by stating that she was moving that weekend, and that this would be our last visit. She had accepted the managerial position and successfully negotiated a salary based on her calculation of a break even point. We discussed her fear of "not making it." We acknowledged that "large scale changes could be scary." We recapped the enormous progress she had made in therapy, and terminated.

This case demonstrates how, in the context of a confiding relationship, an individual trapped in a situation could problem-solve effectively and make an important life decision over the course of sixteen cognitive therapy sessions. Naomi made a significant life change and was able to achieve an outcome that had appeared to be beyond her reach.

Thursday Afternoon, 2:00 P.M.

Today's primary care physician is not adequately trained in recognizing the patient or situation that predictably benefits from a referral

for brief psychotherapy. Besieged by pharmaceutical salespeople, he or she doesn't typically receive input from psychotherapeutic "salespeople." This results in some patients missing out on the benefits of combining a psychotropic drug with brief cognitive therapy. That psychotherapy alone could be therapeutic is, typically, not even considered.

Dr. Katherine St. Germaine describes a case in which the physician's expectations for a drug trial strongly affected the patient's decision to remain in treatment and not seek a "second opinion." When the patient consulted her and received a more balanced "prescription," a period of constructive life change was initiated.

Your final patient today is Andrew*, a 36-year-old man, married for ten years with two sons (ages 10 and 14), who is currently completing a bachelor's degree. Simultaneously, he is working in a retail store. Andrew was being treated in primary care for depression for a period of two years. He was prescribed a variety of antidepressant drugs and, each time, told to return in about one month's time. He claimed that his doctor registered surprise on each occasion that he was not feeling better. While he noticed a positive effect on mood, the side effects of sweating and sexual dysfunction had defeated the only two successful trials. At his request, he was referred to our clinic for further evaluation and treatment.

At our initial visit, Andy's chief complaint was "continuing to feel depressed." He reported previous drug trials with Wellbutrin (bupropion) and Prozac (fluoxetine), each at a therapeutic dose for a reasonable period of time. He told me that he was "tired of feeling so bad about himself, feeling guilty, and being a failure." He acknowledged that his marriage was now over, and that he and his wife were discussing a divorce. He related that they "could never see eye to eye" and so the marriage had been "doomed from the start." When they tried to talk with each other, the result was "ineffective yelling." In addition, Andy was frustrated because his younger son never listened to him, and he and his wife disagreed on disciplinary options for the child.

My working diagnosis was: major depression. I recommended brief cognitive therapy to start, with additional medication trials to follow, if necessary. Andy contracted to work with me. In session two, we set

---

* This case is adapted with permission of *Primary Care Companion to the Journal of Clinical Psychiatry*. The case originally appeared in K. St. Germain & D. Schuyler (2001). Psychotherapy clarified the diagnosis and treated the problem. *Primary Care Companion to the Journal of Clinical Psychiatry*, 3(1), 30–31.

goals for treatment. He grandiosely stated that he wanted to be the "funniest, smartest man he could be" and " the best dad, the best student, the best of everything." Our first task was to work together to define more realistic goals. Challenged to do so, the patient focused on changing his tendency to impulsively criticize others. As a recent example, Andy cited being strongly and openly critical of a supervisor at work when he was upset with the way an assignment had been planned. He believed that the major result had been a poor evaluation from this supervisor. Subsequently, he blamed himself, and labeled himself a failure.

In session three, we focused on Andy's easily evoked anger and impatience, which seemed to lead to impulsive outbursts. We identified thoughts that triggered the feelings and the behavior and linked them to their negative consequences. We noted physical signs that served to indicate a rapid progression to uncontrolled anger and could serve as *alerts* to lead to better self-control. We redefined as an asset his capacity to find problems in a system, and worked on finding ways for him to communicate in a different fashion.

By session four, it was clear that Andy had absorbed the key points in our discussions and was actively applying them both at work with his boss and at home with his son. By interrupting what he called "this cycle," the patient increased his tolerance level, curbed his impulsive tendency, and thereby diminished the subsequent guilt and failure he was experiencing. Statements indicating that he was doing the work to identify the meanings related to his distress suggested therapeutic success was likely.

The following two sessions focused on *catastrophizing*, the cognitive error of constantly anticipating the worst possible outcome. We discussed a variety of situations using the triple-column format of examining situations, feelings and thoughts. In relating his son's newfound interest in the opposite sex, he stated: "If he got a girl pregnant, it would be all over." He quickly labeled the errors in thinking as jumping to a conclusion and catastrophizing, and we worked on finding a more reasonable alternative approach to his thinking.

Next, we took on his tendency to compare himself with his brother, and then to judge his performance a failure. Together, we reviewed his beliefs about his wife and that of his brother, with the aim of finding a more realistic understanding. By the eighth session, Andy told me that he and his wife were no longer contemplating divorce. He had written down the issues that bothered him and asked his wife to do the same. He found that they could talk now, without their interaction becoming a "shouting match." He suggested marriage counseling, and his wife readily agreed.

For the following three sessions, we decided to meet every two weeks and work on polishing the skills Andy had acquired. After a period of four months and a total of eleven sessions, we mutually agreed to terminate

therapy. I did not believe that antidepressant medication was necessary, and none was prescribed. My final diagnosis was generalized anxiety disorder (GAD), with secondary depression.

I understood Andy as a man who would become easily overwhelmed and then act impulsively, with resultant guilt, self-criticism, and lowering of self-esteem. If our treatment had been limited to medication management, I believe that I would have missed the diagnosis, and quite likely failed to help Andy. Time spent getting to know Andy and establishing an agenda for psychotherapy facilitated his dramatic life changes and therapeutic benefit.

Friday Morning, 9:00 A.M.

Before there was brief therapy, *psychotherapy* implied a long-term venture that focused on childhood origins and conflicts. The therapist was more often passive than active, and the procedure occupied a lot of time. Brief therapy made specific alterations on this standard model, including a here-and-now focus, a problem-solving approach, and a deliberately collaborative process. Little time was spent in the past, and origins were no longer considered to be highly significant.

But, what about duration? When must a therapy end to be considered as *brief*? The case presented by Dr. Andy Kozel revisits the issue of *medication versus psychotherapy*, but also defines *brief* as a format, not necessarily as a length of time. One successful "brief segment" may beget a second therapy, and even a third. The total duration may extend to 20–30 sessions, well beyond most therapists' definition of *brief*.

Your first patient today is Ellen*, a 56-year-old employed, widowed mother of two children, who had been treated with medication for depression and anxiety by her primary care physician for two years. (Does this sound familiar?) Because of worsening symptoms, a psychiatric consultation was obtained while the patient was still in the primary care clinic. The evaluating psychiatrist diagnosed a bereavement reaction and noted a history of major depression and panic disorder. A recommendation was made for brief therapy to help her in the task of "recreating her life."

---

* This case is adapted with permission of *Primary Care Companion to the Journal of Clinical Psychiatry*. The case originally appeared in F. A. Kozel & D. Schuyler (2000). When brief therapy worked and medication did not. *Primary Care Companion to the Journal of Clinical Psychiatry, 2*(5), 181–182.

Ellen had been widowed thirty years prior to being referred to me. Recent stresses in her life included the cancer-related death of a man with whom she had had an intimate relationship for twenty years. Owing to circumstances beyond her control, Ellen was unable to be with him during the latter part of his illness and death. She was also denied an opportunity to grieve openly. In addition, her daughter, who was suffering from bipolar disorder, and her daughter's two young children, had been living with the patient for the past three years, creating added stress and life disruption.

The initial evaluation by the treating psychiatrist revealed a long history of difficulty with depression and panic attacks, but no treatment until two years earlier. The treatment provided some relief, but not complete control of her symptoms. The recent stress of the lost lover had significantly worsened the depression and increased the frequency of panic attacks. Ellen's depression manifested in worsening sleep, low interest in daily life, low energy, intense guilt feelings, poor concentration, and weight gain. There were no thoughts of self-harm. Her general level of anxiety was elevated, and she was having severe panic attacks three times a week. She had begun to avoid malls and crowds, thus restricting herself from activities previously enjoyable for her. Ellen had no history of substance abuse, suicide attempts, or mania.

Ellen's past psychiatric history revealed the onset of panic attacks in her teens. She had an episode of postpartum depression following the birth of her second child, who died soon after birth. Her current medications were: paroxetine (Paxil) 40 mg. per day, Premarin (conjugated estrogen), trazodone (Desyrel), 50 mg. at bedtime, and clonazepam (Klonopin), 0.5 mg. per day. Ellen was a high school graduate, marrying soon after graduation. Her husband had died in a fishing accident ten years after their marriage. She was currently unemployed, having stopped work as a restaurant manager, two years earlier, due to "nerves."

The psychotherapy began by encouraging Ellen to talk about the events and emotions associated with the loss of her lover. By providing an opportunity to focus on her loss and establishing a framework in which to understand it, some of her depressive symptoms rapidly abated. At the second session, she requested that Klonopin be taken only at night, due to daytime drowsiness. This was the only medication change made. Ellen next addressed the current stresses in her life, as they impacted her well-being. She was encouraged to express and deal directly with feelings, even if they were negative or painful. Together, we examined her thoughts to see if they were reasonable.

By session three, there was a dramatic improvement in her depressive symptoms and a diminution in the frequency of panic attacks. From the fourth through the sixth sessions, the focus was on stresses in Ellen's past and present life, and how to cope with them. By session six, her panic attacks had ceased, and her depressive symptoms were gone. The ther-

apy had achieved what medication alone had not, even prior to her recent loss. She was able to begin a job caring for a young child. Treatment could reasonably have been terminated at this point, because the agreed upon goals had been met, but a decision was made to help Ellen reclaim those elements of her life that had been lost during her illness.

Sessions seven through twelve changed focus and were devoted to helping Ellen reconnect with lost social contacts. She became more active in church, and began to go out and take part in social activities. With a support network now reestablished, Ellen experienced a return of preoccupation with her lost love. Bereavement, therefore, became our focus from sessions twelve to sixteen. She was able to deal with the loss, and begin to orient toward the future. This progress led to the next focus which involved her relationship with her adult daughter and her wish for the daughter to move out. Using techniques she had learned earlier, Ellen worked on this for sessions seventeen to twenty-three, finally achieving her goal.

Although problems remain, Ellen has learned ways to help deal with them. She is currently working, and is planning a return to school. She has an active social life and participates in a number of organizations. Ellen has experienced no return of depressive symptoms or panic attacks. We are increasing the intervals between visits, leading to periodic meetings for medication management. If Ellen finds herself in a situation in which her coping techniques are overwhelmed, I have assured her that we can reinitiate a brief therapy to help her deal with that circumstance.

Friday Morning, 10:00 A.M.

A visit to a primary care physician with symptoms of persistent anxiety is likely to result in a prescription for anti-anxiety medication. Benzodiazepines (like Xanax or Ativan) lead to tolerance (the same dose no longer works) and dependency (problems with discontinuation). Seventy-five percent of anxiety disorders present in primary care settings. There is the additional concern of the diagnosis being missed and treatment rendered for individual physical symptoms of the anxiety disorder. Sometimes this route is bypassed when a parent or a knowledgeable source refers the patient directly for brief therapy. Brian's father, a medical researcher, helped his son to take a successful path to relief.

Your second patient today is Brian, a 25-year-old single male research analyst, who has had problems with excessive nervousness. His father suggested cognitive therapy, and Brian called for an evaluation appointment. Brian's history began five years prior to our first session while he was in college. He became so nervous he couldn't fall asleep the night

before an exam. One year later, he had his first panic attack, after starting his first job. Six months later, Brian was in "panic mode" for two months after starting a new project in another job.

One year prior to coming to me, Brian broke up with a woman after a two-year relationship. Subsequently, he was in a state of "paralysis"— anxious, indecisive, and insomniac. He recovered over a six-month period, and remained well until one month ago. In the interim, Brian met the woman who is now his fiancee. One month ago, he became acutely dissatisfied at work once again, was constantly nervous, and had a return of initial insomnia. He consulted a primary care physician in his insurance plan who prescribed a sleeping pill, temazepam (Restoril, 30 mg.) which was of no benefit. He was referred to a psychiatrist who prescribed Prozac, which was likewise unhelpful. He called his father who suggested he buy David Burns's book *Feeling Good*, and if it made sense to him, consult a cognitive therapist.

Brian's father is a medical researcher and is healthy. His mother sells real estate and was depressed at age thirty. His two older sisters are "bright" and are doing well. My diagnosis for Brian was: generalized anxiety disorder (GAD). I explained the cognitive method at the outset of session two. It made sense to him, and seemed similar to what he had read about. We identified an appraisal "below his usual standard" for himself that seemed to trigger several of his anxiety episodes. Further conversation revealed a consistent cognitive error of polarization, and a self-standard of perfectionism. This was reframed as a *choice* instead of a trait or habit. I asked in each instance: "Does this make sense to you?" and "Does this further your progress toward your goals?" For homework, I asked Brian to keep a memo book, with triple-column tables logging anxiety-evoking situations.

Examining Brian's homework in session three, we traced how he proceeds from an initial automatic thought to arbitrary inferences (i.e., jumps to a conclusion) and then to over-generalizations. I defined two modes of functioning that seemed to be at play: problem-solving mode (for him, typically healthy) and evaluative mode (for him, the process that often leads to anxiety).

In session four, our focus was his thinking in a work setting. We noted how Brian distorted the past and I encouraged him to describe the past more accurately to me. Once again, we found multiple instances of arbitrary inferences: conclusions he couldn't support with data.

The next hour was devoted to decentering. It seems that his focus too often "got stuck" on himself, without considering the impact of, or consequences for, others. For example, what explained negative judgments made about him? How often was it really a problem of his, and how often did it meet the need of another?

In session six, Brian reported using the cognitive approach often during the past week. "It worked," he said, "and things seemed less fear-

some." We noted another group of polarized meanings. We worked to separate *right versus wrong* from *differences in an individual's style.* His belief was: "If I don't do better than someone else, that means that I am inferior."

The seventh session focused on perfectionism. We worked to identify and separate *what really mattered* from his belief that "everything matters." We discussed making his own choices as opposed to "following past habits." Brian's progress to date suggested that we lengthen the interval between sessions to two weeks.

In session eight, Brian brought up his tendency to procrastinate. It seemed clear to him, after a little discussion, that procrastination related directly to a "need to do things perfectly." The next hour led to a discussion of discrimination and generalization as these processes related to how he processed data. He offered: "I'm learning some different ways to think . . . ways to converse with myself." He noted that he was doing much better, with few anxiety episodes.

We scheduled session ten for one month later. Brian discussed the changes he had made. He was grateful for reaching the goals he had set at the outset. He was hopeful that the changes made "would stick." Brian called me six months later as we had arranged. He believed he had gotten a "new lease on life."

Friday Morning, 11:00 A.M.

The supervisee, Jeff Cluver, had already proved his mettle delivering the cognitive model effectively (see Tuesday Morning, 9:00 A.M.). Now, he had a dilemma. Dr. Cluver said:

> I completed an intake for a patient I believe would be a good candidate for cognitive therapy. He has a clear case of obsessive-compulsive disorder, and a pretty rigid personality style. I didn't think I'd get anywhere with him doing a structured therapy, with triple columns, homework, and regular weekly appointments. What I wound up doing with him over five monthly sessions "worked," and I want to tell you about it. But, I really don't know what to call it.

The conceptual model Dr. Cluver employed was surely cognitive therapy. To emphasize the omission of structure, we decided to call it *cognitive therapy lite.*

Obsessive-compulsive disorder (OCD) is a common and potentially disabling illness. It is thought to be the fourth most common psychiatric diagnosis after specific phobias, substance-related disor-

ders, and major depression. It may well have a strong biological component, and the treatment of OCD has been modified by the development of the selective serotonin reuptake inhibitors (SSRIs). There are some cases in which the response to medication is inadequate, and the clinician is called upon to supplement pharmacotherapy with other, complementary modes of treatment.

Your third patient today is Richard, a 55-year-old divorced white man who was diagnosed with OCD seventeen months prior to this session when he first presented to our psychiatric outpatient clinic. At the time of his initial presentation, he reported persistent and intrusive thoughts about harming other people. Specifically, he described having thoughts about placing sharp objects in others' food. Richard stated that if he saw any food that was unattended, he would immediately have the thought that he may have placed something dangerous in the food. He recognized that these thoughts were strange and often absurd, yet he could not rid himself of them, and would often spend hours agonizing over whether he should act on his impulses to throw the food in the trash can. Richard lived with his elderly and sick father, and he would often have thoughts that he was somehow responsible for his father's illness, that he had harmed him with some food that contained sharp or harmful objects. A large proportion of the patient's time was spent at home with his father as he closely monitored, and often discarded, food that may have been "contaminated."

Richard described his early childhood as unremarkable, and he graduated from high school near the top of his class. His mother stayed at home to raise Robert and his two brothers. His father worked in a factory. Richard was married at age twenty-one, and he and his wife had two children. He worked as a salesman for several different companies over the course of almost thirty years. Richard and his wife divorced thirteen years ago, after their youngest son had moved out of their home. At the time of his presentation in the clinic, he was living with his father and reported using alcohol only on rare occasions, and he denied the use of tobacco or illicit drugs.

Richard had been having intrusive thoughts since his early twenties. The thoughts had grown more persistent and bothersome over time, although Richard had never sought treatment in the past, not knowing that what he was experiencing was a treatable disorder. Five years ago, his father had been diagnosed with colon cancer, and this seemed to trigger a worsening of his obsessions and resulted in ruminative worrying and some compulsive behavior, such as throwing away food and inspecting and washing the cups, plates, and bowls found in the house. Two years ago, Richard, himself, was diagnosed with prostate cancer. This further heightened his symptoms, as he grew increasingly con-

cerned about his health. His rumination, checking, washing, and discarding increased to the point that he was unable to do much else. Richard eventually reported these problems to his urologist, who made the referral to the psychiatric clinic.

After unsuccessful trials of paroxetine (Paxil) and fluoxetine (Prozac), a dose of 80 mg. per day of citalopram (Celexa) led to a modest symptomatic improvement. Although not occurring as frequently, when the obsessions did occur, they were just as intrusive, troublesome and difficult to ignore. In addition, Richard's worrying and rumination continued to consume vast amounts of time, and his washing and discarding had both continued to the point where he was spending inordinate amounts of money on food and cleaning supplies. After almost a year in our clinic, he had achieved only a mild improvement in his OCD symptoms through the use of high dose SSRI therapy.

Prior to my first appointment with him, Richard had been coming to the clinic once a month for thirty-minute medication management appointments. During our first meeting, I suggested to him that we meet more frequently to initiate a course of brief cognitive therapy, explaining that this might help to augment the effects of his medication. I explained the principles of cognitive therapy in general, and he seemed very interested. However, due to transportation problems, he stated that he would be able to come only once monthly. He did offer to stay for hour-long appointments once a month, and we contracted for extended once monthly appointments, combining medication management and brief cognitive therapy.

We started the initial hour-long session by reviewing the obsessions that were becoming more intrusive to Richard. He explained that the thoughts about placing objects in people's food, specifically his father's, were becoming more and more prominent. We discussed the origin of these obsessive thoughts, and Richard clearly stated that he felt as though they came from his own mind. He felt the need to act on them, because he would be responsible if something bad did happen and he could have stopped it. I provided some education on OCD and attempted to normalize some of his experiences. I explained that many people had impulses to do things that may be out of character for them, but that their brains did not allow them to dwell on the thought, so that a fleeting thought or strange idea came and went without a second thought. He laughed at this and explained that it was not the "second thought" that he was worried about, but rather the third, fourth, fifth, and so on.

We then went on to discuss the concept of *automatic thoughts* in the context of what he was experiencing. I defined an automatic thought for Richard and explained that, with OCD, there are essentially two types of automatic thoughts. The first is the *obsession*, and the second is the thought one has after the obsession has intruded. The obsession itself is difficult to control, as by definition it enters awareness without much

prompting or warning. We began to focus on the *second automatic thought.* These included thoughts such as: "What if I put something in his food? He may get even sicker, or I may cause him to die." Identifying these thoughts was easy for Richard to do, and he went on with other examples, such as, "What can I do about it? What can I do to be certain that I haven't put anything in there?" He explained that these thoughts would scroll through his head for hours at a time, until he absolutely had to do something about it, or was forced to move on to something else. I explained that these thoughts were the cause of his problems, more so than the obsession itself. I asked what would happen if he was able to keep from thinking in the manner that he had just described. Richard thought for a moment and said, "Honestly, I have no idea."

I began the second therapy session by describing an example of an old and long abandoned treatment for OCD. A patient would sit in a chair in an otherwise empty room, with the therapist standing behind him or her. The patient was instructed to let the therapist know as soon as an unwanted thought entered into the patient's awareness, at which point the therapist would hurl a fragile plate or glass against the wall behind the patient, making a resounding crash. Invariably, the patient would jump out of his or her chair and ask what was happening, concerned more about his or her safety than the thought that had just crossed his or her mind. I explained that this was a method of interrupting the thought process that led to excessive rumination and sometimes compulsions that were time consuming and often debilitating. "It gives you something else to think about," Richard interjected. "It gives you time to think about something else," I offered. We went on to discuss the idea of creating a *window of opportunity* after the obsession, so that he could dispute and interrupt the self-talk that would invariably follow. We then looked at the probability of his having actually placed something in his father's food, and he was readily able to determine that there was very little likelihood that this would ever actually happen.

Richard began the third session by describing an incident that occurred at a neighbor's birthday party, when he threw away the birthday cake after having thoughts that he may have placed something harmful in it. "And I was really upset with myself for giving in like that," he said. We talked about *giving in* and what he could do to give himself a choice in the future. We created a list of options of what he might do when placed in a similar situation in the future. Richard reported that he was able to "interrupt" and even "avoid" the repetitive thoughts on several occasions over the past months. He gave multiple examples, and it became clear that the birthday cake was the exception to the rule over the past month, as he had averted many potentially similar results. We looked at these successes and examined what he was able to do to avoid the repetitive self-talk, and he began to see more clearly that he was starting to "break some dishes" on his own.

Our fourth session began with another example from Richard. This time he was having guests, and one family member placed an almost-full plate of food next to him and asked him to "keep an eye on it" until he got back from the bathroom. The thought appeared almost immediately: "Did I put something in the food?" Richard reported that his next thought was, "Of course I didn't; Joe just put it down there, and there was no time for me to do anything." This dispute kept the other thoughts at bay, but not completely out of the picture, as he still contemplated throwing out the food. Joe returned and walked away with his plate of food. Richard told himself that everything would be fine and walked the other way. "And, then what?" I asked. "Nothing happened," he responded with a smile, "Everything was fine."

We met again several weeks ago, and Richard told me that he was doing "very well" and that "those stupid thoughts still come and go all the time, but at least now I can get them to go." He talked about his increasingly effective disputing of the previously destructive self-talk, and he offered numerous examples of successfully avoiding the ruminations and compulsions. Richard said that he had only one more problem that he wanted help with. "And, what's that?" I asked. "What do I do with all of this time I have on my hands?" he replied.

Throughout the five sessions described above, we continued to discuss Richard's medication—its effectiveness and side effects—and we also reviewed his other medications and the status of his cancer. The extended medication management sessions gave us time to work on cognitive therapy techniques that he was able to readily understand and apply. No medication changes were made during the five months. Richard was able to apply the principles of cognitive therapy and "try them on" for himself in the intervening weeks, and this resulted in a marked reduction in his symptoms over the course of five monthly sessions.

Friday Afternoon, 1:00 P.M.

Cognitive therapy has been found useful in approaching a wide range of clinical problems. Although my personal work has largely been limited to depression and anxiety disorders, supervision of resident psychotherapy has taught me the value of the cognitive model in a variety of other settings. In this excellent case report, Samantha Symons applies the model successfully to a form of eating disorder. Dr. Symons has studied the treatment of eating disorders during a significant portion of her training. I urged her to write about her success in applying cognitive methodology to the treatment of this difficult group of problems. Here is her report.

Binge eating disorder includes a sense of lack of control over eating, and a feeling of being depressed, guilty or disgusted with one-self after eating. It therefore made sense to me both to screen for depression in this population and to consider short-term cognitive therapy to target guilt and behavior control. Like the other eating disorders, binge eating usually affects adolescent and young adult fe-males who tend to be high achievers. Not surprisingly, this often means a higher prevalence in college and post-graduate programs. The subject of this article, a 21-year-old single white female college student was initially seen in a primary care setting, and then referred to our university clinic for evaluation and treatment.

Your fourth patient today, Eileen*, is in her fourth-year of college and is currently applying for post-graduate programs in biochemistry. She has a good relationship with her parents and younger sister, although all live out of state, and she finds it difficult to visit as often as she would like. Eileen describes an unremarkable childhood marked by her aca-demic success, which she has been able to maintain in college with disci-pline and hard work. With the added stress of studying for the Graduate Record Exams (GRE) and work as a research assistant for the past three months, she reports an increasing number of what she describes as "bad days." These are days that include at least one episode of binge eating, described as consuming an inappropriate number of calories during one sitting until she feels uncomfortable. Eileen believes that she has no con-trol over this eating pattern, which may include eating half a cake or a whole pizza, even when she doesn't feel particularly hungry. She denies using any compensatory behaviors such as purging, taking laxatives, or over-exercising. After these binges, she feels guilty, sad, and often takes long naps that prevent her from getting her work done. During these days she feels depressed, has decreased motivation and energy, reports an inability to concentrate while studying, and suffers frequent episodes of tearfulness. Although her grades and work have not suffered, Eileen feels a great deal of distress about these "bad days," now occurring four to seven days a week, and is concerned that she may have an eating disorder.
Eileen is currently 5'8" tall and weighs 181 pounds. She believes that she is overweight, but she seems more concerned with her pattern of

---

* This case is adapted with permission of *Primary Care Companion to the Journal of Clinical Psychiatry*. The case originally appeared in S. Symons (2003). Binge eating, depression, and cognitive therapy. *Primary Care Companion to the Journal of Clini-cal Psychiatry*, 5(1), 45–46.

eating. Her highest weight in the past was 190 pounds, and this occurred during her freshman year of high school. She has been slightly overweight for much of her adult life, other than an eight-month period at the beginning of college when she was able to maintain a weight of 160 pounds. She describes this time as "happy and stress-free." She has had several episodes of dieting, none lasting more than a week, and she denies any purging behaviors. She has binged occasionally throughout the past six years, and this is usually associated with periods of depression. Eileen has never been formally diagnosed with depression, nor treated with medication.

My diagnostic impression was: eating disorder (not otherwise specified) and major depressive disorder. Eileen agreed to a course of weekly cognitive therapy sessions. We discussed the possibility of treatment with antidepressants, but, as Eileen was reluctant to start a medication and had no thoughts of self-harm, we agreed to re-visit this in a later session, if necessary.

During our second session, I asked Eileen to describe in some detail one of her recent "bad days." She was able to identify a trigger of worrying about an upcoming test. She came home from school and sat down to eat. After eating until she was uncomfortably full, she felt guilty and worthless. She described a voice that "puts her down" by saying things like, "You're not good enough." We discussed negative self-talk and she observed that she could frequently identify thoughts that attack her self-esteem or abilities. She realized that she is often listening to this voice when she sits down to eat. The cognitive model of automatic thoughts leading to feelings and behavior was explained to her. Towards the end of the session, Eileen described what she did on her "good days," such as walking her dog and talking with her sister on the phone. For homework, she agreed to listen for negative self-talk, identify triggers, and attempt to replace eating with those activities she does on her good days.

During our third session, it was apparent that Eileen had started to recognize how her thoughts, feelings, and behavior are linked. She was able to successfully prevent a binge by leaving the house to visit a friend. She continued to discuss her cognitions, and described thinking that if she does poorly on the GRE, she will "be a failure and never get into graduate school." This is an example of the cognitive distortions of over-generalizing and catastrophizing. I asked her how realistic this statement was, and Eileen was able to discuss the possible outcome of doing poorly on the exam, and the low likelihood of this occurrence based on her academic success in the past.

In subsequent sessions, we continued to identify and discuss cognitive distortions. Eileen gave examples of all-or-none thinking and mind-reading, which she was successfully able to refute by identifying a range of possibilities and reality testing. Although her "bad days" were becoming more infrequent, she continued to have tearful episodes, and agreed

to a trial of Prozac (fluoxetine), 20 mg. per day. With further evaluation of her binge eating, Eileen was able to state that, "I equate what I eat with my value as a person." This realization led her to change her diet to include more healthy choices and to gain more control over binge eating. It became clear that her binge eating was a behavior stemming from a distorted cognition of low self-worth. As her self-esteem continued to improve, her binge eating episodes decreased, and disappeared by session five. By session eleven, Eileen's depressive symptoms were in remission, and we decreased the frequency of our sessions to once every two to three weeks.

For Eileen, binge eating was inextricably linked with depression. As cognitive distortions were examined and refuted and negative thinking re-framed, self-esteem improved and binge eating diminished. Psychotherapy, in combination with anti-depressant medication, alleviated symptoms of depression. Over time, binge eating behavior was eradicated.

Friday Afternoon, 2:00 P.M.

Typically, psychotherapy follows a traditional format. Therapist and patient meet for a *fifty-minute hour.* The frequency is once weekly. Although I know of no research data on the subject, it seems legitimate to consider the consequences of briefer sessions. What if the patient can only stay for thirty minutes? And, what if the frequency of meetings is reduced to every two weeks or once monthly?

At what point is the continuity of the process compromised, and the value of the therapy lost? Daniel Varon's post-graduate training combines psychiatry and neurology. I was mildly surprised, but pleased, when he expressed a desire to learn to do cognitive therapy. "I want to make it a part of my repertoire," he said. Dr. Varon proceeded, then, to describe a case that didn't fit the typical format. The outcome was a testimony to his skill in delivering the cognitive model.

Social phobia is a relatively common disorder. The prevalence of social phobia in primary care settings ranges from 2.9% to 7.0%. Brief therapy has been used successfully in patients with this disorder, alone or in conjunction with medications. The therapy is usually done once a week or sometimes twice a week, if necessary, which can be difficult to afford for some patients. This patient presents a case of major depressive disorder, with comorbid generalized social phobia and some obsessive-compulsive personality traits He was treated for ten brief therapy sessions every other week with significant benefit.

This case demonstrates the usefulness of bi-weekly psychotherapy for a subset of patients with whom weekly meetings are not an option.

Tony*, a 31-year-old Asian-American single male, had been treated for five months for depression and anxiety with pharmacotherapy at the university clinic. Tony's depressive symptoms had improved, but he continued to experience marked anxiety. He had moved from Rhode Island to Charleston six months prior to his visit with me, in order to start a new job at an insurance company. Tony said that he frequently felt anxious, particularly around his boss and female coworkers, because he was fearful of saying or doing "the wrong thing" in front of them. He had to do monthly presentations in front of his coworkers and, although he usually did fine, he would worry for two weeks prior to the presentation about his performance. He also had difficulties interacting with people in social situations, unless he had a drink or two beforehand. He considered himself a loner, preferring to stay at home watching television or taking care of his car. Tony also mentioned having a motor vehicle accident soon after moving to Charleston, in which his car was badly damaged. He had to purchase a new car due to the accident. He had become very careful with his new car, spending a great deal of time washing it on the weekends, making sure the paint was in good condition every day when he returned from work, and fixing minor scratches as soon as they occurred. He would also drive the car as little as possible to decrease the chances of it getting scratched or damaged, and he would avoid going to places where the parking spaces were too close to each other. Tony would spend a good bit of time looking for a parking space at work where the car would be safe from careless drivers. He denied any flashbacks from the accident, or undue concern about his safety. He thought his care of the car might have been a little excessive, but he really enjoyed doing it and he did not think this was impairing his daily activities.

During his initial evaluation, Tony made poor eye contact and seemed mildly anxious, but his affect had a full range. His speech was normal and his thought process was goal-directed, with no evidence of depressive, suicidal, or psychotic content. Tony described his symptoms of depression, including low energy, decreased appetite, poor sleep, and decreased motivation. All had improved after three months of drug treatment. However, his symptoms of anxiety were unchanged.

My diagnostic impressions included generalized social phobia and

---

* This case is adapted with permission of *Primary Care Companion to the Journal of Clinical Psychiatry*. The case originally appeared in D. Varon (2003). Biweekly cognitive therapy for social phobia. *Primary Care Companion to the Journal of Clinical Psychiatry*, 5(2), 89–91.

major depressive disorder (in remission). Tony felt comfortable on the medication he was taking at the time, which included paroxetine (Paxil) and bupropion (Wellbutrin). We discussed other options for treatment, and I briefly reviewed the cognitive therapy model with him. I explained that we needed to start by identifying automatic thoughts, which in turn could affect the way he felt about certain situations. He was not able to afford weekly sessions, so I agreed to see him once every two weeks.

During our second session, I discussed the cognitive model in more depth, and we started examining situations in which he was uncomfortable. Tony stated that he felt most anxious in the days prior to his presentations at work. During this time, he would have thoughts of losing his job, of his coworkers not being able to understand what he was presenting and ridiculing him, and of his boss thinking he had done a poor job. These thoughts represented two common cognitive errors: catastrophizing and polarization. When asked what evidence he had to support these thoughts, he realized that there had not been any times in the past when his boss or coworkers had done what he was concerned about. He was able to refute his thoughts by generating alternatives, including: "If my boss thought that I had done a poor job in the past, he would have said so," "I have done well in the past, so therefore this time shouldn't be any different," and "I usually prepare well, so I should do fine in the presentation." At the end of the session, we discussed the use of triple columns in order to record distressing situations, the associated feelings and thoughts or meanings that accompanied the feelings.

During our third and fourth sessions, we reviewed the triple column contents, looked for distorted cognitions, and proposed alternative thoughts. We also discussed Tony's anticipatory anxiety prior to public presentations, his concerns about talking to his boss, and his fears of ridicule by his coworkers.

During session five, Tony commented that he had been preparing for a presentation and was able to overcome his anxiety and fears of failure. He seemed pleased with the outcome of his talk. He mentioned a situation in which he had gone to a bar the week before, with his coworkers. Tony looked for a parking space for 15 minutes, and although he did not feel comfortable with the space he found, he decided to park his car there. He had to leave the place 30 minutes later because he feared his car might have gotten scratched. He also mentioned that he would look for minor alterations in the paint on his car every day after work, and try to have them touched up the same day. I asked what would happen if he waited until the weekend to "fix the defects?" He replied: "Probably nothing." We were able to identify several distorted cognitions regarding his car, by looking for evidence to support or disprove his thoughts.

We evaluated his progress during session six, noting how comfortable he had become with the cognitive model. It clearly made sense to him, and he would employ it frequently when he felt anxious. We continued

to work on situations that evoked anxious feelings, including interactions with people in social gatherings, and his belief that people noticed his anxiety in these situations.

By session nine, Tony said that he was no longer feeling excessively anxious about presentations at work, discussing issues with coworkers, or approaching his boss. He had substantially decreased the amount of time he spent caring for his car, was no longer obsessed about minor issues, and although he was still careful about parking, he did not spend as much time finding a spot as he used to. Tony felt that he had made a lot of progress and thought he could continue to apply the cognitive model on his own.

We agreed to meet four weeks later to review how he was doing. On his return visit, Tony reported that he was doing well. He had been on a trip with a friend from college, and attended a wedding where he had been able to talk to several people with less difficulty than ever before. We agreed to continue to meet every two months for medication management only.

Final Thoughts

This completes a simulated week of twenty-five hours of cognitive therapy treating patients with a range of clinical problems. Ideally, the clinician will complement his or her psychotherapy work with other tasks that are stimulating. These may be within the field of psychiatry or psychology, and include teaching and research opportunities. They may be outside of the profession—I have taught college students and worked as a sports reporter—as well. Diversity, for me, counters the ills of burnout, and maintains fresh enthusiasm for a variety of challenges.

I hope the cognitive caseload exemplified (and the different voices who narrated the cases) encourages the reader to consider a career that incorporates doing cognitive therapy. If you have questions, please email me at schuyled@musc.edu.

BIBLIOGRAPHY

Bach, R. (1979). *Illusions: Confessions of a reluctant messiah*. New York: Dell.

Beck, A. T. (1961). A systematic investigation of depression. *Comprehensive Psychiatry*, 2, 163–170.

Beck, A. T. (1963). Thinking and depression. *Archives of General Psychiatry*, 9, 324–333.

Beck, A. T. (1967). *Depression: Clinical, experimental, and theoretical aspects*. New York: Harper & Row.

Beck, A. T. (1976). *Cognitive therapy and the emotional disorders*. New York: International Universities Press.

Beck, A. T. (1988). *Love is never enough*. New York: Harper & Row.

Beck, A. T, Emery, G., & Greenberg, R. (1985). *Anxiety disorders and phobias: A cognitive perspective*. New York: Basic Books.

Beck, A. T., Freeman, A., & Associates. (1990). *Cognitive therapy for personality disorders*. New York: Guilford.

Beck, A. T., Rush, A. J., Shaw, B. F., & Emery, G. (1979). *Cognitive therapy of depression*. New York: Guilford.

Budman, S. (1985). *Forms of brief psychotherapy*. New York: Guilford.

Burns, D. D. (1980). *Feeling good: The new mood therapy*. New York: William Morrow.

Dattilio, F. M., & Padesky, C. A. (1990). *Cognitive therapy with couples*. Sarasota, FL: Professsional Resource Exchange.

Davanloo, H. (1976). *Basic principles and techniques in short-term dynamic psychotherapy*. New York: S. R Medical & Scientific Books.

Dobson, K. S. (1988). *Handbook of cognitive-behavioral therapies*. New York: Guilford.

Ellis, A. (1962). *Reason and emotion in psychotherapy*. New York: Lyle Stuart.

Emery, G., Hollon, S. D., & Bedrosian, R. C. (1981). *New directions in cognitive therapy*. New York: Guilford.

Erikson, E. H. (1963). *Childhood and society*. New York: Norton.

Frank, J. D., & Frank, J. B. (1993). *Persuasion and healing: A comparative study of psychotherapy*. Baltimore: Johns Hopkins Press.

Hoehn-Saric, R., Liberman, B., Imber, S. D., Stone, A. R., Pande, S. K., & Frank, J. D. (1972). Arousal and attitude change in neurotic patients. *Archives of General Psychiatry*, 26, 51–56.

Johnson, S. (1998). *Who moved my cheese?* New York: Putnam.

Klerman, L., Weissman, M. M., Rounsaville, B. J., & Chevron, E. S. (1984). *Interpersonal psychotherapy of depression*. New York: Basic Books.

Kopp, S. (1979). *What took you so long? An assortment of life's every-day ironies.* Palo Alto, CA: Science and Behavior Books.

Linehan, M. M. (1993). *Cognitive-behavioral treatment of borderline personality disorder.* New York: Guilford Press.

Mahoney, M. (1974). *Cognition and behavior modification.* Cambridge, MA: Ballinger.

Malan, D. H. (1963). *A study of brief psychotherapy.* New York: Plenum.

Mann, J. (1973). *Time-limited psychotherapy.* Cambridge, MA: Harvard University Press.

McMullin, R. E. (1999). *The new handbook of cognitive therapy techniques.* New York: Norton.

Meichenbaum, D. (1974). *Cognitive-behavioral modification: An integrative approach.* Morristown, NJ: Gener Learning.

Meichenbaum, D. (1977). *Cognitive-behavior modification.* New York: Plenum.

Orne, M., & Wender, P. (1968). Anticipatory socialization for psychotherapy: Method and rationale. *American Journal of Psychiatry, 124,* 1202–1211.

Perris, C. (1989). *Cognitive therapy with schizophrenic patients.* New York: Guilford.

Sank, L. I., & Shaffer, C. (1984). *A therapist's manual for cognitive behavior therapy in groups.* New York: Plenum.

Schuyler, D. (2000). Prescribing brief psychotherapy. *Primary Care Companion to the Journal of Clinical Psychiatry, 2* (1), 13–15.

Schuyler, D. (2002). Short-term cognitive therapy shows promise for dysthymia. *Current Psychiatry, 1* (5), 143–149.

Schuyler, D., Basco, M., & Thase, M. (2002). Cognitive therapy for affective disorders. *Psychiatric Update, 22,* 1–8.

Schuyler, D., & Clyburn, E. B. (2003). *Teaching psychiatry in primary care.* Unpublished manuscript.

Schuyler, D., & Davis, K. (1999). Primary care and psychiatry: Anticipating an interfaith marriage. *Academic Medicine, 74,* 27–32.

Sifneos, P. (1972). *Short-term psychotherapy and emotional crisis.* Cambridge, MA: Harvard University Press.

Simons, A. D., Garfield, S. L., & Murphy, G. E. (1984). The process of change in cognitive therapy and pharmacotherapy for depression. *Archives of General Psychiatry, 41,* 45–51.

Viscott, D. (1977). *Risking.* New York: Simon & Schuster.

Watzlawick, P., Weakland, J., & Fisch, R. (1974). *Change: Principles of problem formation and problem resolution.* New York: Norton.

Wilkes, T. C., Belsher, G., Rush, A. J., & Frank, E. (1994). *Cognitive therapy for depressed adolescents.* New York: Guilford.

Wolpe, J. (1958). *Psychotherapy by reciprocal inhibition.* Stanford, CA: Stanford University Press.

Index

Academy of Cognitive Therapists, xiii
acceptance, therapist's, of the patient, 17
addiction, to a relationship, 80
adjustment disorder
  with anxious and depressed mood,
    case example, 178–80
  of a cancer patient, case example,
    156–58
  with depression, case example,
    141–43
  sertraline (Zoloft), use of with, 178
  stressors and, 141–43, 153
adolescent patients
  cognitive therapy for treating, 20
  reparenting model for treating,
    105–14
Adult Primary Care Clinic, consultant's
    role in, 135
affect
  in being in love, 67–68
  in being out of love, 68–69
  changing, with mastery over assump-
    tions, 44
  driven by cognition, 18
age
  and change, 85–92
  and success in cognitive therapy, 20
agoraphobia, panic disorder with, case ex-
    ample, 181–82
Akiskal, H., 14
Alcoholics Anonymous, 102, 171
alcoholism
  case example, 170–73
  follow-up in, example, 125–27
  in a long-term cognitive therapy pa-
    tient, 100–103

triple-column table, use of with,
    171–72
all-or-none thinking, cognitive distortion
    of, 198–99
alprazolam (Xanax), 180
alternatives
  generating
    by the patient, 46
    as a teaching method, 17
    in therapy, 18–19, 50, 57–62
    in therapy, long-term, 97
  in responding to automatic thoughts,
    63–64
American Psychiatric Association, xiii
analogy, for shifting the set, 52–54, 169
anger
  expressing in a relationship, 117–18
  management of, case examples,
    159–63
  in separation, 78
anxiety
  anticipatory, automatic thoughts rele-
    vant to, 103–4
  duration of short-term therapy for, 21
  providing structure for managing, 17
  about public speaking, personal exam-
    ple, 39–40
  relabeling physical symptoms as, exam-
    ple, 47–48
  skin rash related to, case example,
    180–82
anxiety disorders, treating, 19
appraisals
  generation of, from data, 34
  patient's, of performance, 43
  see also evaluation; self-appraisal